The
History and Mystery
of the
Menger Hotel

Docia Schultz Williams
with special recollections of
Ernesto Malacara

D1026054

REPUBLIC OF TEXAS PRESS
Dallas • Lanham • Boulder • New York • Toronto • Oxford

Library of Congress Cataloging-in-Publication Data

Williams, Docia Schultz.
  The history and mystery of the Menger Hotel / Docia Schultz Williams.
      p. cm.
  Includes index.
  ISBN 1-55622-792-2 (pbk.)
  1. Menger Hotel—History.   I. Title.

  TX941.M465 W55 2000
  647.94764'35101—dc21   00-040292
                                                              CIP

Published by Republic of Texas Press
An imprint of The Rowman & Littlefield Publishing Group, Inc.
4501 Forbes Boulevard, Suite 200
Lanham, MD 20706

Distributed by NATIONAL BOOK NETWORK

⊖™ The paper used in this publication meets the minimum requirements of American
National Standard for Information Sciences—Permanence of Paper for Printed Library
Materials, ANSI/NISO Z39.48-1992.

Manufactured in the United States of America.

Contents

Part 1
The Menger Hotel: Its Illustrious History

Contents

Part 2
The Menger Hotel, Its Haunting Mystery

Acknowledgements

A number of people shared their historical knowledge with Ernesto Malacara, Roy Williams, and me as we sought information for this book. Without their help, the project would have never reached its completion, and we are truly grateful to them all.

First of all, to my husband Roy Williams, a tremendous "thank you" for hours of work at the computer preparing and correcting the manuscript for publication.

To historical researcher Robin Ellis, for the collection of articles about the hotel from newspapers and magazines he collected over many years and so generously offered to us, a great big "thank you!" This book would not have been nearly as complete without this material.

A big verbal bouquet to Ms. Joyce Dundee, corporate secretary of the Gal-Tex Corporation, Galveston, for providing us with historical and biographical information on the Moody family and the Moody Foundation.

Thanks, too, to Tom Shelton, photo archivist, Institute of Texan Cultures, who went the extra mile time and again to ferret out special photographs for use in this volume, and to Ingrid Kokinda, who shared her antique postcards from the collection of the late Ilse Griffith for publication in this book. Also, a thank you to Jeremy Gretencord and Esmarelda Ruzicka at Wolf Camera for their extra attention in making special photo prints for this book.

Martin L. Malacara provided us with many excellent Menger Hotel photographs.

In addition, our gratitude goes out to a number of staff members at research facilities who greatly aided in our search for material about the Menger. These helpful individuals include: Ms. Chris Floerke, program co-ordinator, library, Institute of Texan Cultures; Ms. Nellie Weincek, librarian for the San Antonio

Conservation Society, and her staff of able volunteers; and the capable staff at the Daughters of the Republic of Texas Library including Jeannette Phinney, Martha Utterbach, and Melinda Loomis. Warren Striker, Archivist at the DRT Library, as well as at the University of the Incarnate Word Library, was especially helpful and informative. We also want to thank Mr. Wendell Morgan, dean of library sciences at the University of the Incarnate Word.

Frank Faulkner, librarian, and Clarissa Chavera, library assistant, at the Texana Collection at the San Antonio Central Library, went out of their way to find needed information. Amy Fulkerson, of the archival staff, Witte Museum also lent her expertise to the project.

Galveston's Roberta Sullivan at the Moody Mansion Museum and Casey Edward Greene at the Rosenberg Library sent us needed photographs and information.

San Antonio columnist and historian Frank W. Jennings, author of *San Antonio: The Story of an Enchanted City*, provided information about John W. Gates and the barbed wire story.

A number of military historians were especially helpful in compiling information about the various military greats who have visited the hotel, including Teddy Roosevelt and his volunteer Rough Riders. Lt. Colonel (U.S. Army Reserve, Rtd.) John Manguso, director of the Fort Sam Houston Museum and dean of San Antonio's military historians; Colonel George Weinbrenner of the Army Retirement Community; and Sam Nesmith, military historian, formerly curator, the Alamo Museum and the Institute of Texan Cultures Museum all gave us their able assistance. Lt. General Beverley Powell was responsible for the information about Colonel Tommy Tompkins used in chapter eight. All of these people deserve our heartfelt thanks!

A special thanks to Peggy Green, of Weatherford, Texas, for sharing the Spanish American War memoirs of Clifton David Scott, one of her relatives, for inclusion in chapter nine. Bryan Snyder III of Austin kindly supplied information about Celeste Willis Snyder, the subject of a painting hanging in the main lobby.

A number of San Antonio writers were cooperative in allowing us to quote from their works. These helpful individuals include: Frank W. Jennings, Ted Fehrenbach, Cecilia Steinfeldt, Donald E. Everett, Grant Lyons, and David Bowser.

Personal interviews always come into play in a work such as this, and a number of individuals were more than cooperative in granting us their time, either by way of personal interviews or telephone interviews. I wish to thank the following: Mr. Ike Kampmann Jr., son of former owners of the hotel; Mrs. Robert McCormick, great-great-great-granddaughter of William and Mary Menger; Mrs. Hubertus Strughold; Mrs. William O. Bowers III; Charles Schreiner III of the YO Ranch, Mountain Home, Texas; Mrs. Lewis Moorman; Mr. Frates Seeligson; Dr. Don Newell, D.D.S.; Reverend and Mrs. Mike Cave; and Mr. Maury Maverick Jr., noted columnist. These interviews brought forth much valuable information.

Lastly, a special thanks to the Menger executive staff, who showed such keen interest in this project and cooperated in every way possible. Mr. Hector Venegas, general manager; Ms. Lisa Meng, administrative assistant to the general manager; and Ms. Anita Younes, director, historical preservation and decorative arts. Thanks also to Mr. Winfried Heumann, executive chef, for sharing some of his fine recipes for chapter ten.

A special thanks, as always, to the publishers, editors, and staff at the Republic of Texas Press for their continual encouragement and good faith!

Prologue

This book is the result of nearly three years of researching local libraries, poring over old newspapers, going through ancient hotel registers and ledgers, and interviewing a number of individuals. It is presented as a tribute to San Antonio's oldest, most historic hotel property, the Menger Hotel.

Ernesto Malacara, assistant general manager of the hotel, has been employed there for over twenty-three years. He "lives, eats, and breathes" his position at the Menger. A devoted innkeeper, he is also a dedicated researcher and historian. His sharing of personal experiences connected with his years at the hotel and his assistance in locating valuable material for this book have been of immeasurable help.

Personally, I have long been an ardent admirer of the Menger. The very first night I ever spent in San Antonio was spent at the hotel in the spring of 1950. As the Texas A&M Cotton Ball Queen that year, I was a participant in a spectacular river parade sponsored by Joskes of Texas and the American Cotton Council. Along with other Southwest Conference beauty queens, my chaperone and I were housed at the Menger. The hotel pulled out all stops to make our visit memorable. I fondly recall the beautiful reception in the Spanish patio. It was a very glamorous weekend for a nineteen-year-old coed!

Years later, after I married, I came back to San Antonio, this time as a permanent resident. I soon became immersed in historical research, joined numerous clubs and organizations, made lots of friends, and eventually became a professional tour guide. Over the ensuing years I have played hostess and guide to numerous tour groups who have stayed at the Menger. I always include a talk about the history of the hotel as well as the general history of San Antonio.

Over the years, I have seen numerous changes in the hotel, such as the addition of more guestrooms and the magnificent grand ballroom with its adjacent meeting rooms. While boasting the most modern conveniences, the Menger has still maintained its Old World charm and Victorian ambiance. Delving into its illustrious history and its mystery (there are some special ghostly residents at the old landmark!) has been a delightful writing project. But without the collaboration, enthusiasm, and inspiration provided by Ernesto Malacara, this project would not have been nearly so gratifying. And, I might add, without the painstaking task of preparing the manuscript on the computer, accomplished by my long-suffering husband, this book would never have been completed!

It is my sincere wish that the culmination of over three years of research will bring pleasure to you as readers and friends of the Menger Hotel.

Roy Williams, Docia Schultz Williams, and Ernesto Malacara

Introduction

One could say the heart of the great city of San Antonio, America's eighth largest metropolis, is Alamo Plaza, the location of the famous shrine to Texas freedom, the Alamo. There the blood of 189 brave and courageous defenders was shed in the historic battle that took place on March 6, 1836.

Sharing the spotlight with the Alamo Chapel and its surrounding grounds is the venerable Menger Hotel, built just twenty-three years after the battle. During those years, between 1836 and 1859, the sleepy little village on the banks of the San Antonio River had begun to grow into a lively, bustling city on the edge of the western frontier. In fact, for many years, San Antonio was Texas's largest city! Because of its phenomenal growth, greatly buoyed up by the large numbers of German immigrants who came to this area during the Republic of Texas period (1836-1845), there was a real need for a hotel of elegance and distinction. German immigrant and entrepreneur William A. Menger saw this need and rose to the occasion, constructing his fine hotel alongside the Alamo compound in 1859.

It is amazing to think that the Menger first welcomed visitors arriving by carriage or stagecoach, on foot, or on horseback. It was built a number of years before the first railroad arrived in San Antonio. The Menger was in place long before Fort Sam Houston graced Government Hill, before the first public schools were established to educate the children of the community, and before the city had a hospital or a university. The Menger was built before a devastating hurricane destroyed the seaport city of Indianola on the Gulf of Mexico, where many of the first German settlers of Texas arrived from Europe.

Putting the information we collected about the hotel in any kind of chronological order was challenging. Many of the old news clippings we found in library files bore no dates. In some instances, names of the publications were handwritten in the margins. Other articles had been cut out, with no date and no newspaper name noted, and we could only make an educated guess about the time frame. Some old documents, photographs, and ledgers were so fragile we had to wear white gloves as we leafed through them. The whole project was like putting together a huge jigsaw puzzle. Unfortunately, some pieces are still missing.

Through the years, the hotel has become a favorite stopping-off spot for scores of weary travelers. And while becoming a favored home away from home for the living, the Menger has also become home to a number of other-worldly spirits, mostly former employees and guests, who loved the place so much they've no desire to move on! The well-documented ghost stories you will find in Part II provide charming glimpses into the dimension of the supernatural.

This wonderful old hostelry still charms visitors today, just as it has for nearly a century and a half. The Menger story is very much a story of San Antonio's illustrious past, as the hotel has been closely connected to just about everything and everybody who have played a part in making San Antonio the great city it is today.

Part 1

The Menger Hotel: Its Illustrious History

Chapter 1

The Menger Years, 1859-1881

A few years after the Battle of the Alamo, which took place on March 6, 1836, the small hamlet of San Antonio began to grow rapidly, with the arrival of immigrants from abroad and settlers from all parts of the United States. The government of the new Republic of Texas had sent out the word, far and wide, that newcomers were welcome and choice land was available for homesteading.

On the other side of the Atlantic, the invitation to come to Texas had reached Germany, where it was of special interest to many young men living in that country. The custom had long been for only the eldest son in a family to inherit money, property, or title, upon the death of the parents. Younger and middle sons just had to fend for themselves, often joining the Prussian army, or signing up for the priesthood. Sometimes the young men would apprentice themselves to a craftsman in order to learn a trade. Seeking a more prosperous lifestyle, a large number of ambitious young men from Germany began to arrive in the new republic.

William Achatius Menger was one of those young German men who decided to seek his fortune in Texas, far removed from his native land. He was born in Bei Hanau, Hessen, Germany on March 15, 1827. He had become a skilled cooper, making casks and barrels for the beer and wine industries. He also knew quite a bit about brewing beer. While Menger had very little money, he was armed with ambition, his tools, and his talent, when he arrived in San Antonio in 1847. He was only twenty years old and only five feet tall! However, this little man had big ambitions, a big heart, and he made a big and lasting impression on the community he had chosen to be his new home. Not much is known of Menger's very first years in San Antonio. It is known that in 1848 or 1849 he took rooms in a boardinghouse, which was run by a young German widow, Mary Baumschleuter Guenther. Mrs. Guenther was noted as being a fine cook and housekeeper, and the fact she was German and spoke William's language must have been especially helpful. Theirs was not an overnight love affair, because it was not until 1851 that William and Mary were married. William had, in the meantime, gone to work making kegs and barrels, and he had opened a small grocery in partnership with a man named Charles Degenard. By the time William and Mary were married, the young German had already begun to prosper!

Mary was an industrious and ambitious woman. She was no stranger to long hours and hard work, so she made an ideal partner for young Menger. She and her mother, a sixty-year-old widow named Anna Baumschleuter, had come from Germany in 1846. Mary, who was born in 1818, was twenty-eight years old at the time she arrived in San Antonio. The two women had a difficult and dangerous journey. It had taken six months to cross the Atlantic from Bremen. They had been the only passengers on a schooner loaded with lumber. Caught by a severe storm, the ship's masts were destroyed in the gales, and they had to sail to Liverpool, England for repairs.

The travelers finally made it across the Atlantic, but when they arrived at the port of Galveston, it took ten days for the tides to rise high enough for the ship to pass safely over the long sandbars surrounding the port city. By then, the ship was running low on supplies, and the two women, unaccustomed to life at sea, must have been extremely uncomfortable.

From Galveston, Mary and Anna took a little boat up the Buffalo Bayou to the small settlement of Harrisburg (now absorbed by Houston) where they camped and waited for a train of covered wagons drawn by oxen to arrive. This wagon train was to bring them, eventually, to their final destination, San Antonio. It is difficult to imagine in these days of freeways and fast automobiles how it must have been in those times. It took the women six weeks to make the trip that today could easily by made in three or four hours. There were heavy rains along the way, which created swollen, impassable streams, and the road was nothing but a muddy path through heavily wooded areas. Since there were no bridges, streams had to be forded. One river along the route rose so rapidly that only half of their little wagon train was able to reach the far side. The rest of the party had to wait several days until the water subsided before they could cross and join the rest of the wagon train, which had been impatiently waiting for them. That portion of the train had all the food supplies!

Then, while another river was being forded, the swift current washed the trunks belonging to many of the travelers out of the wagons into the depths of the river, and the poor people barely got out with their lives. There were also a couple of Indian attacks along the way, and several of the people took desperately ill. The trip to San Antonio was a tumultuous beginning in a new country for Mary and her mother.

Just a couple of weeks after the two women arrived in the small village, Anna took to her bed with a high fever. She was totally exhausted from the long journey and did not have enough strength to recover. Mary also came down with the flu. Anna died, and Mary could not muster enough strength to attend her mother's hastily arranged funeral and burial. A priest who was just passing through the town en route to Mexico conducted the service. Anna Baumschleuter was buried in the Catholic cemetery located where the Santa Rosa Hospital is now situated, in an unmarked grave. Mary was never able to find the exact location of her mother's final resting place.

Mary was left to fend for herself in a town where there were very few people who spoke either German or English. Most of the population of San Antonio was either Mexican or Indian. After Mary recovered from the flu, she went to the little market in the town to buy some provisions. While she was away from her lodgings, someone broke open her small trunk and stole all of her money. She was alone, penniless, and in frail health. Somehow, she survived through the kindness of the people she met in the town. What a difficult beginning!

Not much is known about what Mary did from the time of her arrival in 1846, until a couple of years later. One account stated she was in ill health much of the first year she was in San Antonio. She later obtained employment, possibly as a domestic worker. In 1848 she married a man named Emil Guenther, who was also a German immigrant. Only six months after the couple married, Guenther died, leaving Mary widowed and pregnant at the age of thirty. Her baby was born in 1849 and died that same year. We could find no other records and do not know whether the infant was a boy or a girl.

Mary's husband must have left her some money, because it was only a short time after his death in 1848 that she began to run a boardinghouse. Will Menger had been living elsewhere during his first year in San Antonio, but he moved into the widow Guenther's establishment, on St. Mary's Street near the river, sometime in 1848 or 1849.

It is interesting to note that in a time when women generally married men a great deal older than themselves, William Menger, a twenty-four-year-old man, would marry a woman who was nine years his senior. It has been suggested that Mary was a motherly type and a wonderful cook, and perhaps this was the attraction. At any rate, the couple were married in 1851. Will had a local livery stable dispatch a horse to Castroville so his friend the Reverend Claude M. Dubuis could ride to San Antonio to conduct the nuptial rites. When the priest rode up, Menger was aghast at the broken down nag upon which the minister was mounted. He apologized profusely to the priest, saying, "I am so sorry they did not send you a better horse." Reverend Dubuis, who later became the bishop of Galveston, replied, "I'm glad you didn't. If you had, the Indians along the way would have certainly killed me to get my horse."

Menger bought a small piece of property adjacent to the old Alamo mission, and there he established his small brewery around 1855. He always said the time to buy land was after a heavy rain. If there were no standing water, it would be a good buy! The plot he chose was uphill from the San Antonio River and proved to be a good choice. Menger hired a fellow German, Carl Degen (some historical accounts say the man's name was "Charles" Degen), as his brewmaster. The little brewery, which he called The Menger Brewery, was very successful. He made his own kegs, and he had the malt and hops shipped from New York, via water, to the port of Indianola. From there, the supplies were transported by ox cart to San Antonio.

The beer project was an immediate success, but still Menger realized he could do better. Many people didn't want to buy a whole keg or barrel of beer. They would have no way to transport it to their homes. So, he decided to build a small tavern so people could enjoy a few steins of beer and then go on their ways. However the Menger beer was quite strong. A couple of big mugs would be enough to put a traveler in the precarious position of being unable to saddle a horse and ride it home in the dark. Some of his hard-drinking patrons just curled up on the floor or swept the mugs off a table and stretched out there to sleep it off. Menger and Mary, his wife, decided something must be done! They built a one-story rooming house adjacent to the brewery and tavern, so over-imbibers could sleep off their drinking bouts. Mary always had plenty of strong black coffee and good food on hand. The boardinghouse, built in 1855, was an immediate success! How Mary ran a boardinghouse, did most of the cooking, and at the same time raised a family is remarkable. She and Will were loving parents to four children: Louis William, born in 1852; Mary, born in 1854;

Peter Gustav, born in 1857; and Catherine Barbara, who was born in 1860. Little Mary died in 1856 when she was only two years old.

It wasn't long until the Mengers decided something better was needed. Settlers from surrounding communities who came to San Antonio to buy their supplies needed a place to stay. There were no elegant hostelries in the town, which was still very much a rough and ready frontier settlement. The Mengers decided to pull out all stops and build a fine hotel adjacent to their popular brewery and tavern.

In 1858 William Menger hired John M. Fries as the architect for the project, and he settled on J. H. Kampmann, another fellow German settler, as the general contractor. The two-story building, a fifty-room inn, was built of limestone from the quarries located where the Sunken Gardens in Brackenridge Park are today.

The *San Antonio Herald* on January 18, 1859, reported on the hotel project:

The Menger Hotel is rapidly drawing towards completion. The main room on the second floor is unsurpassed for beauty. The finishing of the walls and ceilings being developed and executed by our fellow citizen P. C. Taylor. The walls and ceilings unite the smoothness of glass to the whiteness of alabaster, whilst the mouldings are conceived in fine taste and executed in the best style of art.

Mr. Menger ran the following ad in local newspapers:

Menger Hotel.
(Alamo Plaza   San Antonio.)
THE UNDERSIGNED HAS
With great care and expense
built and fitted out a large & commodious Hotel on Alamo Square
which be opened on the 1st of Feb. 1859
He flatters himself that his establishment will be found by the travelling public generally as fully equal to the wants of all. He will spare no pains to have his TABLE, and all the accommodations of his house, at least, equal to those of any hotel in the West
Attached to the establishment will be a large and well ventilated
STABLE,
which will at all times be kept supplied with the best provender, and attended to by experienced hostlers
W A MENGER

MENGER HOTEL
ALAMO PLAZA   SAN ANTONIO

The undersigned has with great care and expense built and fitted out a large & commodious hotel on Alamo Square which [will] be opened on the 1st of February 1859.

He flatters himself that his establishment will be found by the traveling public generally as fully equal to the want of all. He will spare no pains to have his table, and all the accommodations of his house, at least, equal to those of any hotel in the West.

Attached to the establishment will be a large and well ventilated stable, which will at all times be kept supplied with the best provender, and attended to by experienced hostlers.

W. A. Menger

The Menger Hotel, which was built for $15,712, was opened to the public on February 1, 1859. The day before, Monday, January 31, Menger held a special open house for invited guests.

The citizens of San Antonio heralded the most exciting event of its day, the opening of the fine new hotel, with much jubilation. The *San Antonio Herald* edition of February 1, 1859 stated:

Opening of the Menger Hotel

According to previous announcement, the opening of this splendid new hotel took place on Monday evening. The turn out of our citizens was exceedingly large, all seeming disposed to applaud the enterprising proprietor for the liberality displayed by him in the erection and fitting out of a hotel that would be no discredit to any city of the Union, as well as to assist him in getting through with some of his sparkling wines and incomparable lager. Every portion of the building was brilliantly illuminated and showed to great advantage from the street, whilst the new and shining furniture, fine carpets, and beautiful curtains, presented a spectacle of exceeding brilliancy. We heard but one expression during the evening as to the character of the display, and that was of universal praise and admiration.

The Menger Hotel is a monument to the enterprise of its proprietor, and we trust will prove for him a valuable investment, as we feel sure it will be the means of greatly benefiting our city, especially that portion of it in which it is located. He has set a noble example to some of the "old fogies" in our portion of the city, in the matter of a first class hotel, it remains to be seen when they will follow it. If not soon, we shall all see that business will gradually begin to leave the far-famed Plaza; for nothing does so much to attract business as a good hotel (not merely a well kept establishment, such as we have ever had), but a building of commanding appearance and one provided with most comfortable rooms and plenty of fresh air.

Menger Hotel, taken between 1865 and 1875

Photo courtesy Texas University Institute of Texan Cultures, photo by Thomas W. Cutrer

In just a short time, the Mengers realized that their new hotel was not large enough. The hostelry had been a success since its opening day and was generally filled to capacity. But there were only fifty rooms available. Mr. Kampmann was engaged to add on another fifty rooms, to the rear of the building. Just eight months from the initial opening, on September 13, 1859, the *San Antonio Herald* announced:

> The large addition to the Menger Hotel we believe is finished, making the Menger not only the handsomest hotel in the State, but the largest, also. Great credit is due to the enterprising proprietor for the liberality displayed by him in the direction of so magnificent a public house in our city.

It was certainly obvious that the hotel had met with great success from its day of opening. The registers read like a virtual who's who of the Southwest. Even the great Robert E. Lee is known to have stayed at the Menger, and it is said when he registered he rode into the lobby astride his faithful steed Traveler. There are those of us who might doubt this, as Lee was known to have been a real gentleman, and we find it hard to believe he would have ridden a horse into the Menger's beautiful lobby! Menger family members swear that the story is true and that Lee even swept up little Catherine Barbara, the only Menger child born in the hotel, into his saddle and placed a gold locket around the toddler's neck. Lee's sister, who was with him at the hotel, gave little Catherine a set of gold earrings set with coral. These items are still in the possession of some of the Menger descendants.

Another early guest of the hotel was the first president of the Republic of Texas, General Sam Houston. He signed the guest register, "Sam Houston and horse!"

During the Civil War, the hotel did very little business. The Menger Hotel closed down its guestrooms for a short period, because help was hard to get, and business was slow, anyway. However, meal service continued, and many soldiers and officers took their meals at the hotel during the war years. Some remodeling was accomplished during the closure. As soon as the conflict ended, the hotel was back in business again! Soon after the war ended, on October 26, 1865, Western Union opened an office at the hotel. The Menger was once more the scene of the most gala events in San Antonio. Will Menger became one of the most dedicated civic leaders in the city. He had already served as an alderman from 1857 to 1859 and had a great interest in the city government. In 1867 he and Mary went to Germany and then to Paris, to purchase furniture (most of it is still at the hotel) for their inn. Upon their return to the United States, while they were in New York, William witnessed a fire. There was a steam engine pumping water, and Menger, who was a captain with San Antonio's volunteer fire department, thought it would be just wonderful if San Antonio could have a pumper like New York's! He found out where the factory was located and went there, where he purchased a Silsby Rotary engine for his fire department. It cost him $4,000, which, in those days, was a tremendous amount of money. He never expected to be reimbursed, as the city had little money for such "extras." Later, however, the money was returned to him.

The engine was the first steam engine to be used in Texas. It had to be shipped to a port on the Texas coast and then overland by ox cart. It was so heavy, it took three yokes of oxen to haul the equipment to San Antonio, and the freight bill alone ran to over $900.

The *San Antonio Express* heralded the arrival of the engine with the banner headlines: *NOW WE ARE SAFE!* The engine was even given a name! It was christened "The Alamo."

When the steamer arrived in San Antonio, a military band serenaded Menger in front of the hotel, and the innkeeper invited the gathered assemblage inside where refreshments were laid out for the enthusiastic crowd. Later, a parade headed by a brass band and a procession of firemen and prominent citizens marched to Main Plaza, displaying the marvelous new engine. The parade terminated right in front of San Fernando Cathedral.

It is interesting to note, prior to the opening of the first hospital in San Antonio, when people from surrounding small

William A. Menger, chief of the Alamo Fire Company No. 2, in uniform

From the San Antonio Conservation Society Collection, courtesy of University of Texas Institute of Texan Cultures. Photo by Henry Doerr, San Antonio.

communities or far-flung ranches took ill, they were often brought into San Antonio where they took rooms at the Menger. The local physician could call on them there. The hotel was comfortable and clean, and the staff was efficient and considerate. Many young women who were anticipating difficult childbirth also came to the hotel to deliver their babies, where the physician or midwife might tend to them in comfortable surroundings. The hotel was a place where lives began, and where some lives ended as well.

In 1869 there was a terrible cholera epidemic in the city. There were only a few doctors and no clinic or hospital at all. The Catholic bishop of the diocese, Bishop Dubuis (the same priest who had performed the nuptials for William and Mary in 1851) wrote to the Order of the Incarnate Word in France, known for its fine nursing sisters. He urged some of the sisters to come as quickly as possible to San Antonio to provide help for the stricken area. Three young nuns made the long, arduous trip, first by ship from France to Galveston, then to San Antonio by wagon. They started a little clinic on Military Plaza, which they called the Santa Rosa Infirmary. William Menger became their chief benefactor. He actually "passed the hat" among some of the city's wealthiest citizens and asked each one to give at least $200 or more, which was quite a sizeable sum back in those days. This money was used to help fund the clinic, buying medicine and much needed supplies.

This tiny infirmary was the beginning of the Christus Santa Rosa Medical Center we have in San Antonio today, which is one of the country's largest and finest Catholic hospitals.

There is another example of William Menger's being a good citizen of his city and his adopted country. The U.S. Army, after the Civil War, was back in San Antonio, but the military had no property of its own. The army leased several buildings; some were used as barracks, another as a hospital, and still another as a guardhouse. These buildings were not really sufficient for the needs of the military, and the army could not afford to go out and buy property and buildings. The decision was made to move the military out of San Antonio. William Menger decided he could, and would, do something about the situation! Since another building was needed, he would build it and lease it to the army. They could pay him whenever they had the funds. Menger's great-great-great-granddaughter, Marguerite McCormick, told us that William Menger actually rode his horse all the way to Washington, D.C., to plead to the government officials for the army to remain in San Antonio. His building was erected at the corner of Crockett and Lasoya Street. After William died in 1871, his widow, Mary, continued to rent the building to the army until 1878. By then, Fort Sam Houston had been built on land the city donated to the army.

It is not known just how wealthy William Menger was at the time of his death. He was generous with what he had, never turning away anyone who needed help, so he may not have had all that much money. However he had made such a name for himself that he was considered among the "nobility and true builders" of San Antonio. His hotel was a success, and his brewery was by all accounts a thriving business. In 1868 he bought out a competitor, Naylor's Brewery. Menger became known as the "Beer King."

A tedious search through old records has brought no substantial information as far as the cause of William Menger's death is concerned. When William became gravely ill in March of 1871, the March 18 edition of the *San Antonio Daily Express* commented:

William Menger, circa 1870

Photo courtesy Menger Hotel

Our community can ill spare a gentleman of such public spirit, such enterprise, such generosity and such wonderful energy.

Unfortunately, Menger died that very evening, March 18, 1871, at the age of forty-four years. Autopsies were seldom performed in those days when someone passed away, and so the cause of his death remains a mystery. There were a number of epidemics back then and many diseases for which there were no cures.

The stocky little man, who had served his community as a brewer, an innkeeper, a chief of the Alamo Fire Department, an alderman, a hospital benefactor, and a friend to the U.S. Army, was mourned by the whole city. The funeral rites were conducted by the Odd Fellows Fraternity assisted by Reverend Grossweiler of the German Lutheran Church. The mile-long procession to City Cemetery 1 included the mayor and aldermen, the members of the fire department he had served so faithfully, officials of civic and cultural organizations, and military officials. A long line of one hundred carriages full of mourners as well as many citizens on foot followed the hearse to the cemetery. Many of the assemblage recalled how Menger had helped them personally at one time or another. This little man with a great big heart had prospered in his adopted city. And he had also earned the love and respect of his community in the short period of time, only twenty-five years, he had lived in San Antonio. His generosity and thoughtfulness had earned him an enviable place among the founding fathers of San Antonio.

The obituary for William Menger ran in the *San Antonio Express* March 21, 1871:

San Antonio met with a severe loss in the death of one of her most valued and enterprising citizens. Nearly 30 years ago W. A. Menger came to San Antonio, a stout, healthy young man with no other capital save a willing heart and strong arms. By economy and prudence he soon made headway in a then sparsely settled country and gradually through the drift of all those years worked himself until he became one of our leading citizens. His extensive business, his mammoth hotel, and surrounding buildings speak of his untiring energy.

On March 28, 1871, the *San Antonio Express* printed the following notice:

The death of the late owner and proprietor will cause no change in the affairs of the hotel as well as the brewery.

Signed, Mrs. W. A. Menger, March 21, 1871

After William died, Mary and her eldest son, Louis William, who was only nineteen, carried on with the management of the hotel as best they could for another ten years.

Mary had three children, ranging from nineteen to eleven years of age to take care of and support. They all lived in the hotel, in their own private quarters. Mary had lived a hard life and had ably helped William manage the hotel. She was a very down-to-earth German housewife, who apparently was completely devoid of "putting on airs." It was not unusual to find Mary, the hotel owner, sitting on the patio, peeling potatoes or shelling peas, which seemed rather shocking to some of her wealthy and socially prominent female patrons.

As the hotel proprietor, Mary bought all the provisions for the hotel during her ten years at the helm. She had a bookkeeper, but she was the chief buying agent. Ledgers unearthed from 1876 show she bought a Wilson sewing machine for $76.90 for use by her family and the hotel. She also bought four bales of New Orleans moss. This was Spanish moss used for stuffing mattresses and upholstered furniture. She paid $7.20 for 960 pounds. She bought two bales of cotton at 11½ cents per pound, and feather pillows that weighed 3½ pounds apiece and cost $3.25. She bought hair pillows that were evidently of lesser quality since they weighed 3 pounds and cost only $1.65 each. The same purchase order noted she also bought four dozen brooms and "several" well buckets.

Mary purchased many of the food items that were not grown in her own kitchen gardens from the firm of Honore Grenet. This was a fancy grocer located where the Alamo property is today. Ledgers show one purchase order for "110 pounds of garlic for $1.25, smoked beef and corned beef at 10 cents a pound, 100 pounds dried buffalo meat at 9 cents a pound, 110 pounds of dried El Paso pears." There were also the following items included in the order: Texas Irish potatoes, sweet potatoes, onions, turnips, green corn, green peppers, lard, sausage, and veal. Mary frequently purchased pecans from Gus Duerler for 25 cents a pound. These nuts were often harvested by nearby Indian tribes. Duerler eventually went into the candy business and opened a confectionery on Alamo Plaza. He is credited with inventing the ice cream soda.

There was also a city market in the middle of the plaza in front of the hotel where Mary purchased fruits and vegetables.

The Menger was known all over the country as well as in many foreign countries. It appealed to travelers all over the globe. An old 1874 register, which is owned by the Daughters of the Republic of Texas Library, bears the signatures of travelers from all over the United States and numerous foreign countries. The month of April and May 1874 listed such diverse hometowns as Albany and Brooklyn, New York, New York City; PawPaw, Michigan; Boston, Massachusetts; Hannibal, Missouri; Denver, Colorado; St. Louis, Missouri; Baltimore, Maryland; and New Orleans, Louisiana, to name but a few. Foreign countries included Mexico, Canada, India, Ireland, Scotland, and England. Two priests from France were also among the guests registered. Texans frequented the hotel and signed in from Austin, Fredericksburg, Indianola, Waco, Sherman, Galveston, Honey Grove, and Dallas. Since there was no railroad, all of these travelers had to arrive in San Antonio by stagecoach, horseback, or private carriage.

The hotel was not keeping up with the times, however; if one might believe the remarks made about the then sixteen-year-old inn in the *San Antonio Express News*, May 24, 1875 edition:

The Menger has no bells, no bathrooms, no proper water closets. Although excellently kept, and ample board provided, it is not the type of hotel that is endorsed by travelers from cosmopolitan cities of the world who live at the hotels and judge them by New York standards, and shoals of people coming to spend the winter months: They expect to find modern hotel accommodations or else they will come today and bid us good-bye tomorrow.

At this time gaslights illuminated all the rooms. In 1879 Mary Menger had equipment installed so the hotel might manufacture its own gas. A large cistern west of the Alamo supplied the guests with water.

It was noted in an old ledger that Mary had in her employ a laundress or washerwoman named Mrs. Liebenmann, who worked on a "per piece" basis. She worked at the Menger for a number of years. Records show that in 1876 the trusty employee was docked $1.50 for losing a Mr. Hall's undershirt.

Apparently, Mary was good to her help. When the common-law husband of Sallie White, a chambermaid, murdered the young servant on March 28, 1876, the Menger hotel ledgers show that the hotel paid for Sallie's coffin and burial.

Other records showed that Mary regularly made ten-dollar payments for "Babette's tuition." This was the family nickname given to Catherine Barbara, who was only eleven years old at the time of her father's death. She rode her pony every day from the hotel's stables to Ursuline Academy, where she was schooled by the Catholic sisters.

Mary was generous and charitable. Old records show that in 1874 she donated money to the Democratic Executive Committee, contributed to "R. R.'s election," aided Indianola storm sufferers, and contributed $100 towards the building of a Jewish synagogue (and Mary was Catholic).

It was noted that Mary was considered a "solid citizen," just as her late husband had been. She was not at all the frivolous, helpless type female that seemed to be in vogue during the Victorian era. She managed her hotel well, involved herself in civic affairs, and was a good parent to her fatherless children. Her oldest son, Louis, was a great deal of help to her in the management of the hotel. Although he was very young, Louis was a good businessman. He wanted to get more businesses to locate around Alamo Plaza, and he pressured the U.S. government to move the main post office there from where it had long been located on Main Plaza. Postal authorities took up the matter with the post office department in Washington, D.C., and also with the congressman from the district. The government finally approved the proposition, and the new post office was erected in 1877 at the corner of Alamo Plaza and North Alamo, where Dillard's department store is now located. The new building was two stories high and constructed of rock quarried in Medina County. The Yale and Johnson Lock Company arranged and installed the mailboxes.

Later, when this building became too small for the rapidly growing city, a new post office and federal building was erected north of the Alamo on Houston Street, at a cost of $3 million. While it is no longer the main post office, this building is still standing at that location.

In 1881, when she was sixty-three years old, Mary and her children turned the operation of the hotel over to the original contractor, Major J. H. Kampmann.

At the library of the Institute of Texan Cultures, there's a copy of the deed of sale by Mary Menger and her children, which transferred ownership of the hotel to J. H. Kampmann on November 7, 1881. The deed stated: "all those certain lots of land upon which are erected the Menger Hotel and the several buildings connected with said hotel and commonly known as Menger Hotel property." Mr. Kampmann paid $110,000 for the property.

There is another deed, written and signed on the same date, from Mary Menger to J. H. Kampmann for the sale of the Menger Hotel furnishings for the sum of $8,500. The deed listed the furnishings as follows: "chairs, tables, mirrors, wash stands, bureaus, bedsteads, bedding and all and every article of furniture in the bedrooms of said hotel. Also, all the furniture of every description, safes and other matters in the offices, parlors and sitting rooms, also all the furniture, silver and plated ware, crockery, knives, forks and spoons and glassware in the dining rooms of said hotel and belonging to the same, also all the kitchen furniture and cooking utensils of every description used in said hotel, and in fact, all the personal and moveable property used in and about said hotel for the purpose of carrying on the same, except the furniture and bedding used now by the same Mary Menger and her family."

Mary and her children retained all of their personal property and furnishings. There are several pieces still in the possession of Menger descendants. I have seen the beautiful bedroom suite, in the Eastlake style of the mid-nineteenth century, which the Mengers bought for the room of their daughter, Catherine Barbara. This furniture, still in perfect condition, consists of a high-backed carved walnut bed with a marble-topped dresser and matching washstand. It is in the home of Mrs. Robert (Marguerite) McCormick, great-great-great-granddaughter of Mary Menger. The photographs on the following pages show what lovely furnishings the Menger family possessed and the good taste they had in their selection. Catherine Barbara used this furniture during the years she lived in the Menger (she was born in the hotel, and this was the furniture she used until the family moved away in 1881). Marguerite McCormick's great-great-grandmother, Catherine Barbara, had eight children, and all of them were born in that bed!

Another piece of Menger family furniture was Mary Menger's lovely square grand piano, which she purchased in 1876 for $515. It was used for her personal enjoyment and that of the hotel guests. Now the instrument has found its way back into the hotel by courtesy of Menger family member Posie Menger McClung, where it is on permanent loan. It can be seen in the Victorian lobby.

According to records at the Catholic Chancery, Mary Menger passed away on July 3, 1887. Her burial took place the next day, July 4, 1887, at the old city cemetery. Mary was sixty-nine years old at the time.

In 1891 her eldest son, Louis William, and his wife donated a 1,500-pound bell to St. Joseph's Church. The bell, one of a set of four in matched tones, was given in memory of Mary Menger, and this bell is called the "Mary bell." It is still rung on Sundays, Holy Days of Obligation, and other joyful occasions. It was a fitting tribute to Mrs. Menger, who was a loyal charter member of the St.

Joseph's congregation. In fact, at one time, the Menger family provided lodging for the parish priest prior to the building of the
rectory.

There is an interesting book that was published by the St.
Joseph's parish, titled *St. Joseph's, 125 Year History of St. Joseph's
Church and Parish,* that mentions the Menger family numerous
times, citing their many contributions to the Catholic community.

Mary Menger's son Louis William became a charter member
and the first vice-president of the Roman Catholic Benevolent
Association that was founded in 1885. In 1892 he established the
Southern Messenger, which became the official Catholic newspaper
of Texas. He followed in the footsteps of his fine parents, becoming
a pillar of his church and community.

Piano purchased by Mary Menger in 1876.
On permanent loan to the Menger Hotel by
Posie Menger McClung, it is located in the Victorian Lobby.

Photo by author

Victorian bed, circa 1867, that belonged to Menger family.
Now the property of Menger descendant Marguerite McCormick.

Photo by author

Marble-topped washstand that belonged to Menger family, property of Menger descendant Marguerite McCormick

Photo by author

Marble-topped dresser that belonged to Menger family, property of Menger descendant Marguerite McCormick

Photo by author

Chapter 2

The Kampmann Years, 1881–1943

There could have been no buyer for the Menger better suited to take over the management of the hotel than Major John Hermann Kampmann. He was the contractor who actually built the hotel and soon after the 1859 opening was called upon to expand the facilities. He knew every brick and stone, every door and sash, and most of all, the building was his pride and joy. He was proud of all the buildings he had constructed, but the Menger was the one project he considered his best work.

John Hermann Kampmann, like William Menger, a German immigrant, came to San Antonio in May 1848. He came from an interesting and impressive background. Kampmann was born in Waltrop, Prussia, on Christmas Day, 1819. His parents were Peter and Elizabeth (Finniman) Kampmann. Peter had been a farmer prior to his death in 1844. Elizabeth was the daughter of a prominent rural family at Waltrop. Young John Hermann received a liberal education in some of the best schools and academies of Prussia and then studied architecture at the Academy of Builders in Cologne for three years. Along the way and as prerequisites to his becoming an architect, he had become proficient at the trades of blacksmith, locksmith, carpenter, mason, and stonecutter. When he was only fourteen years old, he had already begun his apprenticeship, working each summer and attending the academy during

Major John Hermann Kampmann

Texas University Institute of Texan Cultures, photo courtesy of Ike Kampmann Jr.

the winter months. He also served in the Prussian army for two years. He stayed in Germany until 1848, and for about the last four years he spent in his homeland he was the principal architect for Count Fuerstenburg at Steinheim.

It was often said that Kampmann was a self-made man. His family, while comfortable, was not wealthy, and it was largely through his own efforts and ambition that he was able to receive an education and rise to some measure of proficiency in his chosen profession prior to leaving Germany. Unfortunately, in the German revolution of 1848 Kampmann was suspected of having some republican leanings. And although he committed no overt acts, he decided his safety hinged on leaving Germany, and that is why he came to America.

Kampmann first landed in New Orleans and then took a vessel to Galveston. From that port he came overland to the German colony at New Braunfels in Comal County. While he was there he lent money to someone who unfortunately did not repay him, and by the time he decided to come to San Antonio, he was almost destitute.

Kampmann was well trained to support himself, and it wasn't any time until he had established himself as a stonemason. By 1850 he had prospered sufficiently to begin practice as an architect and master builder. There were many immigrants moving into the frontier city, and there was a great demand for experienced builders. Kampmann rapidly became well known and well established. He accumulated some property and built some of the finest buildings and residences in the city. The Menger Hotel was one of these structures.

In 1849 John Hermann married Caroline Bonnet of San Antonio. They were a popular couple and were involved in much of the early civic and social life of San Antonio. Like many other citizens of his adopted city, Kampmann joined the Confederate army in 1861. He went in as a captain of a company of German troops, which he raised, and throughout the war, his service was within the state of Texas. He was later promoted to the rank of major of the Third Texas Infantry, of which his company was a part. He was very proud of his military service, and when the war was over, he always used the military title of "Major."

After the war Kampmann again became involved in the building business and established a sash, blind, and door factory. He was extremely successful and became one of the city's leading citizens. He built many notable structures, including the Edward Steves home and the Carl Groos home, both located in the King William historic district, the German-English school, and St. Mark's Episcopal Church, which was completed in 1875. He also built the lovely St. Joseph's Catholic Church, located on Commerce Street. The cornerstone for the church, which largely served the German community of Catholics, was laid in 1868, and the church was completed in 1871.

An article that appeared in the January 12, 1872 edition of the *San Antonio Herald* mentions the prominent Kampmann and his beautiful home:

> Happening over in the vicinity of where the Railroad Depots are to be and passing by the residence of Major Kampmann, a day or two ago, that worthy gentleman invited us in to look at his new fountain, which he has just got into operation. It is situated in the South-East corner of the grounds on which his palatial residence is located, and is certainly a perfect beauty, emitting eight or ten streams likened to the branches of the weeping willow, as also one central jet that shoots up in a straight direction to the height of some twelve or fifteen feet. The fountain is of cast-iron, and sets in a basin of same material, some eight or ten feet in diameter, all from Philadelphia. It is well worth a ride over to the Major's premises any beautiful evening to take a look at this charming work of art. Such adornments as these are well calculated to sweeten life to all those who can afford them, as can our excellent friend? Maj. Kampmann is an eminent example of what can be achieved here in San Antonio by enterprise and foresight. By profession, he is a builder; and the Menger Hotel and a majority of the fine business blocks in this city, attest how successful has been his career. The Major is a man of large means and carries on his operations to great advantage, especially through his ample, steam machine works, where, from sawing the largest blocks of stone to the dressing and mortising of the simplest piece of woodwork, everything is done by machinery.

Major Kampmann has hardly yet reached the prime of life, and if health were spared him, *and we could ever get a Railroad,* we shall expect to witness the rising of many a noble structure under his masterly enterprise. He has our best wishes for his continued good health and for an indefinite extension of his career of usefulness.

Caroline Kampmann also received mention in the news media in 1875, when Kampmann was involved in the building of St. Marks Episcopal Church. The *San Antonio Herald*, May 12, 1875, stated:

One of the windows has been promised us by the estimable wife of our worthy contractor and builder, Major Kampmann, as a thank offering for her restoration to health.

Major Kampmann did, indeed, live to see the railroad arrive in San Antonio. The great event took place in 1877. A long and wordy report of the celebration appeared in the February 20, 1877 edition of the *San Antonio Express*. Although Major Kampmann was not yet the owner of the Menger, he took part in the procession, which escorted R. H. Hubbard, the governor of the state of Texas, the railroad officials, and numerous other dignitaries to Alamo Plaza. It was quite a remarkable celebration by all accounts. Large numbers of people from Galveston and Houston and towns all along the railroad route came to the big celebration that ended in a memorable procession from the new depot to Alamo Plaza, where all the dignitaries formed en masse in front of the Menger Hotel. The procession must have been a sight to see! In advance came four tall standards, bearing three small American flags and a festoon of Chinese lanterns and other shining decorations, with hundreds of flaming torches interspersed along the line, making the parade with its undulating lights a thing of great glamour and beauty. Perhaps, without knowing it, these early city fathers planted the seed that would one day become our glorious illuminated Fiesta Flambeau nighttime parade.

Soon after the railroad arrived in San Antonio, the Galveston, Harrisburg and San Antonio Railway opened a ticket office in the Menger Hotel, according to Morrison and Fourmy's *General Directory of the city of San Antonio*. This classified directory for the year 1881-82 showed there were two railroads serving the community. Besides the Galveston, Harrisburg and San Antonio, there was the International and Great Northern Railroad as well.

When Major Kampmann bought the hotel from Mary Menger in 1881, he almost immediately started to remodel the hotel. He added an east wing, including another lobby, and increased the capacity of the hotel dining room to where it could seat 160 people at one time. The kitchen was relocated, and a third story was added to the Alamo Plaza portion, along with a three-story addition to the north. Water was piped to every room, and a laundry was added.

There were quite a few private bathrooms added to guest-rooms, although not all the rooms yet had private baths. It is interesting to note that guests traveling to San Antonio by rail used to make a mad dash, actually running, to the Menger, to get there first in order to secure a room with a bath! There was also a sort of communal bath made available where water was brought in to provide baths for dusty, dirty cowboys and trail riders.

In 1882 the owner established a means of housing the hired help. Cottage-like accommodations were built in the rear of the courtyard. The original Menger cottage, which was probably a part of their old boardinghouse, was used as general headquarters for female employees. A number of small separate cottages served as their sleeping quarters. Male employees had a similar setup in a different part of the courtyard.

Black employees were provided with a central clubhouse for off-duty comfort, but they did not sleep on the hotel premises. In those days there were several blocks of small one-family dwellings located to the east of the hotel, and this is probably where most of these employees lived.

From the September 1983 edition of the *Texas Historian*, Volume XLIX, an 1885 survey had high praise for the Menger:

Every modern convenience and appliance is brought into requisition to justify and support its claims to patronage. An elegant bar room, billiard hall, and barbershop are connected with the hotel, also telegraph, and telephone for the general accommodation of guests. The furnishing is in keeping with comfort as well as style, the 150 sleeping rooms affording ample accommodations for 250 persons. Water is conducted to every floor and the building contains bathrooms and laundry.

Major Kampmann turned the operations of the hotel over to his son, Hermann D., and retired from active participation in his numerous businesses not long after having purchased the hotel from Mary Menger. Major Kampmann was vacationing in Colorado Springs at the time of his death, September 6, 1885. He was sixty-six years old.

Young Hermann was born in San Antonio, September 7, 1857, and was a lifelong resident of the city. He was an astute businessman, having become very successful even before he took over the management of the hotel from his father. He, like his father, became one of San Antonio's most prominent businessmen. He owned extensive properties and was a partner for a time in the Lockwood-Kampmann Bank. He eventually sold his interest in that business to Mr. Lockwood and then purchased the San Antonio Gas Company and the San Antonio Electric Light Company. Later he sold these enterprises to Mr. Emerson McMillan of St. Louis so he could devote all of his time to managing the Menger Hotel. He was dedicated to the hotel and spent much time and money improving its facilities.

Hermann was married in 1880 to the lovely Elizabeth Simpson, whose father was a very prominent San Antonio attorney. The couple had four children: John Hermann, Isaac Simpson, Eda (who married J. H. Frost), and Robert Simpson.

Hermann D. Kampmann

Texas University Institute of Texan Cultures. Photo courtesy of Ike Kampmann Jr.

In 1886 the *San Antonio Light* ran an interesting article about the "capitalists" in San Antonio. Fourteen of the most wealthy and successful men in the city were written about in this article, which ran on September 28:

San Antonio was a Spanish military post in 1716; received its first charter from the Spanish Government in 1733; celebrated as containing the Alamo and as a winter resort for consumptives; population, 30,991; number of children in attendance in the public schools. There are a number of capitalists in the city.

The *Light* article went on to list the fourteen men, all leading citizens. Hermann Kampmann was among those singled out by the newspaper:

> Hermann Kampmann, banker, estimated wealth: $850,000. Assessed $447,090; taxes $5588; consists in real estate, stocks, etc. partly inherited, partly acquired; is engaged in banking, a brewery and many other important enterprises; independent in politics, with democratic leanings; anti-silver dollar; native of this city.

In 1887 Hermann decided that the hotel needed a new taproom, or saloon. He sent an architect to London to sketch and study the famous pub at the House of Lords. These sketches were later implemented into the Menger Bar's design. The bar today is such a famous part of the hotel and is so closely tied with Teddy Roosevelt and his famous Rough Riders, a later chapter is devoted to just this section of the hostelry. The addition of the Menger Bar was one of Hermann's best decisions and certainly was well accepted by his clientele. In the same year that the bar was added, 1887, a fourth floor was also added to the Blum Street side. In addition, a steam elevator, a steam laundry, electric lights (which replaced earlier gaslights), and an artesian well were all amenities added to the Menger.

About this time also, a comfortable reading room was added to the hotel. Here came many early writers and chroniclers of life in the Southwest to wile away their time within the cool rooms of the old hotel. In order to encourage literary pursuit, the hotel provided four copies each of the following publications: the *San Antonio Herald,* the *San Antonio Express,* the *San Antonio Freie Presse,* the *New Orleans Picayune,* the *Galveston News,* the *Kansas City Times,* and the *American Brewer's Gazette.* In addition, the reading tables held copies of the *Texas New Yorker, Oakville Tribune, New Orleans Morning Star,* and the *New Orleans Zeitung.* As time went on the *Gray's Atlas* was offered to readers as well.

A charming tearoom, largely used by the ladies, was also a popular hotel feature. The area, furnished with tufted settees and bentwood tables, was decorated with green plants and ferns, vines, and bouquets of fresh flowers.

On September 18, 1889, the *San Antonio Express* printed the following notice that referred to the Menger Hotel:

> The leading hotel in the Southwest, having been thoroughly overhauled and renovated. Fine billiard and barrooms attached. Hot and cold baths. Large sample rooms for commercial men. Patronage of the traveling public solicited.

In 1896 Kampmann bought all furniture, appliances, and personal property in and around the Menger Hotel from his mother, Caroline Kampmann. In 1897 he had more remodeling and modernizing done at the hotel. The kitchen was again remodeled, and new fixtures and furnishings were added to the dining room. After this remodeling the *San Antonio Daily Express*, August 12, 1897, noted:

> The Menger has been practically rebuilt from basement to capstone since last season and old experienced tourists, who have visited all parts of the world, pronounce the new Menger to be unexcelled by any hotel in the country.
>
> The Menger has been a famous landmark in San Antonio for nearly half a century and is known from the Atlantic to the Pacific and from Canada to South America. Its fame has even traveled beyond the seas and hundreds of England's titled citizens have enjoyed its hospitality. It was the starting point for stages, which were then the mode of conveyance, for the railroads had not at that time reached the great metropolis of southwest Texas. The hotel people never failed to provide their departing patrons with a most appetizing lunch, as eating stations were few and far between.

The hotel, his numerous business interests, and his family obligations were taking their toll on Hermann. He reluctantly made a decision to let someone else take over the management of his hotel. The *San Antonio Daily Express* made the following announcement on August 12, 1897:

> Under new management from September 1, 1897; the many other interests of the owner and previous manager, Hermann D. Kampmann, demanded more time than he could give while managing the hotel. He ended his search for competent successors by reaching an agreement with the experienced and well-known hotel managers J. W. McClean and J. H. Mudge. Kampmann directed the enterprise but left active management to McLean and Mudge.

Although Kampmann had relinquished the management of the hotel to McClean and Mudge, he still made the major decisions. In 1899 Mr. Kampmann initiated the building of a fifty-room addition.

Hermann D. Kampmann, the dedicated innovator, died in 1902 as the result of a fatal buggy accident. He was only forty-five years old. The hotel, as well as the Kampmann Building, stayed in the family. But the days of real dedication were largely over.

There was another attempt, under Kampmann ownership, to improve the hotel. This was accomplished in 1909, when the Kampmanns employed the famous English-born architect Alfred Giles to extensively improve the hotel. The front wall was replaced with a French facade. A fine marble floor was laid in the 1881 lobby, and an arched opening from the lobby to the patio was made. A patterned tile floor, made of tiny octagonal-shaped tiles, was laid in the Victorian lobby, while ornate Corinthian columns were added as a dominating feature of the oval-shaped lobby. With this "face-lifting" the Menger still was in the running among the most elegant of San Antonio's hotels. This refurbishing took place at just the time the Crockett and Gunter Hotels opened. Competition was becoming fierce in San Antonio, and the Menger, being older, had to keep up with the times and with the competition.

Colonnade and front entrance to Menger Hotel, circa 1910
Ilse Griffith Collection, courtesy Ingrid Kokinda

In 1912 the famous architect Atlee B. Ayres was commissioned by the Kampmann family to renovate the dining room and add thirty additional guestrooms.

According to Ike Kampmann Jr., his grandmother, Elizabeth Simpson Kampmann, was a distinguished, elegant lady. She had luxurious tastes in her choice of clothes and furnishings. She loved to travel and was generally accompanied by a French maid. She had enjoyed the luxuries that her wealthy, successful husband, Hermann, had provided for her and their four children. Managing a hotel with all of its accompanying responsibilities were not of paramount interest to her. Her children were not too interested in the hotel either. John Hermann married Mary Melon from Pittsburgh. He became a businessman and investor but had little interest in the management of the hotel. Eda became a part of another prominent San Antonio family, when she married J. H. Frost. Isaac

Menger Hotel facing Alamo Plaza, circa 1920
Ilse Griffith Collection, courtesy Ingrid Kokinda

Simpson (Ike) Kampmann was born in 1882. He graduated from Princeton University in 1905 and Harvard Law School in 1908. He chose the profession of his maternal grandfather, and when he graduated, he came back to San Antonio and became established in the practice of law. Robert Simpson Kampmann served in the U.S. Navy in World War I. He eloped with a Philadelphia girl, but the marriage did not last. After the divorce Robert came back to San Antonio in 1934. He actually moved into the Menger and lived there for a short time. In ill health, Robert did not have much to do with the management of the property. He died at the Menger in 1935, according to Ike Jr., who said he was still in college when his "Uncle Bob" died. Ike Jr. is a graduate of Princeton, class of 1939, and he later graduated from law school at the University of Texas.

In an interesting visit with Ike Kampmann Jr., he recalled that his father, Isaac Simpson Kampmann, struggled for a time with the management of the hotel, since his siblings and his mother were not willing to take charge. He had managers who stayed there, but he never lived there. Isaac was a family man, with three school-aged children, and he was establishing a law practice. Isaac, like his siblings, had a quarter interest in the hotel. Eda, who married J. H. Frost, had two children. She died fairly young, literally working herself to death as a Red Cross worker during the flu epidemic in 1918, succumbing herself to that scourge. Her two children inherited her quarter interest in the Menger.

Robert had no children when he died, so there were no offspring from him to take over his interest in the hotel. Ike said that his father, Isaac, was the only one of the Kampmann children that was involved with running the hotel.

In the years following World War I, the hotel began to decline. It was not big enough for some of the major conventions and social events of the day. That business began to go to the larger Gunter and St. Anthony Hotels, or to the new San Antonio Country Club according to writer Grant Lyons, in his article "The Ghosts of the Menger," which appeared in the *San Antonio Magazine*, March 1979.

By 1929 the hotel was considered so run down it was no longer mentioned in the San Antonio guidebooks. It was fast coming up to the time of the Depression, when people did not have the money to travel and seek out plush accommodations. The business slowed markedly. There was not enough money coming in to make necessary repairs. The hotel entered a state of what one might call "declining elegance" during the thirties and forties as various managers came and went. By the outbreak of World War II, plans were afoot to tear the old hotel down and use the land for a parking area. Lovers of Texas history and Texas tradition and thus lovers of the grand old hotel came to its rescue. Eloquent stories ran in newspapers and magazines. Public pleas were made to save the hotel. It was time for a savior, and one stood in the wings.

His name was Mr. William Lewis Moody Jr.

Chapter 3

The Moody Years, 1943 to Present

New Ownership: New Life

*W*hen the time came for the aging hotel to be saved from the wrecking crew, there was no one in the state of Texas better equipped to come to the rescue than William Lewis Moody Jr.

After the hotel was purchased in 1943, the National Hotel Corporation, which Moody founded in 1928, actually took possession of the property on June 30, 1944. Not much could be done towards restoring or remodeling the old landmark at that time. The country was in the midst of World War II, and there was a shortage of both materials and manpower. But with the end of the conflict in 1945, the wheels rapidly began to turn. Plans were drawn up for the complete restoration of the original building. There was to be new plumbing and electrical fixtures, new decorations, and a complete restoration of the Spanish patio gardens. Worn floor coverings were to be replaced with miles of new carpeting, and guestrooms and public rooms alike were slated to receive a complete face lifting.

A newly equipped kitchen with a $100,000 price tag was also on the drawing boards. The artworks scattered all over the property were to be painstakingly restored by Ernst Raba, a local artist of considerable talent. Antique furniture was to be refinished and reupholstered, and the Colonial Dining Room was to be fully restored to its former splendor.

After all of this was accomplished, in 1948 most of the lobby added by Major Kampmann in 1881 and the guestrooms on the floors above it were completely torn down. A spacious new lobby overlooking the tranquil Spanish patio gardens was built to replace the section that was torn down. Three floors of comfortable air-conditioned guestrooms were added above this lobby. The original portion of the hotel, built in 1859 by William Menger, was left intact and remains so to this day.

Menger Hotel, circa 1950
Photo courtesy Menger Hotel

On March 2, 1951, Mr. Moody was honored by the San Antonio Conservation Society for his outstanding restoration of the Menger Hotel, one of San Antonio's major landmarks.

In 1953 a very large swimming pool was added to the second patio located immediately behind the Spanish patio.

Although W. L. Moody Jr. passed away in 1954, the Hotel Corporation, now headed by Mary Moody Northen, daughter of the late W. L. Moody Jr., continued to successfully operate the hotel. In 1959, when the hotel celebrated its centennial with a gala ball, Mrs. Northen was there to join in the festivities.

In 1968, just in time for the World's Fair held in San Antonio, known as the Hemisfair, the Menger spent over $1.5 million on a five-story addition consisting of 110 guestrooms. This addition became known as the "Motor Hotel," with drive-in convenience and available valet parking. Famous architects Atlee B. Ayres and Robert Ayres were chosen to design this mammoth project. A few years later, in 1977, major restoration work on the original Victorian section of the building was completed.

In 1987 thirty-three new rooms and suites plus a magnificent grand ballroom and adjacent meeting rooms were added to the rear portion of the property facing the Rivercenter Mall.

Hotel Awarded State Historic Marker

Praised as the "oldest continually operated hotel west of the Mississippi," the hotel was presented with the equivalent of the "Oscar" for old buildings when it was awarded a state historic marker in 1980. The marker, establishing the building as a vital part of San Antonio and Texas history, was presented at a special unveiling ceremony held in front of the hotel. The large bronze plaque, which briefly capsules the hotel's history, may still be seen at the entrance to the Victorian section of the building. The inscription reads as follows:

William A. (1827-1871) and Mary Menger, both born in Germany, opened a boarding house and brewery at this site in 1855, when most local business was still clustered around Main Plaza and Military Plaza. The popularity of the boarding house led Menger to replace it with a two-story stone hotel erected at the corner of Blum and Alamo Plaza in 1859. Mary Menger sold the hotel in 1881 to J. H. Kampmann, the builder of the first portion of the structure. Famed for its excellent meals and beautiful patio garden, the Menger was San Antonio's most prominent hotel in the nineteenth century. It attracted many well-known visitors and was periodically enlarged and remodeled to accommodate more guests. Cattlemen such as Richard King stayed here during the era of the great cattle drives. Other guests included Generals U. S. Grant, Robert E. Lee, and John Pershing, Poet Sidney Lanier, Writer O. Henry (William Sidney Porter) and performers at the Grand Opera House located across the Plaza. Theodore Roosevelt recruited his regiment of "Rough Riders" for the Spanish-American War at the Menger in 1898. Purchased in 1943 by W. L. Moody, Jr., the hotel was further expanded in 1966-67 to cover the entire block.

Mary Moody Northen was present for the unveiling. During this visit to San Antonio, the dynamic businesswoman was showered with various honors in appreciation for her support of historical preservation. She had recently presented a grant of $25,000 to San Jose Mission.

Mrs. Northen was also presented with the Alcaldesa Award by Mayor Lila Cockrell, the Hildalgo Award from County Commissioner (now State Senator) Jeff Wentworth, and the Texas Historical Commission Silver Spur of Bexar, a replica of a seventeenth-century spur.

Mary Moody Northen passed away in 1986, and the baton for the vast Moody holdings was passed on to her nephew, Mr. Robert L. Moody Jr. He continues as chairman of the Moody Foundation.

In 1991 the Hotel Corporation completed restoration of an 8,000-square-foot retail space on the Alamo Plaza side of the building. The hotel entrance was restored, uncovering a huge limestone archway at the entrance. By 1992 restoration work at the hotel had been completed to the tune of around $9 million.

The National Hotel Corporation is known today as Gal-Tex Hotel Corporation. Robert L. Moody Jr. is chairman of the board. In 1999 the corporation bought the Crockett Hotel, just across Crockett Street from the Menger.

The Menger Hotel and its neighbor the Crockett are in excellent hands. The ownership is now in the fourth generation of Moodys, a truly distinctive family. To better understand and appreciate the current ownership and operation of the Menger, I would like to briefly acquaint you with three generations of this remarkable family.

Colonel William Lewis Moody

William Lewis Moody was born in Essex County, Virginia, on May 19, 1828. He studied at the University of Virginia and received a law degree from that institution in 1851. He came to Texas in

1852, traveling by boat to the ports of New Orleans and Galveston, and then overland to the then small towns of Houston and Fairfield. He settled in Fairfield and took up the practice of law. As a sideline, he also became involved in the mercantile business. On January 19, 1860, the thirty-two-year-old lawyer married Pherabe Elizabeth Bradley.

Moody left Fairfield and moved to Galveston to become a merchant. Old records imply that ill health forced him to give up his law practice. In 1861, when Texas seceded from the Union, Moody, a devoted

Colonel William Lewis Moody
Courtesy Gal-Tex Hotel Corporation

Southerner, donned the gray uniform of the Confederacy and raised Company G of the 7th Texas Infantry, which was captured at Fort Donelson in 1862. He spent time in Union prison camps at Douglas, Chase, and Johnson's Island and was finally exchanged in the fall of 1862. He was sent with his regiment to Mississippi, where he was promoted to lieutenant colonel. He was commended for bravery at Raymond and gravely wounded at Jackson, Mississippi, in 1863. Lastly, having advanced in rank to colonel, the young officer sadly surrendered his troops to Union forces in Austin, Texas, in 1865. The war was over. It was time to go home to Pherabe and get on with his life.

Moody was proud of having served the Confederacy. He liked to be called "Colonel," and the title stuck with him through the remainder of his life.

The family soon established themselves in Galveston. They had six children: three sons and three daughters. Moody opened a cotton business, and this is where he made his initial fortune. He also became a director for the Gulf, Colorado, and Santa Fe Railway Company and was instrumental in the construction of a deep-water port for the city of Galveston. In addition, he was a member of the Texas legislature in 1874 and a delegate to both state and national Democratic conventions.

Moody served Galveston as an alderman, and in 1875 Governor Richard Coke appointed him as the State of Texas Financial Agent.

Although the Moodys were blessed with six children, the first-born, William Lewis Jr., was his father's favorite. Young Moody was born in Fairfield on January 25, 1865. He was a rather frail child. His father, who still had strong ties to his native Virginia, elected to send the youngster to that state for his education. He first was sent to Roanoke to receive his primary education at Hollins Institute. He later attended two other boarding schools before he completed his studies at the Virginia Military Institute. He then studied for a time in Germany. Finally, he returned to Texas and took up the study of law at the University of Texas. He then returned to

Galveston, becoming a junior partner in his father's cotton factoring firm, W. L. Moody and Company, in 1886.

In 1900 a devastating hurricane almost destroyed Galveston Island. Colonel Moody and young W. L. Jr. were instrumental in rebuilding the island's economy.

Colonel Moody lived a long life, with many fine accomplishments to his credit. He left a mighty legacy to his children and especially to William L. Jr., who always preferred to be referred to as "Junior," by way of honoring his beloved father. Colonel Moody died on July 17, 1920, and was returned to Chesterfield County, Virginia, his childhood home, for burial.

Colonel William Lewis Moody
Photo courtesy Rosenberg Library, Galveston, Texas

William Lewis Moody Jr.

When young Moody returned to Galveston after receiving his education, he was ready to take his place beside his father in business. If anything, he was probably more ambitious than the senior Moody. His main interest was the family business. He persuaded his father to open a private bank in 1889. In 1890 he married Libbie Rice Shearn of Houston. The couple had four children: Mary, W. L. Moody III, Shearn, and Libbie. In 1900 he acquired a beautiful mansion at 2618 Broadway that became the family home. Today it is known as the Moody Museum and is open to the public.

William Lewis Moody Junior

Photo courtesy Rosenberg Library, Galveston, Texas

Although the term "workaholic" had probably not yet been coined when Moody joined his father's enterprises, one might be tempted to use it in describing the late Mr. Moody. He was a human dynamo of energy and ability, and his capabilities were amazing! In 1907 he organized the City National Bank of Galveston, which later was renamed the Moody National Bank. In 1913 he established the Moody Cotton Compress. He also organized the American National Insurance Company, one of the largest companies in the South. In 1920 he established the American Printing Company of Galveston, and in 1923 he acquired the *Galveston News*, the oldest newspaper in Texas. Later he also purchased the *Galveston Tribune* and consolidated the two papers. They remained in the Moody enterprises for many years, until they were sold in 1964. In addition, the dynamic Moody founded the National Hotel Corporation in 1928. At one time the corporation held as many as forty hotels, from the Atlantic seaboard to the Rocky Mountain states. He even built several of these hotels including the Buccaneer and the Jean Lafitte in Galveston. He purchased the famous Mountain Lake Hotel in Virginia and Hotel Washington in Washington, D.C. He purchased the Menger, the subject of this book, in 1943. At the time he bought the Menger, he was already seventy-eight years old. Most men would have long since retired. But Moody was certainly no ordinary man. He seemed to thrive on long hours, big plans, and big business!

As if all these business holdings were not enough to exhaust most ordinary individuals, Moody also owned as many as eleven different ranches in Texas and Oklahoma, numbering several hundred thousand acres. He also had land holdings in West Virginia and Mexico. Although ranching wasn't one of his chief interests, he did enjoy the ranches and used them for duck hunting and fishing. They were also used for cattle, sheep, and goat raising operations. He especially enjoyed visiting the Silver Lake Ranch where he spent the months of April and October as he grew older. He often used it for entertaining his friends at grand house parties.

Mr. Moody and his wife, Libbie, left a great legacy to the state of Texas, the Moody Foundation, which they founded in 1942. At first the foundation focused on several small projects, including the Moody State School for Cerebral Palsied Children. Mr. Moody passed away on July 21, 1954, at the age of eighty-nine. He was active up until two days before his death. The bulk of his fortune was transferred to the Moody Foundation, one of the largest in the nation. The stated purpose of the foundation was to assist religious, charitable, scientific, and educational organizations within the state of Texas.

Mary Moody Northen

Mary, who was born on February 10, 1892, was the oldest child of William and Libbie Moody. She was a frail child and was tutored at home. She didn't have a lot of childhood friends, because she was so sheltered. However her education did not suffer. It was said she was conversant in Spanish, German, and French and was given a fine background in business and economics in order to prepare for the role she would someday play. She never attended a college or university, yet her business career was so outstanding, she was awarded honorary doctoral degrees by five Texas universities. These included: Southern Methodist University in Dallas, Southwestern University in Georgetown, Our Lady of the Lake University in San Antonio, St. Edwards University in Austin, and Texas Wesleyan University in Fort Worth. She was also awarded the coveted Santa Rita Award by the University of Texas in 1976, which is the highest honor the University of Texas system can bestow.

Although William Moody had four children, it was no secret that Mary, the eldest, was his favorite. Although she never worked for a salary, Mary gained tremendous business judgement just by being in close contact with her father. The two seemed to think and react in the same ways, and Mary was intensely interested in her father's businesses. He confided in her, and she became an astute businesswoman. She married Edwin Clyde Northen in 1915. The couple had no children, and Mary did not have to work, so she spent much time with her father, learning about the intricacies of his many-faceted business empire. When William died in 1954, she was the person he selected to become his successor.

Mary suffered two terrible losses in 1954. Her beloved father died, and then, just a few months later, her husband of thirty-nine years passed away as well. She must have been devastated! Mary was sixty-two years old, at an age where most people would have already been retired, and she was handed the responsibility of becoming the president of more than fifty corporations. Her business acumen and her attention to details gained for her the honorary title of "First Lady of Finance." She was truly one of the most intelligent and illustrious women in America and was greatly loved in her home city of Galveston. Even when she was up in her nineties, this dynamic woman still served as senior chairman of the board of Moody National Bank of Galveston. She was a member of the board of directors of the American National Insurance Company and a member of the board of the Gal-Tex Hotel Corporation. She was also chairman of the board of trustees for the Moody Foundation, which was established by her late parents.

Mrs. Northen received such widely diverse awards as the Distinguished Texan Award presented by Governor Dolph Briscoe, the prestigious Silver Fawn Award presented by Boy Scouts of America, and the William Booth Award from the Salvation Army. She was the first and only woman ever to serve on the board of Virginia Military Institute Foundation and was presented an honorary degree by that institution, becoming the only female alumna of that all-male institution. Her accomplishments, philanthropies, and interests would fill pages!

When reading of her life, the term "frail" came back again and again. The Galveston papers stated in her last years she was "like a China doll, fragile, precious, and coveted." I wonder, had she been younger and in robust health, what more she might have accomplished. In fact, she survived a broken hip at the age of seventy-nine and an acute appendectomy at the age of eighty-four!

Mary Moody Northen
Photo courtesy Rosenberg Library, Galveston, Texas

Up until the time of her death, on August 25, 1986, over ninety million dollars had gone out from the Moody Foundation to educational institutions, health care services, to promote the arts and humanities, to cultural and humanitarian organizations, medical centers, and social services, all within the state of Texas. It was little wonder that the city of Galveston and the state of Texas mourned the passing of one so kind, unselfish, and philanthropic.

The "Grand Dame" of Galveston was laid to rest in the Galveston Memorial Park in Hitchcock. Five former governors, including Price Daniel, John Connally, Preston Smith, Dolph Briscoe, William Clements, and Governor Mark White, Lt. Governor William H. Hobby, Governor Mills Godwin of Virginia, Senators Harry Byrd Jr. and Elmon T. Gray of Virginia, numerous judges, generals, admirals, and other notables made up the contingent of honorary pallbearers. All came to pay tribute to a woman who lived a life of giving and sharing.

Robert L. Moody

Robert L. Moody is the present chairman of the Moody Foundation. Moody is the son of the late Shearn Moody Sr. and the grandson of William L. Moody Jr. He is the nephew of the late Mary Moody Northen. Now, at the age of sixty-four, Mr. Moody stands at the helm of not only the Moody Foundation, but he is chairman of the board, Gal-Tex Hotel Corporation, chairman of the American National Insurance Company, and owner of the Moody National Bank. His business interests number in the scores. He is an energetic businessman who has followed closely in the footsteps of his predecessors. He has three sons, two of whom are already actively involved in the Moody interests.

Like those who went before him, Robert L. Moody is not only a successful businessman, but he has provided leadership for a vast number of civic and charitable endeavors. Moody was recently awarded the prestigious "2000 Citizen of the Year" award by the *Galveston Daily News.* In presenting this award, *Daily News* president and publisher Dolph Tillotson stated that Mr. Moody is one of those rare individuals who have the ability and take the opportunity to change the world for the better. Moody, whose forebears are numbered among Galveston's most illustrious founding families, said much of the credit for his work belongs to the Moodys who came before him. He said he just hoped to continue to carry on the legacy.

One attribute the Moodys all seemed to possess is the good judgement to surround themselves with capable, competent lieutenants to run their vast corporate empire. No single man or woman could do so many things so well without help. To comprehend the continuing success of the Menger Hotel as it now moves into a new millenium, one has to be aware of the vast energy, resources, and managerial expertise generated by the Moody family and the Gal-Tex Hotel Corporation. The Moodys are truly one of Texas's first and finest families, and they might well serve as role models for anyone with aspirations of success.

Today's Menger Management

The Gal-Tex Hotel Corporation has placed Mr. Hector R. Venegas in the position of general manager of the Menger Hotel. He has served in that position since his arrival in San Antonio six years ago. He has been employed by the Gal-Tex Corporation for nine years.

Previously, Mr. Venegas served at hotels in Central America, South America, Europe, and Africa during his forty years in the hotel business. He was employed previously by the Inter-Continental Hotels and the Sheraton Hotels: International Division. Venegas, who was born in San Juan, Puerto Rico, holds degrees from Tulane University and New York University. The affable manager and his charming wife, Mari, make their home in the Menger Hotel.

Ernesto Malacara is the assistant general manager and has been with the hotel for almost twenty-five years.

The Menger: A Historic Hotel of America

The Menger Hotel is a registered national, state, and city land-mark. In 1989 the National Trust for Historic Preservation named the Menger as one of thirty-two charter members of a program called the "Historic Hotels of America." The hotels were selected because of their historic architecture and ambiance.

Hotels in the program must be at least fifty years old and be listed in, or be eligible for, the National Register of Historic Places or recognized by a state or local government as having historical significance.

Today's Menger Serves the Community

The current management at the Menger Hotel has instigated some wonderful "happenings" for the children of the community. Mr. Malacara and Mr. Venegas seem to enjoy these occasions as much as the children that they have been designed to entertain.

For the past two years, the hotel has held a grand Halloween party for youngsters. The honorees are from various children's homes and the San Antonio Children's Shelter. These children are unable to go trick or treating in neighborhoods, and so this party gives them their own special Halloween observance. One of the meeting rooms was decked out in Halloween regalia, with spooky sounds and lights. The youngsters enjoyed having a few whole-some shivers as they filed through the display. A number of volunteers helped with the festivities. There were mimes, balloon artists who made animals and special toys out of balloons to delight the small fry, and caricaturists who sketched special pictures for them. Clowns mingled through the crowd of over two hundred youngsters, and there were magic acts as well! Child-oriented refreshments of pizza slices, hot dogs, and hamburgers were the order of the day, and there was a big orange-and-black Halloween cake as well. I have never seen happier, more delighted children. They were on their best behavior, too, and were a completely orderly group. Perhaps their sponsors and teachers had given them fair warning to behave. The delightful evenings closed with the breaking of pinatas as happy youngsters scrambled for the candies that fell at their feet.

I believe the hotel plans to continue this practice of providing a wonderful evening for some of San Antonio's less fortunate youngsters.

And then, there's Christmas! In 1998 the first Children's Music Festival took place the week before Christmas. A choral group of mostly blind or otherwise handicapped children from the LGSM Foundation sang Christmas carols from the balcony outside the second floor Renaissance Room. Passers by on Alamo Plaza were delighted to hear the youngsters. Patsy Torres, San Antonio's popular Hispanic recording star, was mistress of ceremonies, and Archbishop Patrick Flores was an honored guest. The hotel served cookies, empanadas, pastries, and punch to the delighted youngsters, their parents, and a few invited guests.

Archbishop Patrick Flores, at Menger Music Festival, 1999

Photo courtesy Ernesto Malacara

The 1999 event was far more ambitious. It was called "Menger Holiday Memories 1859-1999," celebrating one hundred and forty Christmases at the hotel! Seven outstanding groups performed to a full house in the hotel's grand ballroom. Mr. Hector Venegas, general manager of the hotel, and Mrs. Venegas, and assistant general manager Ernesto Malacara acted as hosts for the gala event. Patsy Torres and Archbishop Flores shared the microphone as joint master/mistress of ceremonies. An enthusiastic crowd cheered and applauded as group after group of gifted performers showcased their many-faceted talents to the gathering.

"Santa Claus," portrayed by the Menger's Jim Humphries, and lovely Patsy Torres pose at the Menger Christmas tree, 1999

Photo courtesy Ernesto Malacara

The hotel hosted a lively reception where refreshments were served to the performers, their parents, and some delighted invited guests. The Zapata Mariachi group played some impromptu numbers, and young Juanito Castillos, a ten-year-old musical prodigy, blind since birth, sang and played his guitar and accordion as the assemblage applauded and "ole'd" the evening away! The hotel plans to continue the Children's Music Festivals on an annual basis.

The most impressive thing about these events is that the hotel does this just so these youngsters can have a good time. The Halloween parties are for children from underprivileged backgrounds. The music festivals give youth groups, some of whom are handicapped, an opportunity to perform for an audience. There was no play for publicity of these events, and the news media probably did not even know they were held. I believe the San Antonio community should know what the Menger does for its youth. The hotel people went all out to show them a good time. Talented staff members painted backdrops, ran spotlights and sound equipment, and served refreshments. Much energy was expended in making these events truly memorable for these youngsters.

Woodstone Elementary School Chorus gathers around the Menger Christmas tree, 1999

Photo courtesy Ernesto Malacara

The Menger Moves Right Along

After reading of the three ownerships of the hotel: the Mengers, the Kampmanns, and the Moody family, you are probably as impressed as I was when I began to research the material for this book. All three families have been solid citizens, with flawless reputations, who have shown great dedication to the hotel and to the community. And isn't it remarkable that in over one hundred and forty years, there have been only three ownerships of the hotel? No wonder so much of the original furniture and artworks are still in place, lovingly tended and kept in mint condition!

Now you are acquainted with the historical background of this grand old inn. In the next chapter you are invited to "take a tour," to view some of the art treasures and antiques that adorn the public rooms of the hotel.

Chapter 4

Let's Take a Tour

———————◄◆►———————

*G*oing back to my earliest recollections, I cannot recall a time when I was not drawn to, fascinated by, and held in spellbound wonder over that period in history known as the Victorian era. It was a time of overabundance. There was great elegance in fine polished and carved woods, plush fabrics, extravagant fringes and tapestries, wonderful floor and wall coverings. Great attention was given to detail, and there were beautiful cut glass and porcelain table appointments, finely chased silver, and brilliant chandeliers. This lavish style reflected what life was all about for the upper classes just prior to the outbreak of the American Civil War.

Lovers of this era must naturally be drawn to the authentically Victorian Menger Hotel, which has presided with such grace and charm over Alamo Plaza for almost a century and a half.

Each time I open the door that leads off Alamo Plaza into the original Victorian lobby, I can imagine the scene. They are there, in my mind's eye. Handsome military officers, dressed in uniform, cattlemen in dusty range clothing and boots, businessmen in impeccably tailored suits, and beautiful women wearing plume and flower bedecked bonnets in the latest fashion all mingle in the beautifully appointed reception area, as they approach the desk to sign the guest register.

It is a return, via one's imagination, to an era of graciousness and decorum far removed from today's mechanized, computerized, insulated, and refrigerated world.

I would like to share a visit to this unique and elegant hotel with you. Let us stroll through the lobbies and dining rooms, the corridors and spacious meeting rooms, and the lovely flower-scented patios. It is the same scene enjoyed by many famous and fascinating personalities who stopped at the Menger over many past decades.

The Victorian Lobby

The Victorian lobby was the location of the registration desk in the first fifty-room inn that William and Mary Menger built in 1859. The patterned tile floor we see today is one that was placed there during a 1909 remodeling by later owners, the Kampmann family. The earlier wooden floors had begun to show wear and tear after fifty years. The beautiful square grand piano we see was purchased for around $500 by Mary Menger in 1876. The instrument was used for family enjoyment and the guests' entertainment. It was removed from the hotel when Mrs. Menger sold the property in 1881 but has recently been returned to the lobby through the generosity of a Menger descendant, "Posie" Menger McClung, who has placed the piano there on permanent loan.

Across the room is a giant painting hung against the wall. It is flanked by a pair of attractive small Victorian reproduction settees. The painting, entitled *Venting Cattle on the Frisco System*, was executed by Chicago painter Frank Lewis Van Ness in 1902. The wide, flat oak frame was made especially for the large work. Van Ness was a well-known painter of portraits and genre around the turn of the century. He studied art under G. P. A. Healy, a leading portrait artist of that era. According to an article in the *San Antonio Express News* on January 22, 1995, written by columnist-historian Paula Allen:

> During the late nineteeth century and until World War II, many competent artists roamed the country and found work as illustrators, as commissioned painters, or muralists. They often worked for minimal fees and room

and board. We suspect this might be the case with F. L. Van Ness.

The giant painting was loaned to the motion picture company that filmed Edna Ferber's great classic *Giant* in 1956. You may recall the film, which was shot near Marfa, Texas, starred Rock Hudson, Elizabeth Taylor, and James Dean. The painting was seen in the set depicting the lavish drawing room of the ranch house.

Painting in the Victorian lobby, *Venting Cattle on the Frisco System*,
by F. L. Van Ness, circa 1902

Photo by author

Moving into the oval-shaped, three-storied main portion of the original Victorian lobby, one's eyes are immediately drawn to the beautiful leaded glass skylight, which was added as a part of extensive alterations and remodeling done in 1909. It is especially brilliant at midday when the sun shines through the many colors of stained glass. The original lobby was two storied, and an added story was included in the 1909 alterations. That is when the skylight was installed.

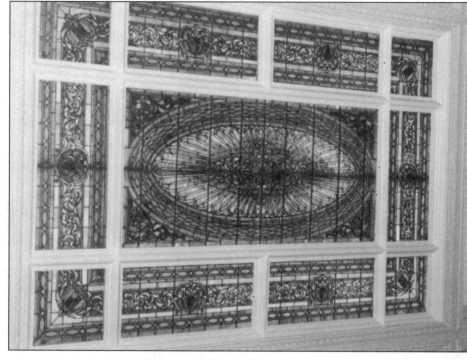

Leaded multicolored stained glass skylight, added to Victorian lobby in 1909
Photo by Martin Malacara

The rooms in this portion of the hotel run off of the circular balconies, which are protected by the original wrought iron balustrades. Guestrooms and suites in this section are most all furnished in their original antique trappings.

The Victorian lobby contains some lovely furnishings. There is a beautiful French bouelle table inlaid with tortoiseshell and brass, which centers the room and always holds a magnificent arrangement of cut flowers or living plants. Often, delicate stems of orchids are included in these floral displays.

There is a stunning French etagere against the wall. It is a beautiful example of elaborate inlay and ebonized marquetry, characteristic of the Napoleon III revival style, which was very popular in the 1860s. It is believed to be one of the pieces that William and Mary Menger had purchased on one of their buying trips to Europe and New York in the late 1860s.

French etagere, circa 1865

Photo by Martin Malacara

There is also a very fine Seth Thomas double-dialed standing clock in an oak case, handsomely decorated with griffin heads. It matches a suite of furniture that was discovered in the basement and restored. The clock still tells perfect time as well as the day of the year.

Seth Thomas wall clock in Victorian lobby

Photo by author

An attractive grouping against one wall of the lobby features a Victorian walnut settee, showing the influence of High Victoria and rococo. It is a rare example of an American made piece circa 1870.

Hanging over the settee and dominating that wall is a painting entitled *Musicians in a Wine Cellar,* by Louis O. Kunz. Kunz was an Austrian painter born in 1833 who came to America in 1848. He was primarily a muralist and landscape artist. A founder of the Chicago Art Institute, he served in the Union army during the Civil War. The painting must have had much appeal to William Menger, a cooper and a brewer as well. It depicts a comely young woman

Victorian lobby painting, *Musicians in a Wine Cellar* by Louis O. Kunz
Photo by author

dispensing wine to a couple of male musicians dressed in cavalier-like attire. The frame is of carved wood and gesso and combines a dozen linear border patterns including ears of corn.

Although it is called the Victorian lobby because it originated in the second half of the nineteenth century, this area actually reflects the sumptuous taste of noted San Antonio architect Alfred Giles, who extensively remodeled the hotel in 1909. This gentleman was the designer of the fine homes on Staff Post Road at Fort Sam Houston and many of the fine mansions in the German residential area known as the King William District. The lobby had always been charming, but it now became even more elegant in the grand neoclassical style, which had become extremely popular.

The room is dominated by eight beautiful Corinthian columns, which soar to the bottom of the third floor balcony. Prior to the remodeling, there were fewer columns and they were made of cast iron. Giles enclosed these earlier columns in hollow plaster, and

Detail on Corinthian column in Victorian lobby

Photo by Martin Malacara

several more columns were added to create symmetry, which was a very important characteristic of neoclassical design. These new columns were accented with garlands, medallions, and acanthus leaves, and were painted to resemble stone. The detail photograph shows the extent of the ornamentation.

This elegant oval lobby leads into a smaller square anteroom where the elevator is located. This brings us to the beautiful main dining room.

The Colonial Room

This room was added to the hotel during the first addition, which closely followed the initial opening. The room later was remodeled extensively by famous San Antonio architect Atlee B. Ayres in 1912. It reflects the neoclassical style of that time. The original cast-iron columns were enclosed by wooden ones in the Greek Revival style. Carved wooden dentils, arched window openings looking out on the beautiful gardens, and decorative millwork, as well as additional mirrors were added.

The unusual plaster mantel, in the rear of the room, has two caryatids, which are supporting columns having the form of a draped female figure; each is topped by an Ionic capital. Decorative scrollwork and a tablet with a nymph motif further embellish the mantel, which originally was painted to resemble wood graining.

This beautiful room has been in continual use since it first opened. It is used as the public restaurant for the hotel, but also has been used for private parties, galas, and balls.

Colonial Dining Room, as it appears today
Photo by author

The Minuet Room

The Minuet Room, slightly smaller than the Colonial Room, leads off the Colonial Room and can also be entered from the rear door leading to the patio. It is often used for overflow crowds in the Colonial Room. It is also utilized as a private party room for special meetings, receptions, and banquets. It was once used primarily as a ballroom, and many a San Antonio debutante made her bow to society in this room. It is, for some unknown reason, in this room that I always feel the pull of another era. I can visualize the scene of elegantly gowned and bejeweled dancers whirling around the room, reflected in the great mirrored walls, as musicians played romantic Strauss waltzes to inspire their graceful movements!

Ming Room

Coming from the Minuet Room through the Colonial Room back into the Victorian lobby, we turn to head into the main lobby. There is a small meeting room done in Oriental décor that we pass at this juncture. The Ming Room, we are told, was so called because the décor was inspired by the way it was once decorated for a debutante's coming out party, a glittering Oriental ball. The entire lobby and ballroom area became a scene straight out of the Far East and *Arabian Nights* on this occasion. Waiters and footmen were colorfully dressed in authentic costumes of the region. It must have been quite a colorful and exotic affair!

The Main Lobby

The main lobby is the result of an extensive remodeling that was taken on by the current owners, the Gal-Tex Hotel Corporation. The old lobby, which was added during the Kampmann ownership of the hotel, was in a deplorable condition, and the new owners found it more feasible to tear down that complete portion of the hotel and rebuild, adding another story and many more guestrooms, rather than try to renovate it. They built the brand new, very long and spacious lobby in 1949, as well as a 125-room, four-story wing and a swimming pool to the east. Although it was a shame that the earlier 1880s portion of the building was destroyed, the architectural firm of Atlee B. and Robert M. Ayres did a fine job of effectively tying in the new main lobby to the original Victorian lobby.

This lobby is extremely spacious, the dimension being one hundred feet in length and fifty feet in width. It is fitted out with several conversation areas furnished with comfortable couches and lounge chairs. There are also a trio of wooden game tables and matching chairs where guests can enjoy a game of cards, write a letter, or just gather 'round for a friendly chat. A grand piano is located at the end of the room opposite the reception desk. It plays

The main lobby, as it appears today
Photo by author

electronically for the enjoyment of hotel guests and visitors as they stroll through the comfortable lobby area.

There are several interesting pieces of furniture worthy of note in the main lobby.

There are display cases next to the fireplace containing memorabilia of all sorts. There are old ledgers and registers and pre-1900 photographs that depict the Menger's past history. There are scenes of the Victorian lobby, the original registration desk, the Colonial dining room, the laundry, and original kitchens. It is well worth the time spent to look over these glimpses into the early history of the hotel.

A beautiful walnut credenza in the Empire style is placed just behind the manager-on-duty desk. It is a fine example of the simplicity of the Empire period and was made in England around 1830. The drawer pulls were added later.

There is a very interesting oil painting, which hangs over this credenza. It is another work by Frank Lewis Van Ness, probably painted about the same time as the large Van Ness hanging in the Victorian lobby was done. The painting, entitled *Woman in Triumph*, depicts a woman who has lifted her arms high above her head, as if to triumphantly say, "The job is done!" At her feet lies a well-roped and tied young steer. This is no mean task for anyone and is not commonly attempted by women. The woman's faithful horse, a white cowpony, stands patiently in the background. A wide, flat oak frame made especially for the work accents the painting.

Until recently, no one at the hotel had a clue who the woman was or why the artist chose to paint such a subject. Then, in July 1999, Ernesto Malacara received the following letter, which clarified the painting's subject:

July 28, 1999
Dear Mr. Malacara:

I was a guest in your hotel June 9-12 for the 68th National Assembly of the Huguenot Society Founders of Manakin in the Colony of Virginia. My wife and I were very impressed by the high quality of service and friendly atmosphere of the Menger. If I am not mistaken, you were the one who spoke to our group explaining the historical background and fabulous preservation of this historic hotel. Thank you so much for your fine presentation.

One day, while sitting in the lobby, I noticed the painting of the *Woman in Triumph* standing on a roped calf. That woman was my grandmother, Celeste Willis Snyder. When I got home I pulled some 97-year-old photographs out of the file cabinet, which my family had saved through the years. Sure enough, there was my grandmother's picture on the calf. My childhood memory was confirmed. Celeste

Willis Snyder was the daughter of P. J. Willis Jr. of Galveston, a wealthy merchant. I could spend a lot of time telling about the Willis family, but one fact I'll tell you. P. J. Willis Jr. was the nephew of R. S. Willis who built and owned the Moody Mansion. The Moody Mansion is now a historical museum and tourist attraction in Galveston. Of course, I am proud of my ancestors, but I wanted to share this information with you.

Sincerely yours,
Bryan Snyder III

A final note: How coincidental! The Moody family now owns the Menger Hotel, and there is a connection to the Willis family who built the Moody Mansion in Galveston.

Bryan Snyder III stands in front of portait of his grandmother. Painting is titled *Woman in Triumph* by F. L. Van Ness.

Photo courtesy Bryan Snyder III

Also in the main lobby is a lovely glass fronted French vitrine, or display cabinet, crafted of gilt bronze, ormolu mounted mahogany. There is a valuable collection of rose medallion Chinese porcelain displayed in it, which dates from about 1840-1860. The use of the famille rose palette combined with rich decoration and extensive use of gilt was very popular at that time. In excellent condition, the porcelain ware was of the type made for export to Europe and America. This beautiful ware belonged to the Mengers. There is also a fine copper samovar displayed in the same case.

On the west wall there is a pair of matching Duncan Phyfe sofas, and hanging on the wall is a fine four-paneled painted French screen, made between 1800 and 1830. The paintings in each panel are scenes done in the late baroque style. Each of the panels is framed in an ornately carved wooden frame original to the oil canvases. It is believed that this piece was one of the items purchased for the hotel by the Mengers on one of their trips to Europe.

Picture Corridor

When you leave the main lobby and head down a long corridor past several meeting rooms, en route to the valet parking garage, you should spend a few minutes viewing a fine collection of framed photographs that have been collected over the years. There are photos of a Fiesta Parade, which took place in front of the hotel, a likeness of former guest Babe Ruth, a good photo of President Harry S. Truman, a picture of famous sculptor Gutzon Borglum and his son, Lincoln, and various others. In the corridor leading into the Menger Bar entrance, there is a fine collection of photographs of Theodore "Teddy" Roosevelt.

The Menger Bar

The Menger Bar, also known as the Roosevelt Bar, is almost as famous as the hotel itself. It may be reached from Crockett Street or via double doors leading into a corridor, which in turn leads into the main lobby. The history of the bar is so fascinating and so complex, chapter nine is devoted to the bar, its historic beginnings, and its close connection with Teddy Roosevelt and his famous volunteers, the Rough Riders.

Menger Grand Ballroom

The beautiful 6,500-square-foot Grand Ballroom, which can accommodate 750 guests, is located in the newest section of the hotel, which was added in 1988. At this time, several meeting rooms, twenty-four luxury guestrooms, and three executive suites were added. This huge ballroom can hold large banquets and gatherings of all sorts, receptions, and grand balls. It can be partitioned off into smaller, more intimate areas as well. This room is most attractive, and the crystal chandeliers are spectacular.

Meeting Rooms

On the first floor there are several meeting rooms of various sizes. These include: The **Cavalier Room** named for the men's social organization that annually selects "King Antonio" to reign over Fiesta Week. This is an organization of outstanding business and social leaders of the city. The **Grant Room** is a small room used for meetings and intimate luncheons and dinners and, of course, is named for General Ulysses S. Grant, who was a guest at the hotel after the Civil War. Then there is the **Lee Room**, named in honor of General Robert E. Lee. It is another room similar in size to the Grant Room and named to honor the Southern leader who, as a colonel in the U.S. Army prior to the Civil War, spent some time as a guest in the hotel. Having rooms named for both

Grant and Lee are proof the Menger shows no partiality as regards the North and the South! Another room often used for parties and meetings, now called the **Patio Room**, was once a private club, the Patio Club. Prior to being called the Patio Club, it was known as the Latin Quarter. It has a definite Spanish flavor in its decor. At one time a number of artists lived and worked in the area just to the rear of the room where the swimming pool is now located.

The Spanish Patio

There has always been a garden attached to the Menger Hotel. References to the gardens go back as far as the early Menger days, when meat was sometimes hung from the trees to cure and was brought to the kitchen via rope pulleys. It has undergone many changes through the years, but is has always been an integral part of the hotel property.

The garden is now called the Spanish Patio. It is centered by a lovely Spanish tiered fountain, which is surrounded by colorful floral plantings. There are numerous shrubs, palm trees, and semitropical plants in the area. Tables are assembled at the south end, near the Colonial Room, and guests often enjoy dining al fresco. It is especially delightful in the balmy spring and summer evenings, when soft candlelight illuminates the tables and refreshing drinks are brought to quench the thirst of guests who have grown weary after a long day of sightseeing. It is said that many couples have "courted" on this patio, and many proposals have been made and accepted in these romantic surroundings. It's such a lovely spot; a young lady would find it hard to say no to any romantic overtures. There is even a "proposal balcony" overlooking the garden. Once, a guest hired a violinist to come and play sentimental music while he proposed to his sweetheart on this balcony. The answer was yes, of course! In gratitude, the young man had a plaque placed on the balcony wall overlooking the patio.

There is a beautifully executed colorful tile mural depicting a courting Spanish couple on one wall of the patio, where a small fountain pool is located.

Tile fountain in Spanish Patio showing a courting couple
Photo by Martin Malacara

Fortunately, we have a number of photographs showing the patio gardens as they once looked. The late Ilse Griffith, a San Antonio resident of the King William District for many years, collected picture postcards. She had many lovely souvenir cards, from years gone by, of the Menger hotel and its gardens, which she gave to her good friend Ingrid Kokinda. Ingrid, learning of this book project, very kindly loaned them to me for use in this book. You will note there was quite a "jungle effect" with a number of banana trees, magnolias, loquats, oleanders, mangoes, tall palms, and a profusion of vines. Today the garden is somewhat more formal, but it is still extremely colorful and beautifully kept. It still has the aura of romance and is a tranquil, peaceful spot in the midst of a busy and thriving city.

There was once an acequia, or irrigation ditch, which passed right through the garden. The ditch was part of the system dug by Franciscan priests in the seventeenth century to bring water from

Spanish Patio circa 1920
Ilse Griffith collection, courtesy Ingrid Kokinda

Spanish Patio circa 1920
Ilse Griffith collection, courtesy Ingrid Kokinda

the San Antonio River to the various missions. Of course, the Menger Hotel sits on property that was once a part of Mission San Antonio de Valero, which was built in 1718. We know it today by its more popular nickname, the Alamo. There is a bronze tablet on the wall of the Spanish patio that marks the site of this old acequia.

At one time the patio was the location of a large fenced pool that housed several alligators. Everyone who went downtown in those days always stopped by the Menger Hotel to see the reptiles. It seems that around 1900 a guest at the hotel had a big 750-pound bull alligator that he asked the management to let him keep in the patio. The 'gator was housed in a large cage. The man had come to San Antonio as an exhibitor at a large international fair that was being held in the city. He evidently did not fare as well as he had hoped. When the exhibition was over, he came up short of cash and was unable to pay what he owed the hotel. He left his alligator as "partial payment." The hotel management named the creature "Bill" in honor of the unpaid tab and put an iron fence around the patio pool to house him. Later, managers Jason Dean and Sally Bourne purchased several baby alligators. These reptiles were named John, Jason, Mary, and Sally. Still later, another alligator named Oscar was added to the menagerie.

Bill lived at the Menger for almost fifty years. It is not known what happened to all the little alligators. We are told that only Oscar survived. A little news item ran in the *San Antonio Express* on August 22, 1936, which stated: "Old Bill, steady boarder for nearly fifty years, was killed by a companion alligator, ending a 15 year struggle for supremacy of the Menger patio pool." Oscar, the killer, was banished from the Menger Hotel and sent to reside at the old alligator gardens, which once were located in Brackenridge Park.

In 1926 a talented poet named Merrill Bishop published a small volume of poetry called *Chromatropes*. The old Naylor Printing Company printed the book. Mr. Bishop included in that volume a charming poem that is just as fresh and true today as it was then. I think you will enjoy it:

The Patio at the Menger Hotel
Merrill Bishop

Soft, cool breezes from the south
Rustle the palms and bend them low;
Languid the gold fish opens his mouth
And takes the crumbs I gently throw
Into the pool, beside my table in the patio.

Listless I play with fork and glass
And keep the rhythm fast and slow,
The violins play. The minutes pass.
And then the moon with silvery glow
Shines down upon the patio.

What scenes fair lady moon have met your eyes
In this quaint spot, so many years ago?
When glasses clinked to ladies heaving sighs,
And lips demurely whispered, "yes" or "no,"
For Romance dwells within the patio.

Don't ever visit the Menger without spending a little time in the patio. It will restore your spirits and bring you a measure of peace and contentment. Lean back in one of the comfortable lounge chairs, inhale the fragrance of the flowers, sip a cooling drink, and be thankful there is still such a place as the Menger's Spanish Patio!

Closeup of fountain, Spanish Patio

Photo by Martin Malacara

Specialty Shops

Rounding out our tour of the ground floor of the Menger, I would like to point out that there are some lovely retail spaces that are leased by various individuals. A Menger guest can enjoy quite a nice afternoon of browsing and buying in these specialty shops, without ever leaving the hotel property.

The Humidor may be entered from Blum Street or from the Victorian lobby. It offers everything the smoker might desire, from fine tobacco blends to imported pipes and cigars and elegant smoker's accessories.

Adelman's Antiques, located right at the corner of Blum Street and Alamo Plaza in the old Victorian section of the hotel, may be entered from the Victorian lobby. It is one of very few businesses of its kind owned by an original old San Antonio family. The shop specializes in magnificent estate antique jewelry, a fine collection of European artworks, antique silver and cut glass, and a wonderful collection of fine Austrian Sworovski crystal costume jewelry.

King's X Collectibles maintains a huge collection of toy miniature soldiers, backdrops, and military vehicles for the serious collector of military memorabilia. These items are imported from Hong Kong, New Zealand, Russia, England, and Wales.

On the Plaza offers an interesting array of artwork and posters, intricately carved and painted handmade animals and figures in the best traditions of Mexican folk art, and some very nice silver jewelry set with semiprecious stones.

The Silver Spur, which may be entered from Alamo Plaza or from the main lobby entrance, offers elegant, upscale ladies' Western wear, jewelry, and accessories. The beautiful beaded collar pieces can transform even the simplest dress or blouse into instant glamour!

San Antonio Style is a nice shop that offers all sorts of novelty gifts, t-shirts, souvenirs, and sundries, and it may be entered via the main lobby or the Alamo Plaza entrance. It has really nice upscale souvenir items that a traveler may proudly take home to recall his San Antonio adventure.

Haagen Däz Ice Cream Shop doesn't need an introduction. The shop occupies the corner space on Alamo Plaza at Crockett Street and is a favorite stop-off spot on a hot summer's day for tourists and locals alike.

The Alamo Visitor's Center occupies the last retail space and is entered from Crockett Street. Here friendly attendants cheerfully dispense tourist information, and visitors can sign up for various sightseeing tours of the city.

One well-known shop in San Antonio had its beginnings at the Menger Hotel. The still very popular Menger Smart Shop, now celebrating its fiftieth anniversary, first opened at the Menger Hotel in the space where the Silver Spur is now located. It was founded in October 1950 by Bernice Cantile and remained at the hotel location until 1969. When it was determined that more space was needed, the shop was relocated to North Star Mall. Today's Menger Shop, owned by Cantile's daughter, Sunny Wager, is located at 4025 Broadway in the Boardwalk, and the name Menger Smart Shop is still synonymous with good taste and good fashion.

Going back through the main lobby, through the Victorian lobby, we come to the elevator just outside the Colonial Dining Room. It's time for a quick trip up to the first balcony, or mezzanine.

The Mezzanine

Stepping off the elevator, we see a round wood table that is said to be the very table that Colonel Leonard Wood used to sign up the volunteer Rough Riders during his visit to the hotel in May 1898.

The Renaissance Room

Even though its name may denote something else, this beautiful second floor reception room is strongly influenced by the neoclassical style, which was very popular in American between 1790 and 1830 and reborn later as Colonial Revival architecture after the Chicago World's Fair was held in 1893. The ceiling of this room is especially noteworthy, with its plaster ornamentation featuring abstracted urns, shells, lyres, and anthemion (honeysuckle) motifs. The mantelpiece is identical to the one found in the Colonial Dining Room. There is a charming balcony outside the Renaissance Room, from which Alamo Plaza can be viewed. The beautiful crystal chandelier is said to have come from an Austrian castle. The room is still a favorite spot for wedding receptions, small dinners, luncheons, and meetings of all descriptions.

Suites

A number of suites at the Menger have been named for celebrity guests who have stayed at the hotel over the years. You will read of these people and the part they played in the history of the Menger in chapter seven. These suites, while named for the notables, are not necessarily the rooms in which the celebrities actually stayed, with the exception of the King Ranch and the Roy Rogers Suites.

The suites are generally always occupied, so unlike the public lobbies, they cannot be visited. They include: the Mary Moody Suite, Teddy Roosevelt Suite, Babe Ruth Suite, General William Tecumseh Sherman Suite, Sarah Bernhardt Suite, Lily Langtry Suite, O. Henry Suite, Oscar Wilde Suite, Sidney Lanier Suite, and the Mae West Suite. There is also the Devon Cattle Suite, named to honor the Devon Cattle Association, which held its meetings at the Menger for many years.

Eastlake Victorian bed, circa 1870 in one of the Menger bedchambers
Photo by Martin Malacara

The King Ranch Suite, on the south side of the Renaissance Room, is definitely the suite where Captain Richard King, the famous cattle baron, always stayed. The four-poster classic canopy bed where he died in 1885 is still in use, as well as Captain King's shaving stand and his desk.

The Roy Rogers Suite, on the north side of the Renaissance Room, is furnished with settee, coffee table, and lamps all covered in cowhide to make the famous Western actor and singing star and his lovely wife, Dale Evans, feel at home during their visits to the Menger. They often stayed in the suite during the years they performed at the San Antonio stock show and rodeo and, again, when they came to perform at the opening of the 1968 Hemisfair. They often said the Menger was their favorite place in all of San Antonio.

Chapter 5

Glitter, Glitz, and Glamour

$\mathcal{J}$ust close your eyes and briefly try to imagine the beauty, the glitter, and the glamour of the noteworthy events that have taken place at the Menger Hotel over the past one hundred and forty years. There have been weddings and receptions, cotillion balls, banquets, and concerts. Debutantes have bowed to society there at sparkling balls. There have been masquerades, military balls, Little Theatre productions, fashion shows, and memorable parties too numerous to mention.

At first, candles and gaslights would have illuminated the scene, causing the chandeliers, accented with hundreds of cut crystal prisms, to sparkle and glimmer. The patio, scene of many parties and romantic dinners, was often lit by the glow of Chinese lanterns and hurricane lamps. Flowers were everywhere, and the fragrance of jasmine and roses perfumed the air as couples danced and whirled to the music of stringed orchestras.

As the years rolled by, musical tastes changed. The minuet and the stately waltz have been replaced with more energetic forms of dance. In the 1940s and 1950s, there was the popular Big Band sound. Often dances were held in the summer months at the beautiful roof garden, now a thing of the past.

Today's parties at the Menger are still among the most elegant in the city. San Antonio's favorite orchestras still set the tempo for debutante parties, the annual Fiesta Week Queen's Ball, and conventioneers bent on having a memorable climax to their meetings at a special evening of dining and dancing. And a quiet time in the lovely lobby is made more enjoyable by the easy-listening music of an electronically played grand piano.

Now, let's take a journey down memory lane! We've selected a few especially glamorous evenings in the long and glittering past of the Menger Hotel to share with you!

Civil War Benefits at the Menger

Just prior to the Civil War, several gala events were held at the Menger. A notable event was a large cotillion party held on July 25, 1860, that was hosted by Captain Richard King, L. R. Evans, J. D. Wade, and H. Wecshler.

After the outbreak of the war, several benefits were held to aid Texas regiments serving the Confederacy. Women desirous of helping the soldiers involved in the Southern cause sponsored them. Money was always needed to buy medical supplies and hospital equipment, and the ladies of San Antonio gladly rallied 'round the Stars and Bars! There was a supper and fair to aid Colonel Pyron's regiment. The San Antonio ladies sent their contributions to the Menger dining room, while people living in the country contributed meat, milk, and poultry. Twelve hundred dollars was raised to benefit the hospital, which cared for Pyron's men. The *San Antonio Herald,* May 2, 1863, stated the social was a brilliant affair attended "by the fairest of the San Antonio fair."

A few days after this gala, a supper was held to benefit General Baylor's Guerilla Company. The tables were laden with delicacies, and the articles that were both sold and raffled made a lovely display. Mrs. W. G. Samuels made a beautiful handmade flag that she presented to General Baylor.

During the Civil War, another gala event took place at the Menger. An elegant ball and banquet was given in honor of Confederate General J. Bankhead Magruder after his victory over the Northern forces in recapturing Galveston.

Celebrations Follow the Civil War, 1867

There wasn't much to celebrate during the War Between the States, and in fact, the Menger guestrooms were closed for a time during the war. The exact date, length of time, and reason for the closure are not known. It is thought some remodeling was done then, and also business would have definitely fallen off during those days of wartime austerity. On April 4, 1865, the *Semi-Weekly News* announced the hotel would reopen and spoke of it as "a large and commodious Hotel for the accommodation of the public and the travelers generally."

In 1867 the Fireman's Ball that celebrated Independence Day (so it must have been on or around July 4) was the first large post-war event held at the hotel. And it must have meant a lot to William Menger for the ball to be in his hotel, since he was always active in the firefighting department. The *Herald* described the supper as "a bountiful and luxurious feast, heartily appreciated by the assemblage." The ball was the largest gathering of a social nature ever held, up until that time, in San Antonio.

Soon after the Fireman's Ball was held at the hotel, the military officers in the city organized the "Army Club." They held their socials at the hotel and included their wives and a few San Antonio citizens in their much sought after invitation lists. One of their most important socials was a reception given by Major Whiteside of the Sixth Cavalry upon his completion of inspection of the cavalry. The *San Antonio Daily Express* of December 12, 1867, stated that in addition to the usual bountiful supper served at affairs sponsored by the Army Club, the Major provided the guests with champagne, which "flowed without reserve." The newspaper observed "The Major leaves many warm friends who regret his departure."

A short time later, three hundred guests honored General John S. Mason prior to his departure to a new station in New Mexico. While a string band played for dancing, the San Antonio Brass band played inspiring airs during part of the festivities. According to the *San Antonio Daily Express,* the guests enjoyed a "superb collation" served at midnight and enjoyed champagne, which flowed freely from Mr. Menger's well-stocked wine cellar. It was reported that E. J. Davis, the Republican candidate for governor, took an active part in the evening's activities.

The *San Antonio Daily Express* reported that the Humbolt *Stiftung,* held on September 19, 1869, which commemorated the hundredth birthday of the German philosopher Alexander Von Humbolt, was one of the grandest festivities of the era. There was a subscription dinner as a sort of preliminary to the celebration. The dining room was reported to have been elegantly decorated, and the entertainment was described as "princely."

Generals Honored, 1871

William Menger personally greeted Generals Shin, Cord, Carleton, and William Tecumseh Sherman, when they paid a visit to the hotel in 1871. They were honored with a fifteen-gun salute on Alamo Plaza in front of the hotel. A gala banquet followed. The *San Antonio Express* said it could not have been surpassed in perfection this side of New York or Washington, D.C.

Washington's Birthday Celebration, February 22, 1872

A gala ball was held on this occasion. The ballroom was decorated with United States flags. The room was "crowded with fair ladies who seemed to enjoy themselves to their heart's content, and the supper was excellent and the wines exquisite," according to the *San Antonio Express*.

Events of the 1870s

The *West Texas Historical Association Year Book*, Volume XXXII, October 1956, contained a fine article about the Menger, written by Inez Strickland Dalton and titled "The Menger Hotel: San Antonio's Civic and Social Center, 1859-1877."

Mrs. Dalton noted in September of 1871 a group of young gentlemen sent printed invitations to their friends to a special party at the Menger. It was noted that although the music and dancing were extremely enjoyable, the fashionable costumes of the lovely ladies in attendance were of prime interest. The *San Antonio Daily Express* of 1871 described the costumes thusly:

The ladies were dressed in the costume of still lingering summer, all the more beautiful for its simple purity. Mrs. Mather, accompanied by her handsom [*sic*] husband, was dressed in black, en train, low cossage [*sic*] white polonaise, hair tastily arranged with a profusion of black curls.

Miss Kitty Mayes, a very pretty brunette, much admired for her graceful dancing, wore a green satin, low cossage [*sic*] white blond pointed over skirt.

Miss Bainridge, sister of Mrs. Gen. Reynolds, appeared in pink tarleton and over-skirt of same material.

Miss Camilla Weir, a hansom [*sic*] demi-brunette with a sweet smile and pearly teeth, shone in a blue silk, trimmed with black lace and scarlet sash.

Miss Maggie Bell looked very sweet in white swiss, pointed over-skirt, trimmed with black lace and scarlet sash.

Miss Bella Bowen, a demi blond with locks of flowing fleece, had on a white tarleton, en train, pearl ornaments in her hair.

Mrs. Doctor Ganslen, sister of Miss Bowen, a petit

brunette with laughing teeth and bashful air, wore a white flowered grenadine and white swiss polonaise, ornaments of scarlet flowers. The graceful walking of these sisters received the united encomiums of all present.

Miss Whiting, a delicate brunette with luxuriant suite of curls, wore a white tarleton tastefully trimmed with a white satin fringe.

Mrs. Dalton noted that after the management changed from Mary Menger's ownership to the Kampmann ownership, the social affairs went right on along just as they had before, with the same careful attention to details. These socials continued to become more exclusive and fashionable as time went on.

General Sheridan Honored, 1873

When General Philip H. Sheridan, accompanied by Secretary of War General William W. Belknap, General Meyers, head of the U.S. Quartermaster Department, and Colonel Loomis, Chief Engineer of the U.S. Army, visited San Antonio in 1873, an elaborate banquet was given for the honorees. Although the City of San Antonio hosted the event, J. H. Kampmann was placed in charge of arrangements. It was noted that he paid F. E. Phillippe eight dollars in coins for the eight bouquets of roses that adorned the tables. San Antonio certainly "courted" these military greats, because the question of whether or not the military would continue to remain in San Antonio was being decided, and much of the city's future hinged on the outcome of the decision made during this visit to the city. The result? San Antonio is considered one of the top military centers in the United States!

General Ranald S. MacKenzie Honored, 1875

Of all the military balls held at the Menger, one was evidently a real standout. General Ranald S. MacKenzie had been around a long time and was highly respected. He was an old-time Indian fighter and won distinction for his successful campaigns against the Kwahadi Comanche, Cheyenne, and Kickapoo. The commander of the Fourth Cavalry led the successful raid against the Kickapoo in Mexico across from Fort Clark, where he was then stationed, in 1873. The brevet general of Civil War fame was very popular in San Antonio. When ill health forced him to make plans to leave and move back East, it was decided he should be honored in a special way.

The *San Antonio Daily Express* mentioned the upcoming ball to its readers, stating it would be "One of the most elegant and recherche affairs of the season." The Alamo Rifles, which was the San Antonio civic militia company, wore their full-dress gray uniform trimmed with red and gold braid, topped off with "pancake hats." The general and his staff and all the military guests in attendance were resplendent in their full dress uniforms.

The *Express* stated that "some of the loveliest faces of San Antonio beauty" were present at the ball. Miss Fanny Williams, a San Antonio belle, was mentioned as being one of the most fashionably dressed guests at this, her first ball. She had chosen a dress with a train, which had black silk cords that laced the back of the dress and "were decorative as well as highly fashionable." The paper concluded, "the dancing was lively, and everything passed off happily and pleasantly."

The Railroad Arrives, 1877

The Menger Hotel was built when the only means of conveyance was the horse. Guests either arrived via horseback or in carriages or stagecoaches. The railroad greatly increased travel in and out of San Antonio. According to the *San Antonio Daily Express*, February 20, 1877, the hotel was decorated and illuminated lavishly for the city's reception honoring Governor R. H. Hubbard, who arrived along with the president of the railroad, Thomas J. Pierce. Mayor J. M. (Jack) French welcomed the huge crowd that gathered in front of the hotel at the conclusion of a huge procession that had come from the railroad station to the hotel. As mentioned in chapter two, tall standards, bearing small American flags and a festoon of Chinese lanterns, and hundreds of flaming torches lit the way. The torch bearers had been followed by the Tenth Infantry Band, the Alamo Rifles, the United States Cavalry, the Turner Association, the fire department, and about ten thousand citizens of San Antonio. In addition, many people had come from as far away as Houston and Galveston to join in the festivities that welcomed the great "iron horse" to San Antonio.

The festivities lasted into the wee hours of the night, and after Governor Hubbard had retired to his suite, the Alamo Rifles returned to the plaza and surprised him with a serenade. The next day a grand reception and promenade took place in the Menger parlors and in the courtyard where elegantly attired guests greeted the governor and his party.

Widows and Orphans Honored, 1880s

No exact date can be found, but it is known that a benefit gala was given for the widows and orphans of soldiers who died, along with General George Custer, fighting the Sioux Indians at the Battle of Little Big Horn.

According to an account of the time, the military and civilian elite gathered, along with the famous Alamo Rifles Militia Company, in full dress uniform. The gathering danced in the "great main hall" (probably the Victorian lobby) which was decorated with gathered sabers with points facing outwards forming pretty star patterns on the side walls. A great deal of bunting, United States flags, and stacked rifles were used as decorations. A stringed orchestra played for what was termed a "terpsichorean exercise" until a late hour, and afterwards a supper was served up in "handsome style."

Militia Balls

It may be noted that down through the years many militia companies, including the Alamo Rifles, the Belknap Rifles, the Maverick, Cresson, Slayden and Milam Rifles, the Alamo Light Infantry Rifles, and the Rough Riders have celebrated their reunions at the hotel, often with "civic militia plume drills." (Note: no one seems to know just what these drills were, but they certainly sound interesting, don't they?)

Driscoll Ball Honors Debutantes, 1905

Miss Clara Driscoll, a prominent socialite and a young woman credited with helping to save the Alamo from destruction by spending some of her own inheritance to save it, gave a memorable banquet and ball in 1905. The event honored two debutantes who were close friends. The ball, a sparkling affair, honored Miss Eda Kampmann, whose family owned the Menger Hotel at that time, and Miss Katherine Yoakum. Miss Kampmann wore a lavender spangled chiffon gown with a train trimmed with violets. Miss Yoakum chose a white silk gown accented with a bertha collar of exquisite lace and diamond ornaments. The hostess, Miss Driscoll, was gowned in yellow net worn over taffeta. She wore a coronet of yellow flowers in her hair, elegant lace, and dazzling jewels. She also carried a bouquet of white hyacinths and maidenhair fern.

According to the *San Antonio Daily Express*, the Menger dining room was elaborately decorated. There were palms, festoons of smilax along the walls, and baskets laden with pink carnations and pink Catherine Mermot roses were actually attached to the walls.

Four hundred and twenty-five guests attended the lavish dinner preceding the dancing. The beautifully gowned and bejeweled guests, the delicious banquet, and the music of the 26th Infantry Band combined to make an outstanding evening in the historic annals of the Menger Hotel. One need not add that Miss Driscoll was wealthy. A party of this magnitude must have cost a fortune!

Dinner Dansant, February 2, 1916

On February 2, 1916, the hotel, no doubt trying to add a bit of gaiety to those World War I years, sponsored a "Dinner Dansant" open to the public. The advertisement stated, "A real Southern dinner of exceptional excellence will be served, and there will be music, palms, flowers, dancing, and happiness included in the festivities." All of this excitement was offered for $1.50 per person.

There were also a number of regular dances and "meriendas" held every Saturday afternoon from 4 to 6 P.M. in the ballroom in those days. They called the events "Baille y Merienda." (Note: a "baille" is a dance, and a "merienda" is a Spanish name for luncheon, or it can also describe a "high tea," which is probably what was served at these affairs.)

Chinese Oriental Night Benefit, July 12, 1917

A large number of Chinese workers had been employed in Mexico, working at building dams, bridges, and railroads for the government when the revolution "starring" Pancho Villa broke out. Villa vowed to hang "every Chino" who was working for the Mexican government. Four hundred twenty-seven of these workers fled to San Antonio and lived in tents, constructed by the Red Cross, that were placed on the Fort Sam Houston reservation. The refugees were given work on construction projects at the fort, but additional money was needed to help them. The Oriental ball held on July 12, 1917, at the Menger was a very colorful and gala event and raised a great deal of money for the men. Many of their descendants have become prominent citizens of the city.

Gone With the Wind Ball, February 1, 1940

Countless debutantes have made their bows to society at glittering balls held at the Menger. One such affair was held on February 1, 1940, in the Minuet Ballroom. Mrs. John Baron Carrington honored her debutante daughter, Pauline, at a masked ball held a week before the local premier of the film *Gone With the Wind*. All of the guests were elegantly dressed to emulate the Civil War era. The ball was a favorite topic of conversation for a long time!

Masked Dixie Ball, honoring debutante Pauline Carrington, circa 1940

Photo courtesy Texas University Institute of Texan Cultures, *San Antonio Light* Collection

Anniversary Gala, September 19, 1959

One of the most glamorous events ever held in San Antonio was the gala staged as a benefit for the San Antonio Symphony and at the same time to commemorate the one hundredth anniversary of the venerable Menger Hotel. It was held on the evening of September 19, 1959.

Fortunately, I was able to interview three people who were there. In addition, I viewed a scrapbook of excellent photographs of the event, owned by Mr. Frates Seeligson. I also read the press coverage in the *San Antonio Express News* written by the late Mildred Whiteaker.

Mrs. Lewis Moorman Jr., who co-chaired the gala with Mrs. Jack M. Bennett Jr., showed me several photographs and some newspaper clippings from the *San Antonio Express News.* Mrs. William O. Bowers, whose first husband, Mr. Jack Bowman, participated in the pageant, was actually the first person who told me about this sparkling occasion, and I was so delighted to learn of this fascinating event in the life of the Menger from Mrs. Bowers.

Mrs. Edgar Tobin and Mr. Walter Mathis headed the invitation committee that sent invitations to prominent socialites all over the country. The response was overwhelming!

On the night of the gala, many guests elected to arrive in horse drawn carriages, setting the stage for the Victorian theme of the ball. King Antonio's carriage, vintage 1859, drew up in front of the hotel to deliver the gala's chairmen, Mesdames Bennett and Moorman and Mr. Walter Mathis who was president of the Symphony Society.

Guests were received by the gala co-chairmen, Mrs. Bennett and Mrs. Moorman, Mr. Mathis, Mr. Ernest Kunz, manager of the Menger, Mrs. Kunz, and Mrs. Mary Moody Northen, of Galveston, chairman of the board of the Moody Foundation.

Elaborate arrangements of foliage and fall flowers were placed in the Victorian lobby, and Minuet and Colonial Rooms. Transparent screens lighted from behind showed sketches of San Antonio before the turn of the century. Mr. Robert Tobin and his committee selected the beautiful decorations. Pre-dinner cocktails were served in the lobby while an ensemble from the San Antonio Symphony played classical music.

The round dining tables were centered with pyramids of fresh fruit and foliage, replicating the type of centerpieces most popular a century past. The Menger used gold rimmed white china and cranberry crystal. The elegant menu included shrimp cocktail, celery salad, Rock Cornish game hen a Sauvain (named for Chef Sauvain), spiced peaches, wild rice with mushrooms, French beans Oriental, Menger mango ice cream, and champagne. Following dinner, a lavish showing of cocktail and evening gowns from Joskes of Texas was presented by professional models.

Female guests were dazzling in their most elegant ball gowns accentuated with sparkling jewels, while their escorts were all dressed in formal attire. A number of San Antonians were dressed as historic figures who had been guests at the Menger over the past one hundred years. They were lavishly and authentically costumed to represent the famous personalities they portrayed. The San Antonio Little Theatre (SALT), directed by Joe Salek, furnished makeup artists to see that each character looked as much as possible like the person they represented. It was an affair of such glamour and magnitude that *Life Magazine* sent photographers and reporters to cover the event, which later appeared on the pages of that magazine. Runways were placed in the Colonial and Minuet Rooms where the participants were introduced. They had been carefully rehearsed by the Tableaux Committee, Mr. Joe Salek, Mrs. Alexander Oppenheimer, and Mr. John Palmer Leeper. Their initial appearances to the assemblage were made through a white painted Victorian gazebo, especially constructed for the occasion. Leeper, for many years the popular director of the McNay Art Museum, served as master of ceremonies in one room; Salek presided in the other.

Some of the historic figures who played a special role in the history of the Menger and who were "brought back to life" through the pageant, included: Teddy Roosevelt (Frates Seeligson),

General Philip H. Sheridan (Lewis Moorman Jr.), Buffalo Bill Cody (Tobin Armstrong), General Ulysses S. Grant (Garland Lasater), Oscar Wilde (Jack Bowman), William S. Porter (Dr. Lewis Tucker), Robert E. Lee (John Bennett), Sidney Lanier (Fidel Chamberlain), Captain Richard King (portrayed by his own great-grandson, Richard "Dick" Kleberg), while King's wife, Henrietta, was played by Mrs. Kleberg. Then, there were General Sam Houston (Donald Duncan) and heavyweight champion Bob Fitzsimmons (Charles Kuper).

Gaslights added to the 1859 authenticity of the event, which concluded with dancing to the music of Bill Mercer and his orchestra.

The *Life Magazine* write-up stated that "four hundred and twenty-five rich Texans" gathered at the Menger and paid $25 a plate for the gala event. All the proceeds went to the Symphony. The Menger Hotel picked up the entire dinner tab. Times surely have changed! Today's benefit galas, still held frequently in San Antonio, usually bear the minimum price tag of $100 a plate and are more likely to cost considerably more.

The Fiesta Queen's Ball

For many years the Queen of Fiesta and her court of beautiful duchesses have been feted at the Queen's Ball, held at the Menger. A small "mini" coronation is usually held preceding the ball, which is staged in the main ballroom. The Order of the Alamo, a men's social organization, stages the elaborate queen's coronations every year. Mr. Frates Seeligson, a longtime member of the Order, told me the ball was always the "best party in town." Then he added, "Why, for years the Menger Bar stayed open until 5 A.M.!"

Although the Order still holds the annual Queen's Ball at the Menger, where her majesty and her court, made up of San Antonio's leading debutantes, are feted during the Fiesta celebration, the bar must adhere to local ordinances, and so it closes much earlier these days.

Chapter 6

Historic and Interesting Trivialities

The Menger Hotel operates on a daily schedule with each employee performing his duties smoothly and professionally. But sometimes strange, amusing, even hilarious occurrences slip in to change the routine. There have been some sad events, too.

Ernesto Malacara, my husband, Roy Williams, and I have gone through many records, file folders, old newspaper clippings, books connected with the history of the hotel, and handwritten notes. We painstakingly singled out a line here, a paragraph or two there, and it took many hours to fit it all together. Our friend Robin Ellis gave us articles about the Menger that he had collected over a number of years. Former employees and guests were interviewed. I spoke with Menger and Kampmann descendants. And many hours were spent at our fine local libraries in pursuit of the Menger story. All the library staff members were extremely helpful. It has been like putting a complex jigsaw puzzle together, and all the pieces still are not in place. But if we wait any longer, the story, however fragmented, will not be told.

Part of the charm of this wonderful hotel lies in the personalities that have both worked there and who have been guests. Some of their fascinating, amusing, and sometimes rather bizarre stories need to be told for a better understanding of what has made the Menger Hotel such a unique place.

Louis William Gets a Pony

When Louis William, the Mengers' eldest son, was about thirteen years old (this would have been around 1865), his father gave him a fine pony with saddle and bridle as a birthday present. The boy started out from the Menger livery stable on Blum Street, turning into Alamo Plaza one morning, when suddenly the pony shied and started running away at breakneck speed. The pony reached the river, with young Louis hanging on for dear life. The horse was running so fast, it could not stop upon finding no bridge across the river. The pony and his young rider plunged into the stream. Fortunately, neither one was seriously injured. Louis William lost all interest in horses after that incident.

Stagecoach Stop at Menger

Can't you just imagine the excitement when the stages would pull up in front of the hotel, bearing weary travelers from all over the country? It must have been noisy, dusty, and entertaining to watch the travelers alight with their luggage and head for the cool comfort of the hotel reception rooms. Four horse coaches arrived daily. They came from El Paso, Fort Concho (which is in present-day San Angelo), Luling, and Austin. The Menger was one of the main San Antonio stops, and here the coaches would both load and unload passengers. Most of the time passengers departing on the coaches would be given nice box lunches to sustain them, since rest stops along the way were few and far between and most of the time less than adequate for the needs of the travelers.

Cowboy Takes a "Bubble Bath"

In his *San Antonio Legacy*, Donald E. Everett quoted from an article in the *San Antonio Express,* May 18, 1909. It seems that a reporter from the *St. Louis Globe Democrat* was in the city attending a cattlemen's convention. He wanted to get some material for his paper that would be a "real Texas cowboy story." He didn't have to wait very long.

The reporter was loafing around the Menger Hotel one hot summer day, when the stage from Laredo rolled up in front of the hotel and off-loaded its passengers. One, the reporter referred to as "old man Wolcott." In later years, as he looked back upon the event, the reporter said Wolcott was probably no more than thirty years old. He had been working down at his ranch on the Rio Grande for six months or so and then, most recently, had ridden on a hot stagecoach for 150 miles or so. He was, to say the least, "aromatic."

Wolcott invited all the cowboys who were standing around the hotel to come in and have a drink with him at the bar. Then he ordered the room clerk to give him a big room with a big bathtub. He said he'd been so busy working and making money he hadn't had any time to bathe in the last six months. He said he wanted a bath that WAS a bath, and he ordered enough champagne to fill the big tub to the very brim. Then he stripped off, got into the tub, and lingered in the bubbly for about two hours. He sent the bellboy out to buy him a brand-new outfit of clothes from the skin out, to replace his filthy attire. He later declared it was the best bath he had ever had and was worth every penny! His friends all said it sure had cost enough.

When Bustles Were the Rage

During the Gay Nineties, bustles were the "in" thing for women of fashion to wear. It seems that young women always took a tremendous interest in the newspapers of the town because, when crumpled up, they made such perfect stuffing for bustles. On the night of a dance at the Menger, the reading room was usually completely bereft of newspapers shortly after they were delivered, grabbed up by fashion-conscious lady guests!

Knowledgeable Waiter

A reporter once asked an elderly waiter, who had worked at the hotel for many years, if he could recall some of the famous people he had waited on. He mentioned various celebrities, entertainers, actors, and musicians. The reporter asked him if he had met any of the "opera stars," and he replied, "Oh yes, I think his name was *FAUST*, but I'm not sure."

English Nobility Visits Menger

In these days, when international news makes the headlines and day by day events at the local hotels would never be mentioned in the news, it is interesting to read of what made the headlines of the *San Antonio Express* on November 19, 1890. The article, which was titled "A COMEDY OF ERRORS," appears in Donald E. Everett's fine book *San Antonio, the Flavor of its Past, 1845-1898:*

> For the two days past there have been as guests of the Menger hotel in this city, two representatives of English nobility in the persons of Sir William and Lady Plowden, who have been visiting for some time in this country. Only recently, they were the guests of Vice-President Huntington, of the Southern Pacific, at San Francisco. In stopping in this city, a special telegraphic request from Mr. Huntington was that they receive the best of attention.
>
> And thereby hangs a tale.
>
> Yesterday morning Lady Plowden, having an idea that the bedding in their suite of rooms had not, on former occasions, been properly aired, undertook to superintend the work of a hotel chambermaid in that direction. The bedding was all hung out without accident, but on the girl making up the beds later on, her ladyship did not like the general effect. To her protests, however, the democratic American girl made a reply. In return she received a stinging box on the ear and amid a tirade from my lady flew down the stairs

to the clerk, where she poured out her lamentations over the nickel plated call-bell.

On the news being communicated to the housekeeper, that functionary gathered her skirts in her hand and went up the stairs for an explanation. My lady was in a genuine pet and the housekeeper was received with a Mrs. Caudle intonation of British freethought that made her ears tingle. She came back down the stairs with a lagubrious expression that an American baggageman couldn't handle with a brass check.

Presently the bell in the office rung for a boy and there was a panic among the collection of boys of Senegambian extraction who gathered about the indicator. One of them, however, was singled out to respond to the ice-water call and as if to appease her ladyship, he departed so far from the usual forms as to place the pitcher and glass on a platter. His knees unconsciously smote together as he climbed the stairs, and over-awed, as he entered her ladyship's apartments with the platter raised on high, he tripped upon a rug and fell headlong. He had approached very closely to her ladyship and in a mighty effort to stop his fall, he grasped her skirts with both hands, tearing the garment of delicate text half in twain.

It was the coup de grace to a comedy of errors and the terrified bell-boy, with the whites of his eyes rolling, fled down the steps, followed by her ladyship who appeared in the corridor in a white heat of outraged dignity, with her torn skirt held up as a mark of American domestic stupidity.

Everything pacific which could be conjured up by the clerk's imagination was used in pacifying the indignant gentlewoman, who finally returned to her apartments to brood over her trials in secret.

The by-play in the corridor attracted the attention of a number of guests who were vastly amused thereby. Sir

William and his lady will leave this morning via the Southern Pacific for New Orleans.

José, the Shoe Shine Boy

This story has been around a long time. Whether it is true or just a much loved, oft told legend is beyond our means to know.

It seems in the 1880s there was a lot of trouble brewing down along the Texas-Mexico border, and it was rumored that plots were being made to recapture Texas.

At this time there was a youngster, a little Mexican boy about twelve years old, who made his living shining shoes and boots in front of the Menger Hotel. A tall Texan, one of the early Texas Rangers, befriended the youngster. He used to stop and chat with young José while the boy polished his boots. He told the youth that he should keep his eyes and ears open, because he was first and foremost a Texan, not a Mexican, and he could serve his state well. If he saw or heard anything suspicious, the ranger instructed José to let him know.

At that time, a Mexican general was staying at the hotel. One day the general, who had spent several days perfecting his take-over Texas plot, called on José. He asked the lad to deliver a note to a man who would figure in the plot. He gave José a peso for running the errand.

Remembering the admonition of his Texas friend, the ranger, José first went to the Texan's house and let him read the note before he ran on to deliver it to the man to whom it was addressed.

That night, the general had a meeting in his room at the Menger. Most of the men he had called in were mercenaries, working for pesos, not for patriotism. They were willing to figure in the plot in exchange for money.

After the men left the room, the ranger, who was waiting outside in the corridor, slipped inside. Beside him stood little José, who had led him to the general's room. The ranger informed the general he would not be able to carry out his plot to take over Texas because he was placing him under arrest.

The general quickly reached for his pistol and aimed at the Texan. He fired. But little José had stepped in front of his friend and took the bullet intended for the ranger. The ranger pulled the trigger on his pistol, and the general dropped to the floor.

The ranger took the dying boy in his arms and asked him why he had jumped in front of him. The little shoe shine boy gasped his last words, "Because, señor, you are my friend." Then he closed his eyes and died. Young José gave his life for his friend and for Texas, and in the doing, probably stopped what might have been a bloody war.

Carrie Came to Texas

The story has been bandied about the hotel for a long time that Carrie Nation put a gash in the beautiful Menger bar during a visit to San Antonio on one of her temperance treks through the country. Well, a gash WAS inflected on the bar at some time (see chapter nine), but it was NOT inflicted by the little "Kansas Cyclone."

According to a lengthy story which appeared in the *Southwestern Historical Quarterly*, Volume 63, July 1959 to April 1960, written by noted columnist Sam Woolford, Carrie Nation came to San Antonio on January 10, 1908. She arrived by train from Guadalajara, where she had preached on the evils of tequila. A Mr. Hill, a male cousin, who had been pressed into service to help carry her baggage, accompanied her. Amongst her other accouterments, Mrs. Nation had one piece of luggage loaded with little gold hatchets, which she sold at her temperance lectures.

Mrs. Nation was a small woman with piercing eyes, who dressed in plain, severe clothing. She had what Woolford referred to as "a determined mien."

The tiny activist and her escort checked into the old Bexar Hotel. Having heard of her imminent arrival, a reporter from the

Gazette awaited her in the lobby, hoping to get a good story. She told the reporter she wanted to see Mayor Callaghan right away, to gain permission to use the Market Hall for her upcoming lecture that evening. The reporter offered to accompany her to the mayor's house, on Crockett Street. Mr. Hill, Mrs. Nation's cousin, was in ill health. He elected to stay at the hotel while Carrie ran her errands.

The hotel desk advised Mrs. Nation that the San Antonio police department had sent a message for her. The department had issued a statement saying she was to be allowed all the liberties of the city, but she was not to break any furniture or otherwise destroy any property. The message stated that "the saloon men in this city pay their taxes."

Mrs. Nation and the reporter from the *Gazette* hailed a cab and set out for the Crockett Street address of the mayor, whom they found "not at home." Next, they went on to the Menger Hotel, which was just a short distance from the mayor's residence. The elegant Menger Bar, adjacent to the beautiful flower-filled patio, was doing a brisk trade that afternoon. In those days, the management provided a nice light lunch snack with the price of a liquid libation. A buzz of convivial conversation filled the taproom. Then, suddenly, there was silence! The bartender, Fred Lockwood, was pouring whiskey from a large container into a cut glass decanter, using a funnel. He suddenly looked up, and there she was. Fred had never seen Carrie Nation before, but he knew her instantly from having seen her pictures in the papers. He was so startled to actually see Mrs. Nation in the flesh that he dropped the jug. The fiery liquid slowly spread across the barroom floor.

The *Gazette* reporter, who seemed to be enjoying himself tremendously, announced, "Gentlemen, this is Carrie Nation."

Mrs. Nation then hurled a few choice epithets at Fred, but he stood his ground. A few of the younger men in the bar tried a little rough humor, but Carrie stared them down and put them in their places with a few suitable retorts.

A large crowd of curious bystanders had gathered around the entrance to the bar, and Mrs. Nation had some difficulty making her way out of the bar and out of the Menger Hotel. She went on from there to numerous local "watering spots" that afternoon, but she kept her famous hatchet out of sight.

The little firebrand delivered her lecture that evening and left the next day, leaving the city verbally chastised but otherwise unscathed.

House Rules

At one time there were signs posted around the hotel that stated: "If you use the bathtub, please leave it clean for the next guests." We wonder if there was a shortage of chambermaids!

We uncovered a set of house rules that have no date available. We presume they were in use around the 1920s, since fans in the rooms were mentioned.

House Rules

No pets allowed in room.

No gambling allowed in room.

No C.O.D. packages received unless previous arrangements are made.

Weekly rates will only be made when room rent is paid in advance.

Delivery of whiskey or other intoxicating liquors to rooms prohibited.

Laundry or cleaning going out must be left at office.

Parties occupying rooms with connecting baths should cleanse tub after bathing.

Ironing board and iron, furnished free, inquire at office.

All visitors staying over night with guests are requested to register.

Guests are requested to lock their doors, on retiring, also when going out.

Guests vacating rooms must notify office before 6 p.m., otherwise a charge will be made for the following day.

We do not loan money or cash checks for strangers.

Stoves or electrical devices not allowed in rooms.

Trunks or other baggage must not remain in halls.

Baggage or other property stored at owner's risk.

Music not permitted before 10 a.m. or after 10 p.m.

Disorderly conduct absolutely not countenanced.

Not responsible for loss of, or damage to, wearing apparel.

Damage to furniture will be charged for.

Do not drive tacks or nails in walls or woodwork.

Please turn out lights and turn off fan when leaving room.

Please deposit money, jewelry, and other valuables in the safe in office.

San Antonio Little Theatre Producing Company

We found an application for membership in the San Antonio Little Theatre Producing Company, which was simply called the Little Theatre, Menger Hotel, for the year 1928-29. It appears that theatrical productions were presented in the hotel at one time. Membership, which entitled the holder to "admissions to each of the five plays and the regular meetings," were five dollars for individual memberships, and patron memberships were twenty-five dollars. Checks were to be made payable to the Little Theatre, Menger Hotel.

Just imagine! Five live plays for only five dollars! Downtown parking to see just one play runs more than that.

Russian Bathhouse

At one time there was a Russian bathhouse located where the valet parking area is today. There were all sorts of services available to pamper the weary traveler. Today, there is a full service spa at the hotel, so the amenities are still in place!

Hijinks in the Patio

Natalie Tompkins Gooch, a resident of Albuquerque, related a story that her late father, Colonel Daniel Tompkins, had an adventure at the Menger when he was a young cavalry officer stationed at Fort Sam Houston. Tompkins was the brother of the famous Colonel "Tommy" Tompkins of the Seventh Cavalry.

It seems that a group of young officers were enjoying an evening of conviviality at the Menger Bar, when they got just a wee bit inebriated. They started daring one another to do this or that, and finally Daniel Tompkins was dared to jump into the alligator pond in the Menger patio. A very large bull alligator named Bill inhabited the pond at the time. Daniel, fully clad, climbed over the barrier to the pond and jumped astride the very startled 'gator! Of course, the "ride" in the cramped quarters only lasted a minute, but it was long enough for Daniel to win the dare. Natalie said this was sometime in the early 1920s. Natalie's mother died when she was just a baby, and her father, a young widower at that time, still enjoyed having some evenings out with "the boys."

Remembrances of Ike Kampmann Jr.

During a recent visit with Mr. Ike Kampmann Jr., whose family formerly owned the Menger, he reminisced about some of his experiences at the hotel. He said as a youngster, he spent a lot of time at the hotel. When the family went there for lunch or dinner, he always headed straight for the patio so he could see the alligators. They would have been quite a curiosity for any young-ster, I should imagine!

Kampmann fondly recalled his friend Jim Rainey, the head bell-man. He was a black gentleman who Ike said was one of the "finest, nicest men in the world." He worked at the hotel for forty or fifty years. Ike recalled him being there in the 1920s and '30s.

When Ike's father, Isaac, married his mother, Margaret Adams of Ft. Worth, Isaac leased a private railroad car to go to the wedding. This was to provide transportation for his ten groomsmen. Isaac took Jim Rainey with him to act as his valet to help him dress for the wedding. Rainey also acted as a sort of maitre d', serving food and drink to the young men in the traveling party.

When Ike's uncle, Robert Kampmann, lived at the Menger Hotel, he wrote a letter to young Ike. He told him that he and Jim Rainey had gone dove hunting on a farm that belonged to the Stanusch family, who were friends of the Kampmanns. "Uncle Rob" wrote that Rainey had gotten his limit in short order. He just shot his doves right out of the trees! Rob, who was used to follow-ing the more acceptable rules of dove hunting, which was flushing the birds and then shooting them on the wing, said all he got "was a bad cold."

Kampmann told me the whole family had a great affection for Jim Rainey, and although they were of a different race and social strata, they often included him in various family events.

When Ike Kampmann Jr. married his first wife, Flora Cameron, in 1947, their wedding reception was held in the Colonial Room at the Menger. They spent their wedding night in the King Ranch Suite. Kampmann, who has a delightful sense of humor, started to chuckle. He said in the middle of the night a fire alarm went off at Joske's department store just across Blum Street from the Menger. Fire engines came charging down Blum right under their second floor window. Ike ran to the window to see what the com-motion was all about. In his haste, he knocked the screen out of the window, and it fell to the street below! He said fortunately, there was no one in its path when it fell.

Kampmann fondly recalled that there was one suite on the mezzanine level that fronted onto Alamo Plaza. Major Tom Armstrong rented it annually during Fiesta Week. The Armstrongs are an outstanding South Texas family. The Major had served in the army in World War I. Although he was always called "Major," he was not a career military man. According to Kampmann, he was an executive with Standard Oil Company. His wife was Henrietta Kleberg, the granddaughter of Captain Richard King.

Armstrong's friends were always invited to come and enjoy drinks and refreshments from the comfort of the suite, while they watched the Fiesta parades that used to pass by on Alamo Plaza. Kampmann said Major Armstrong gave "fabulous parties." The friends who gathered there in that same suite for many years affectionately referred to it as "Uncle Tom's cabin."

An Interesting Recollection

Recently, when I was visiting with a group staying at the Menger Hotel, a gentleman in the group said he had something he would like to tell me. Dr. Don Newell, a periodontist, was visiting the city during a convention. He told me as a young man he had once been stationed at Ft. Sam Houston. This was in the early fifties, he recalled. He was drafted, as were so many young men.

Dr. Newell said there was another draftee in his outfit named Shearn Moody Jr. He said at the time he met him, he believed that Moody was a specialist 4 (about a corporal). In those days, all the enlisted men lived in barracks. They could live "on the economy" only if they owned property in town, which of course, none of them did. Moody told his commanding officer he would really like to live in town. The officer explained what the stipulations were. Moody, the heir apparent to the vast Moody holdings, suggested that he wanted to live at the Menger Hotel and he would commute to work at the fort every day. This was a strange request, indeed, certainly the likes of which the C.O. had never heard before. When the officer said "Son, you'd have to own the hotel to be able to live there," young Moody replied, "Well sir, you see...I do."

Another time Newell said Moody requested some leave time. He had enough leave accrued, so that wasn't a problem. Asked exactly when he wanted the leave, he explained to his commander than he wanted time off to attend the Olympic games, which were being held in Europe. The C.O. agreed that getting the time off was no problem, but he asked the young soldier just how he planned to pay for such an expensive journey. He explained that tickets to all the events would be costly, and the cost of transportation to Europe would be prohibitive. But young Shearn had it all figured out. He would just charter his own plane to go and see the games!

At one time during his tour of duty at Ft. Sam Houston, Dr. Newell was invited to a very lavish party that Moody had at "his" hotel, the Menger. He stressed that Shearn was completely down to earth and very friendly to everyone, and that most people with whom he served in the military had no inkling that he was from such a prominent and wealthy family.

One of Gal-Tex Hotel Corporation's newest hotels is the elegant new Moody Gardens Hotel in Galveston. One of its fine amenities is the lovely "Shearn's," named after the late Shearn Moody Jr. This beautiful restaurant at the hotel reflects his appreciation of fine accouterments. He would have loved the polished walnut and cherry paneling, Wedgewood china, Reed and Barton silver flatware, etched glass, and hand-painted murals of the sea, coupled with the exquisite Continental cuisine and flawless service offered by the restaurant.

Cardinal Visits Menger

His Eminence Patrick Cardinal Hayes, Archbishop of New York, came to San Antonio in March 1932. He had been invited to attend the celebration of the two hundredth anniversary of the founding of the municipal government of the city and the establishment of the Spanish missions. He also officiated at the dedication of the restored Spanish Governor's Palace, on Military Plaza.

At a reception in the parlors of the Menger Hotel, the Cardinal was extended the invitation to address the Texas Legislature by the Senate Committee. Governor Ross Sterling was among the dignitaries introduced to His Eminence by the Most Reverent C. E. Byrne, Bishop of Galveston. The Cardinal received the committee most cordially and accepted their invitation.

Sid Fisher's Music Will Be Missed

For many years, beginning in January 1986, Sid Fisher was a fixture in the Menger lobby every evening, where he played the grand piano and sang for guests. The accomplished musician could play almost any request. He had composed a number of beautiful pieces as well, which he often played. Blind since his birth in 1920, the musician was schooled at the Texas School for the Blind in Austin. He learned to play the piano there. When he graduated he went to work in Galveston where he and four friends had a band. They played at the Texas Alamo Club. Then he went to Austin and played for a catering company that owned a boat used for excursions. He said he stayed in Austin a long time, free-lancing as a musician, playing conventions, and appearing at the Talley Ho Restaurant.

While Sid was living in Austin, he met his wife, Theresa. The devoted couple were married in 1943. They have one daughter who makes her home in Seattle, Washington.

I first met Sid when he played for style shows that were presented at Oak Hills Country Club. I was a fashion commentator then. Sid said he was playing at Oak Hills when Art Abbott, who was then manager of the Menger, asked him to come play at the hotel. This was in 1986, and he played at the hotel until the end of 1999, when he retired. He is a remarkable man and a gifted

musician. His friendly smile and distinctive piano style will certainly be missed.

This Lady's a Lovely Fixture

The Menger must be a good place to work, because so many of the employees stay for a long, long time. Many current staff members have been there for twenty or thirty or even more years. One employee tops them all in longevity! Marie Pierce came to work at the hotel in 1947. At first, she worked as a hatcheck girl for banquets and parties, and then she began to do room decorating for banquets. She also began to sew the banquet table skirts, tablecloths and napkins, and draperies for certain hotel functions. She still does these things, plus she sometimes sews staff uniforms as well.

Classified as "hotel decorator," Marie does anything and everything she is called upon to do. She knows just about all the employees by name, and she can describe in great detail all of the furnishings in the hotel. Marie takes tremendous pride in seeing that her job, after fifty-three years, is still done cheerfully and professionally.

Two Old Friends Met at the Menger

The Menger's Colonial Dining Room was a favorite coffee-klatsching spot for two old friends who often dropped by to chat with one another. Famous San Antonio gentlemen Maury Maverick Jr. and former Congressman Henry B. Gonzalez, both liberal Democrats, spent many an hour discussing their favorite subject, politics, while sipping the Menger's delicious brew. There was a special table where the two always sat, deep in animated conversation, and Ernesto Malacara can still point it out. He still calls it "Mr. Maury's and Henry B.'s table."

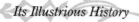

Sidney Brooks: A Tie With the Menger

Flying Cadet Sidney J. Brooks Jr. never had the chance to become a general. Had he lived, he just might have been. The young aviator died in a fiery crash when his JR-4A airplane crashed on a final approach into Kelly Field, where he had been undergoing pilot training. He had made a cross country solo, to Hondo and back. Just before bringing the plane in to the home field, it turned nose down and crashed, killing young Brooks. The flyer had received a typhoid shot early in the morning of the day he died, and doctors speculated that he might have had an allergic reaction, fainting in the cockpit as a result. Physicians knew little about the stress and strain that flying can place on the human body at that time. Three months after his death, a military installation, Brooks Air Force Base, was named in his honor, as he was the first man from San Antonio to die in World War I.

Brooks was from a prominent San Antonio family. His father was Judge Sidney J. Brooks Sr. The family lived in the prestigious King William District in a lovely old Victorian home. Sidney graduated from high school in San Antonio in 1913 and then attended the University of Texas in Austin. For a short time he also served as a reporter for the *San Antonio Light.*

Brooks was killed on November 13, 1917. The very night before he died, he went down to the Menger Hotel to visit with close friend Stuart McManus, who was the night desk clerk. Sidney told his friend he had a strange feeling that he might not be able to solo successfully. McManus told him not to worry, that he would do just fine. Brooks seemed to be very concerned when he left the Menger, McManus later recalled. Little did he know it would be the last time he would see his friend Sidney alive.

Sidney Brooks' premonition was to come true before the sun set on the following day.

Brook's fiancee, Lottie Jean Steele, later said she knew when Brooks died. She was in the backyard of her Terrell Hills home when she distinctly heard his voice calling out to her, not once, but twice! A short time later she received the message he had crashed, at the exact time she heard his voice.

Rosenthal-Kallison Rites

When my dear friend Frances Kallison mentioned that her wedding had been held at the Menger, I begged her to tell me all about the event, which took place nearly seventy years ago.

When Frances Elaine Rosenthal of Fort Worth and Perry Kallison of San Antonio decided to get married, they chose the Menger Hotel as the place where their nuptial vows would be said.

Frances, a recent graduate of the University of Chicago, met Perry Kallison in May of 1930. She was visiting friends in San Antonio over the Decoration Day (now called Memorial Day) weekend. Her hostess invited her to go on a picnic and swimming party outing to New Braunfels' popular Landa Park with a group from the Temple League. This was a group for young people that the rabbi of Temple Beth El and his wife had organized. Frances had not brought a bathing suit with her, so she had to rent a very baggy, unattractive swimsuit that was riddled with moth holes! Perry Kallison was among the group of young folks, with another young lady as his date. But Frances, moth holes and all, must have captivated the young bachelor, because it wasn't long before the two were dating. Frances recalled he visited her on July 4th and again over Labor Day, while letters flew back and forth between the two cities in the meantime. The Kallison family invited the Rosenthals for a Thanksgiving visit in San Antonio. By New Year's Eve, December 31, 1930, the couple announced their engagement, choosing March 8, 1931, as their wedding date.

Perry Kallison's father was quite ill at the time, and so Frances and her family elected to come to San Antonio for the wedding in order to accommodate the Kallison family.

Rabbi Ephraim Frisch of Temple Beth El performed the marriage rites in the parlor of the King Ranch Suite, which was sometimes referred to as the Bridal Suite. The families of the

Frances Elaine Rosenthal Kallison as she appeared on her
wedding day at the Menger Hotel on March 8, 1931

Photo courtesy Mrs. Perry Kallison

couple and a number of close friends witnessed the ceremony. The bride was lovely in a peach colored silk chiffon gown accented with floral motifs. She carried a bouquet of spring flowers. After the nuptials, the party retired to the adjoining Renaissance Room where a seated seven-course champagne dinner was served. It was a gala affair!

When the newly married Kallisons departed from the festivities, they were driven to the Missouri Pacific station where Perry had reserved a Pullman for their wedding trip to Mexico City.

The Perry Kallisons and their three children became one of San Antonio's most prominent and respected families. Perry was one of the founding fathers of the San Antonio Stock Show and Rodeo, and his picture hangs in the Hall of Fame Museum on the stock show grounds.

Chapter 7

Notable Guests

*T*he Menger Hotel has long provided lodgings and warm hospitality to guests from all walks of life. Its registers down through the years have carried the signatures of many famous people, from U.S. presidents to celebrities of the stage and screen. There have been military leaders and captains of industry, great numbers of writers, poets, entertainers, cattle barons, philanthropists, and educators. They all must have departed greatly impressed with the ambiance, delighted with the comfort of their accommodations, and refreshed by the excellent food and service provided by the hotel.

The San Antonio daily newspapers started printing lists of arriving hotel guests in 1855. Since the early hotel registers have been lost or destroyed, these newspaper records have helped us establish that certain personages actually stayed at the hotel.

A number of interesting individuals actually lived at the hotel, for weeks, sometimes months, and sometimes years at a time. All have imprinted their personalities on the very fiber of the place.

Today, the Menger no longer provides accommodations for residential guests. Only the general manager and his wife make their home at the hotel. Many of the former long-term suites, which were equipped with kitchenettes, have been subdivided into standard sized guest accommodations.

We have doubtless overlooked some former guests. There have been so many, and the list is extremely impressive. But included in the following are several of the famous personalities who have crossed the threshold of San Antonio's oldest hotel.

U.S. Presidents

A number of American presidents have been either guests or short-time visitors to the Menger. Some have come while still in office, while others have visited after they left that high place in government. Still others have appeared at the Menger as just presidential hopefuls, while campaigning.

Ulysses S. Grant

The *San Antonio Freie Presse Fuer Texas* reported on March 27, 1880, that general of the army and former president Ulysses S. Grant, Mrs. Grant, and their party arrived for a visit to San Antonio. A handsome procession of carriages, in which rode many local celebrities and civic leaders, met the couple at the train station. Mayor James H. French awaited them, and they were handed into an elegant carriage pulled by a team of four high-stepping horses. The party was escorted by the city band, the San Antonio colored band, and the fire department. The firemen were decked out in blue flannels and helmets with red visors. In addition, two companies of the U.S. Infantry and Battery F of the Second Artillery from Fort Sam Houston were on hand. After a slow trip to the Menger, which was caused by the large crowds all along the way, the general reviewed the troops and then retired to his rooms, which consisted of the entire front of the first floor.

The Grant party remained in San Antonio for four days. On the last day of their visit, it was reported that the general was entertained with a concert of sacred songs by Blind Tom, the slave-born Negro whose genius on the piano had won him great acclaim throughout the nation.

Benjamin Harrison

President Harrison visited the city in 1891 and was a guest at the Menger during that visit. A big parade, planned to welcome the president, was the forerunner of today's gala Battle of Flowers parades, which are held during every Fiesta week. A delay in Harrison's train arrival actually caused the president to miss the parade staged in his honor!

Theodore Roosevelt

Theodore "Teddy" Roosevelt visited the hotel several times in 1892, 1898, and 1905. His stays there and the ties with the Menger Bar made such an impact on the Menger's history that chapter nine is devoted entirely to the Roosevelt story.

Woodrow Wilson

Wilson visited the Menger when he was president of Princeton University and later, president of the United States. A veteran waiter, Robert Fairley, recalled that Wilson was "a fine gentleman, but he was very quiet."

Dwight David Eisenhower

Eisenhower was stationed in San Antonio twice during his military career. In 1916, fresh out of West Point and at Fort Sam Houston as a lieutenant, he met a lovely young lady from Colorado, who was visiting relatives in the city. Eisenhower was very smitten with Mary Geneva "Mamie" Doud and liked to bring her to the romantic patio of the Menger to dine under the stars. He successfully wooed and won the hand of Mamie. After the couple married, Eisenhower, by now a captain, brought his bride of less than a year to the Menger Hotel where they made their temporary home until quarters were available at Ft. Sam Houston. At this time, in 1917, Captain Eisenhower was training the 57th Infantry for their eventual transfer to France.

Later, the Eisenhowers returned to San Antonio when "Ike" was a colonel. He was promoted to brigadier general while at Fort Sam Houston just prior to the outbreak of World War II.

In 1951 General Eisenhower, the newly elected president of the United States, again visited the Menger Hotel. Waiters who attended his table in the Colonial Dining Room were required to wear white gloves while serving him. Secret Service men analyzed his food before it was served to him. Ike required meticulous service, and he demanded the housekeepers turn down his bed nightly long before the service became a common practice.

A number of other presidents have visited at the Menger at one time or another. Unfortunately, we do not have the dates of their visits available, as many of the old registers have been lost or disposed of over the years. But it is known that **William Howard Taft**, **William McKinley**, **Harry Truman**, **Richard Nixon**, **Ronald Reagan** (who visited during the days he was an actor), **Lyndon Johnson**, and **George Bush** were either overnight guests at the hotel or attended special social functions there. **William Jefferson (Bill) Clinton** first visited the hotel while campaigning for Walter Mondale's unsuccessful bid for the presidency. Later, as a presidential candidate himself, he returned. He was greatly impressed by the famous mango ice cream!

Military Greats

Almost from the beginnings of the city, when the first Spanish presidio was situated on Military Plaza, San Antonio has been a real military community. Today, with its four air force bases and the huge army post at Fort Sam Houston, it is indeed "Military City, U.S.A." It is natural that many famous military figures have either been stationed here or have visited the city at one time or another. Many of them have left a lasting mark on the community. Even today, the city is literally awash with military retirees who have chosen to spend their last days in this city so cordial to service personnel. The Menger Hotel over the years has provided hospitality to many of America's most famous military figures.

General Sam Houston

Shortly after the hotel opened, a very tall, stately gentleman signed the guest register as "Sam Houston and horse." The Texas hero was in town to address an audience that gathered in San Pedro Park to hear him speak against secession. Of course, it did no good, as Texas was soon to leave the Union, and Sam Houston became quite unpopular because of his pro-Union views.

General Robert E. Lee

Lee, while a lieutenant colonel in the United States Army, stayed at the Menger several times prior to the outbreak of the Civil War. Lee was stationed at Fort Mason but made frequent trips to San Antonio prior to the time he resigned his commission to serve as commander of the Army of Northern Virginia in 1861. He was a charter member of St. Mark's Episcopal Church and a member of the famous old Casino Club in San Antonio. The story is told that Colonel Lee once rode his famous horse, Traveler, into the Menger lobby, and he placed a gold locket around the neck of the Menger's young daughter, Catherine Barbara.

William Tecumseh Sherman

In 1871 Sherman was greeted with a fifteen-gun salute on Alamo Plaza in front of the Menger Hotel. This ceremony was followed by a banquet so deluxe that the *San Antonio Express* wrote it up the next day as an affair that could not have been surpassed "in Washington, D.C., or New York City."

General Philip Sheridan

The most elaborate social affair of the 1870s was the elegant banquet honoring General Sheridan and then Secretary of War **General William W. Belknap**. With Sheridan and Belknap was

Colonel Loomis, Chief Engineer of the U.S. Army, and **General Meyers**, head of the U.S. Quartermaster Department. The military contingent was in San Antonio to decide where the permanent location of Texas troops would be, and the city was the host for the banquet at the Menger. J. H. Kampmann was placed in charge of the arrangements. Later on, the city also feted the group with a spectacular barbecue held at San Pedro Springs. A seventeen-gun salute greeted the famous generals upon their entrance to the park, which was illuminated by paper lanterns.

General Ranald Slidell Mackenzie

General Ranald S. Mackenzie was a famous old-time Indian fighter and hero of many skirmishes when the West Texas forts offered the only protection the settlers had from the Indians. He was honored with a huge ball at the Menger in 1875. The brevet general of Civil War fame and commander of the Fourth Cavalry led the devastating raid on the Kickapoo Indians in Mexico across from Fort Clark in 1873. MacKenzie was a popular hero who lived in San Antonio after this time until illness forced him to return East.

General Kirby Smith and General Joseph Shelby

After the Civil War, many of the Confederate soldiers drifted towards San Antonio, especially officers who had been deprived of their citizenship and their hope. It was truly a desperate time for them. One famous Confederate general, Kirby Smith, stayed at the Menger in disguise. However a fellow officer, General Joseph Shelby, of the Missouri Cavalry, who was not in disguise, was seated on the balcony when Smith registered, and he recognized him. Shelby had over one hundred men with him in San Antonio. He called up his bandmaster and ordered a serenade and also told all his men to get under arms and parade in front of the balcony. Assembly blew and Shelby ordered his band to play "Hail to the Chief." There was no sign of life from General Smith's room. So Shelby ordered his band to play "Dixie." Shelby told his men, "If the old man were dead it would bring him back to life! That old man up there is Kirby Smith!"

General Smith came forth, undisguised. Shouts and music filled the air. Smith tried three times to speak, and each time he was overcome with emotion and driven to tears. It is doubtful the Menger Hotel was ever witness to a more emotional moment.

The next day General Shelby and the remnants of his Missouri Cavalry marched out of San Antonio, on the way to exile in Mexico. He and his men had never surrendered. When Shelby and his men reached the Rio Grande, they stopped and ceremoniously lowered their beloved flag, the Stars and Bars they had so proudly fought for, into the muddy water. It was the last Confederate flag to fly unsurrendered. Then they sadly marched into Mexico.

Colonel Charles Anderson

Colonel Anderson was a Menger "guest" with a strange twist. He had built his ranch home here in San Antonio. He was an anti-secessionist in rabidly rebel San Antonio. Just prior to the outbreak of the Civil War, when tempers and emotions ran high, he spoke out his sentiments on Alamo Plaza right in front of the Menger Hotel. He was branded "a black Republican and a traitor" when Texas seceded, and he was arrested and confined in the Menger Hotel. Later, he escaped and fled to Mexico. He never returned to his beautiful plantation home that later became known as the Argyle, one of San Antonio's most prestigious private clubs.

General John "Black Jack" Pershing

General Pershing commanded Fort Sam Houston prior to his leaving the city in 1917. He lived in quarters number six on Staff Post Road at Fort Sam Houston, which now bears his name, *The Pershing House*. The city of San Antonio chose the Menger as the perfect place to honor the great American general with a gala farewell ball before he left the city to take command of the American Expeditionary Forces in France during World War I.

General John Lincoln Clem

General John Lincoln Clem was known as "the Drummer Boy of Chickamauga." He lived on Staff Post Road at Fort Sam Houston but attended many parties and dinners at the Menger when he was stationed at the fort. On one occasion, the San Antonio chapter of the Daughters of the Republic of Texas gave a charity card party to benefit the restoration of the Alamo. General Clem won the first prize, a silver matchbox.

Colonel Tommy Tompkins

The flamboyant commander of the Seventh Cavalry actually lived in the Menger Hotel for several years, and his story follows in the next chapter.

General William Hood Simpson

Famous four-star general Simpson, commander of the Ninth Army during World War II, lived at the Menger for a number of years. His story follows in the next chapter.

General Frederick Denham Grant

In 1902 General Frederick Denham Grant, son of President Ulysses S. Grant, was honored by a banquet at the Menger, given by the San Antonio Businessmen's Club. Grant had seen service with Sheridan on the frontiers and had served as a diplomat in European courts. He also served with Teddy Roosevelt in Cuba and later became governor of Puerto Rico, before going to the Philippines, where he again distinguished himself.

Other Military Greats

Other famous figures in military history visited the Menger at one time or another. These included: **Colonel Leonard Wood**, **General O. C. Ord**, **General Frederick Funston**, **General James Henry Carleton**, and **General Nelson A. Miles**. Also, not to be forgotten are **General Hap Arnold**, **General George**

Patton, **General James Doolittle**, and **General Walter Krueger**. All of these distinguished military figures frequented the Menger at one time or another during their tours of duty in San Antonio or on visits to the city. The original "Flying Tigers" have held reunions at the Menger with the famous **Colonel Tex Hill**, and many military units from all branches of service regularly hold their annual reunions at the famous hotel.

Literary Luminaries

Over the years many writers, poets, orators, and playwrights have spent time at the Menger during their visits to San Antonio.

William Jennings Bryant

The famous orator stayed at the Menger during a speaking engagement to the city.

Frances Parkinson Keyes

The famous Louisiana novelist chose the Menger as the setting for a scene in one of her novels, *All That Glitters*. She depicts a young newly married couple as they entered the Menger bridal suite "all decorated with white flowers by the hotel management, according to custom."

According to *San Antonio's Menger*, by Mrs. Franz Stumpf, Mrs. Keyes once wrote a letter to a friend in which she stated, "I first went to the Menger Hotel many years ago and I have always insisted on staying there whenever I have been in San Antonio. It has, in my opinion, more atmosphere than any hotel in the world."

Sidney Lanier

The beloved Southern poet spent six months at the hotel in 1872-73, while recovering from ill health. His story follows in detail in the next chapter.

Joaquin Miller

Miller was known as the "Poet of the Sierras." After a lecture tour of the East, he spent a few days in San Antonio at the Menger and was very impressed with the city. He spoke to students at a school operated by Dr. W. B. Seeley and gave a public lecture at the Madison Square Presbyterian Church. His lecture, named by the *San Antonio Express* as the "best of the season," was entitled "Lessons Not in Books" and included readings of his own poetry.

William Sidney Porter

In 1895 William Sidney Porter, whose pen name was O. Henry, spent some time at the hotel. Several of his short stories were written in his room, which was warmed with a wood-burning fireplace. He did not stay at the Menger the whole time he lived in San Antonio, because he could not afford it. He did frequently visit the bar and dining room even after he moved out of the hotel into less expensive quarters. Several of his short stories refer to San Antonio and to the Menger Hotel. In "Seats of Haughty Hygeia at the Solita" and "The Higher Addiction," Porter had his characters make direct references to the Menger Hotel and its famous bar.

Oscar Wilde

The flamboyant playwright visited the hotel in 1882 while on a lecture tour. It was reported that the dandified Wilde arrived in a carriage that was literally filled with sunflowers tossed into it by admirers as he made his way to the Menger from Sunset Station. Now, you have to picture this: The hotel was often home to ranchers and cattlemen. In fact, many a cattle deal was struck over two fingers of rye and a handshake at the Menger Bar. Just imagine the shock to some of those rough and tough frontier types to see the Englishman arrive, costumed in a dark velvet jacket, white waistcoat, blue cravat, white lace ruffles adorning the collar and sleeves of his blouse, and light drab knee-length trousers. He wore scarlet stockings and black slippers, the toes of which were adorned with shiny silver buckles. His long black hair hung in corkscrew curls to his shoulders. He delighted in smoking long foreign cigarettes fitted into silver holders, while sipping ice cold spiked lemonade as he strolled through the lobbies and patio.

After giving his lecture on "Decorative Art" at the Turner Theatre, Wilde went sightseeing. He was especially delighted with the Spanish missions. He said of San Jose that it was excelled by nothing else he had seen in America.

Menger Hotel Designated Literary Landmark

Because the hotel has hosted so many literary figures throughout its long history, the Friends of Libraries USA and the Friends of the San Antonio Public Library named the hotel an official Literary Landmark on January 12, 2000. This program was established "to preserve and attract the attention in America to sites forever linked to authors' lives. Such sites include residences, sites described in their work, and significant sites of inspiration throughout the country."

A bronze plaque was presented to the hotel management for having provided hospitality and ambiance conducive to the writing efforts of such literary giants as William Sidney Porter (O. Henry), Oscar Wilde, Theodore Roosevelt, and Sidney Lanier.

Ernesto Malacara receives bronze plaque from Mr. Dan Arbour, president of the Friends of Libraries USA, commemorating the Menger being named an official Literary Landmark

Photo by author

Cattle Barons, Ranchers, and Such

Captain Richard King

Captain King, founder of the famous King Ranch for whom the King Ranch Suite at the Menger is named, and his friends **Peter Gallagher** and **George West** often met at the Menger to make arrangements for their spring cattle drives. You will read more about Captain King, who spent much time at the hotel, in chapter eight.

Two other figures who were prominent in the cattle industry were **John Warne "Bet a Million" Gates** and **Pete McManus**, who, while in San Antonio to introduce barbed wire to the local ranchers, chose the Menger as their headquarters. A detailed story about Gates and McManus appears in the following chapter.

Stars of the Entertainment World

Unfortunately, many of the old registers which bore the signatures of famous entertainers, singers, and theatrical figures were tossed aside, probably landing in the trash heap, when the more modern system utilizing registration cards was employed. There are sketchy facts available about some of them, and we have included what little we have been able to find out about their visits to the Menger. So many glamorous figures! What excitement they must have brought to the hotel by their very presence in its lobbies and guest chambers.

From the earliest days of the hotel, when the old San Antonio Opera House was located just across Alamo Plaza from the Menger, glamorous celebrities have stayed at the famous inn. One might have encountered such famous actors as **Sir Henry Lauder, George Wilkins Kendall, Richard Mansfield**, and **Edwin Booth. "Buffalo Bill" Cody** also made several appearances in San Antonio and often frequented the Menger. Vaudeville and stage actresses added a touch of pulchritude to the lobbies and dining rooms as they strolled about the hotel. In 1860 the lovely

Anna Held appeared at the opera house, with its red plush and gilt ambiance. The gifted **Sarah Bernhardt**, known as the Belle of Europe, stayed in San Antonio while passing through en route from a theatrical tour in Mexico and Central and South America in 1887. She was absolutely adored everywhere she went. When she was in South America, the Argentinians were so captivated by her charms they presented her with a gift of 13,000 acres of land! In San Antonio the great lady was feted with a fabulous dinner party held in the Renaissance Room. It was hosted by local dignitaries. Her admirers transformed her room, suite 343, into a "bower of flowers." Beautiful **Lily Langtry**, the famous English actress, visited the Southwest in 1888. She displayed her considerable beauty, talent, and elegant wardrobe to admirers in Houston, Galveston, and San Antonio. She stopped for lunch at the Menger and favored the guests and staff by singing "Dixie" in the hotel lobby. **Maude Adams** and **Lillian Russell** also enjoyed the hospitality of the Menger. The girl with the gun, **Annie Oakley**, also stayed at the hotel along with **Buffalo Bill Cody** and other stars of his Wild West Show.

Of the many theatrical guests who stayed at the hotel prior to 1877, the **Peak Family**, a troupe of Swiss bell ringers, was the most famous.

A great number of twentieth-century stars have headquartered at the Menger. Western star **Roy Rogers** and his lovely wife, **Dale Evans**, spent so much time at the hotel that a suite was named for them, and it is still furnished in the Western style furnishings they loved. They frequently performed at the San Antonio Fat Stock Show and Rodeo. And in August of 1968 the couple came to San Antonio to perform at the opening of the Hemisfair. During this particular visit, the entourage included **Pat Brady**, Roy Rogers' "sidekick," as well as the **Sons of the Pioneers** and the couples' German shepherd dog, **Bullet**. They gave four performances at the fair, filling the audiences with nostalgia with their renditions of "Tumbling Tumbleweeds," "Cool Water," and "Happy Trails."

The provocative **Mae West** also has a suite named for her at the Menger. Whether or not she ever invited anybody to "come up and see me sometime" while staying in that suite is unknown! **Joan Crawford**, who was actually born in a boardinghouse on Crofton Street in the King William historic district, often made her way to the Menger on return visits to her old hometown. Known to have enjoyed the occasional toddy, she especially enjoyed the Menger Bar. **Pola Negri**, the famous silent film star, once the mistress of Rudolph Valentino, lived at the hotel for a couple of years. Her story appears in the next chapter.

Ernesto Malacara recalls chatting with **Linda Evans** when she visited the hotel. He said she was a very lovely and gracious young lady.

Beverly Sills always stayed at the Menger during those grand days when San Antonio still had an opera season. I fondly recall meeting this charming, down-to-earth lady when she performed here in *Norma*, and my daughter, Sarah, was chosen to be a handmaiden to Miss Sills in the production. As a member of the Opera Guild, it was my privilege to help entertain the famous star.

A number of male actors have enjoyed the comfort of the Menger Hotel while in San Antonio to make films or public appearances. **Jose Ferrer, Ronald Reagan, Sean Connery, Robert Mitchum, Steve McQueen, Sonny Tufts**, and **James Stewart** are some of these. When comedian **Bob Hope** stayed at the hotel, he was having severe back pains, and Dr. Anthony Mendicino was called in to minister to the popular star. **John Wayne**, while staying in a suite on the mezzanine, dropped in at the old Patio Club one evening. Uninvited, he sat down at the table with some regular patrons and proceeded to drink their whisky and smoke their cigarettes, all the while totally charming them with his friendliness and affable personality. The people said Wayne even invited them to come up and visit in his suite! **"Happy" Shahan**, who owned the ranch at Brackettville where Wayne's movie *The Alamo* was filmed, also was a frequent Menger guest.

Sports Figures

There have been a number of sports figures who availed them-selves of the Menger accommodations, too. Baseball great **Babe Ruth** is shown in a photograph in the corridor leading from the lobby to the parking garage. Professional fighter **John L. Sullivan** also stayed at the Menger. **Bob Fitzsimmons**, heavyweight champion, stayed at the Menger in 1896 while in training for a fight with **Pete Maher. Eddie Joseph**, veteran of 159 professional fights, started spending his winters at the hotel in 1953.

Other Notable Menger Guests

Many other notables came and went...and still do, at the Menger. You surely must have heard of **Gutzon Borglum**, one of America's most famous sculptors, who executed the famous *Faces of Mount Rushmore*. He lived at the Menger and had his studio there, just off the patio, at one time. You will read more about him in the next chapter.

Clara Driscoll, a young woman who was often referred to as the "Savior of the Alamo," frequently stayed at the hotel. She was known for some of the lavish parties she gave while a guest in the Menger.

Jane Addams, of the celebrated Chicago Hull House, visited the hotel during World War I days. A great social reformer, Addams won the Nobel Peace Prize in 1921. Her San Antonio admirers filled her suite with American Beauty roses during her stay at the Menger. **Hettie Green**, one of the richest women in America, also stayed at the Menger. During Jimmy Carter's presidency, first lady **Roslyn Carter** delivered a speech at the hotel.

Although she wasn't exactly a guest, one lady who was quite an "item" back in her day, the famous temperance activist **Carrie Nation**, once visited the Menger Bar. She gave the bartender and his customers a good tongue lashing over their evil ways before departing.

Even the outlaw **Frank James**, of the infamous Quantrill Raiders, once registered at the hotel.

G. W. Kendall, who pioneered the sheep industry in Texas and for whom Kendall County was named, signed the guest register September 10, 1860. He also became a famous journalist and founded the *Picayune* of New Orleans.

Early German settlers, known in this part of the world for their noteworthy contributions, stayed at the Menger whenever they were in the city. Two of the best known include **John O. Muesebach**, a Prussian baron who founded Fredericksburg in 1845, and **Eugene Lindheimer**, the brilliant naturalist who made his home in New Braunfels.

Another noteworthy gentleman who signed his name **E. Madero** came from Monterrey, Mexico. He was the father of Francisco Madero, the famous revolutionary who triggered the Mexican Revolution in 1910.

Chapter 8

Resident Guests of the Menger

For a long period of time, the Menger Hotel had a number of accommodations designed for long-term residential guests. Some people lived there for periods of weeks, some for months at a time, and a few lived there for many years. Often, these were retired people, some widowed, who no longer could keep up a large residential property. Many were very lonely, and the hotel could be counted on to provide instant company. The Menger provided a home and a place where these people had a sense of belonging. The service personnel were thoughtful and efficient, and there was always good food available. Many of the suites had small kitchens, so guests could also enjoy their own cooking when the occasion or desire arose.

A number of out-of-town patrons maintained suites for their fairly frequent visits to San Antonio during the days when the city was the only place in this part of the state where they might shop, seek medical or legal assistance, or transact business.

Many resident guests were famous people, well-known personalities of their days. Others were just good, substantial citizens, lured to the Menger by the comforts it offered. Just who some of the former resident guests were is not now known, as many old records have been lost. There are no longer any employees there who might remember some of the earlier residents. From what we have been able to find out, most of these people were fascinating individuals, whose very presence in the lobbies, the dining rooms, the bar and patio, added character and personality to this fine hotel.

We would like to share with you the stories we have managed to uncover about some of these interesting personalities.

Sidney Lanier

When Sidney Lanier arrived at the Menger Hotel on November 25, 1872, for a five-month stay, he was as yet unknown, a melancholy young man bent on regaining the physical strength he had lost during his days in a Union prison camp during the Civil War.

Lanier was born February 3, 1842, in Macon, Georgia. From early childhood he had shown a great talent (some called him a genius or prodigy) for music. Before he could even read, he had taught himself to play the piano, violin, and flute. His father, who was a lawyer, discouraged young Sidney's musical interests since he had already decided that his son should become an attorney like himself. Sidney loved music and poetry, and he read every book he could find. In order not to upset his strong-willed father, he concentrated on playing the flute, because he could conceal that instrument in the folds of his clothing.

Sidney entered Oglethorpe University when he was only thirteen years old. By the time he was eighteen, he already held a tutorship at the institution. Then, in April of 1861, he enlisted in the Confederate army. He was soon captured and confined in a Union prison camp, where he wiled away the time by entertaining his fellow captives with impromptu flute concerts. His health was greatly affected by the dampness, lack of nutritious food, and filthy conditions. He had already contracted "consumption," now known as tuberculosis, from the wretched days he spent in confinement.

After Lanier got out of the army he held several jobs. He was for a time a hotel clerk, then a country schoolteacher. Then, to please his father, he went back to school to study law, eventually going into practice with his father. In 1867 he married Mary Day of Macon.

Lanier's heart was not in the practice of law. He was artistic and highly intellectual. He went through what might today be classified as an identity crisis. He couldn't decide what he really wanted to do. From an early age he had written poetry, which seemed the most natural way he had of expressing himself. Some of his best poems, written around 1865, included "The Dying Words of Stonewall Jackson," "The Tournament," and "Psalm of the West."

Always frail, Lanier tried several cures for his illness with no real success. Finally, in 1872 he decided to try a change of climate. Reluctantly leaving his beloved Mary behind in Georgia, he traveled to Texas. He came from Georgia to Galveston, Texas, by boat. Next he went by rail to Houston and thence to Austin. In Austin he took a stagecoach to San Antonio, which was a thirteen-hour drive in those days.

That November evening of his arrival, he wrote to his wife in Macon. He described the Menger Hotel in his letter as follows: "The hotel at which I am stopping is of stone, with a fine paved court in the rear, after the manner of the Cuban hotels, and a fair broad pavement in front where we sit in armchairs and look out upon Alamo Plaza."

Lanier was assigned to room 64. The original furniture from this room has since been moved to room 102, which is designated as the Sidney Lanier Suite. It is often chosen by newlyweds as a honeymoon suite.

When Lanier arrived he appeared as a tall, gaunt, young man, with a slender frame ravaged by illness and fever. He knew no one in San Antonio, but during his stay he managed to make a few friends in the community, people who were kind to him and sympathetic with his poor state of health. He often gave impromptu private flute recitals at the hotel or in the homes of acquaintances. He wrote to his family that ladies in hooped skirts and gentlemen in silk vests enjoyed listening to his music while they sipped mint juleps!

Lanier wrote only a few letters during his stay at the Menger. In one, he wrote of visiting the Beethoven Mannechor (still located at 422 Pereida Street) with his friend Mr. Schudermantel and being "moved to tears by the fine singing."

In February 1873, while still at the Menger, Lanier wrote "Nature Metaphors." He also wrote to Mary, his wife, "I have writ the most beautiful piece (for the flute) called 'Field Larks and Blackbirds.'" This work soon became famous and still is regarded as one of the real classic masterpieces for wind instruments, especially the flute.

Lanier loved to visit the San Fernando Cathedral and Mission San Jose, and he often took walks or rode horseback to San Pedro Park, where he delighted in visiting the small zoo located there.

One acquaintance, H. Kerbes of Comfort, recalled that Lanier was "a refined gentleman, handsome of a French type, with black hair, mustache, and goatee. He was slender of build, pale of complexion, and had the eyes of a dreamer." He was also described as "no Prohibitionist," evidently meaning he enjoyed a drink on occasion.

Lanier had very little money and lived frugally while in San Antonio. He did manage to pick up a few dollars for his flute concerts. He seemed content to write poetry, play his flute, and take long walks about the community. He loved the San Antonio River and enjoyed strolling along its banks. He poetically described the river as "a green, translucent stream, flowing beneath long sprays of weeping willows."

Lanier composed a famous classic essay about San Antonio in 1873. He declared, "If peculiarities were quills, San Antonio de Bexar would be a rare porcupine."

Describing a particularly enjoyable day, Lanier wrote to his wife, "Hadst thou been here, then how fair and happy had been my day, for I mostly have great pain when music, or any beauty, comes past my way, and thou art not by."

Lanier finally left San Antonio in April of 1873, his state of health somewhat improved. He moved to Baltimore, a city steeped in music and literature. He and Mary seemed to enjoy those days. By 1879 he had gained quite a reputation as a poet and was called the "South's greatest poet." (Poets were more appreciated then than they are now!) He gave lectures on English literature at Johns Hopkins University and was well respected. He and Mary had become the parents of four sons by then.

Lanier never fully regained the strength he had lost during the Civil War, and finally his frail body gave up when he was just five months short of his fortieth birthday. He died on September 10, 1881. Among his last great works were: "Sunrise," "The Symphony," "Night and Day," and "Life and Song."

In the "quite a coincidence" department, it is noted on the eighty-seventh anniversary of Lanier's birth, February 3, 1929, a special event took place in Macon, Georgia, the city of his birth. A bust of the poet executed by another famous Menger resident, Gutzon Borglum, was unveiled at Macon's Washington Memorial Library, the gift of the Sidney Lanier Memorial Association.

It is interesting to think about, had Lanier not had his five-month-long stay at the Menger, where he regained some of his physical strength due to a stress-free existence, good nutrition, and mild climate, he might not have lived to write much of his most beautiful poetry. Thanks to his recuperative stay at the Menger, he was able to share his talent with the world, becoming one of America's best-loved poets.

John Warne "Bet a Million" Gates

He wasn't rich, nor was he famous, when he stepped off the stagecoach in front of the Menger Hotel that February day in 1876! But one day all Texans would recognize the name of John Warne "Bet a Million" Gates, because that young man was destined to become a big man and a big name in the Lone Star State!

Young Gates was sent to San Antonio to join a friend and colleague, Pete McManus, on a business trip. The Illinois born Gates had recently become a salesman for a company that was manufacturing a new product called "barbed wire." The fencing material had been invented in France in 1860. It was later made in this country by Joseph F. Glidden, who made the fencing material in DeKalb, Illinois, having been granted his patent in 1874. Glidden's partner, Isaac Leonard Ellwood, who was known as "Colonel Ike," bought out Glidden. Ellwood hired Pete McManus, a friendly, outgoing Irishman, as a salesman for his company. McManus knew Gates, who had a little hardware store in Turner Junction, Illinois. He talked Gates into abandoning the store and temporarily leaving his wife to go on the road selling barbed wire. McManus told Gates he could "make big money" with this new product, according to Lloyd Wendt and Herman Kogan, who wrote the book *Bet a Million! The Story of John W. Gates.*

In 1876 Ellwood sent McManus to Texas to introduce barbed wire to the ranchers and cattlemen, and he hired young Gates to assist the veteran salesman.

Gates and McManus checked into the Menger Hotel and then went about deciding how they would introduce, and hopefully sell, a product that had never been seen or heard of in Texas before. Gates, always an innovator, decided to "scout out" the local cattlemen, see what made them tick, and then decide on the best procedure to get them to order his product.

Although the men were staying at the Menger, they started spending most of their time in a local watering hole called the Hole in the Wall Saloon, which was located on Military Plaza. They had noted that mostly silk-stockinged trade drank at the Menger Bar, and they needed to meet a lot of ordinary ranchers, who seemed to stay at the less impressive old Southern Hotel on Military Plaza and drink at the nearby Hole in the Wall. Finally, Gates and McManus decided on a clever scheme to attract the attention of the cattlemen and hopefully sell a good order of the barbed wire for their firm. Gates, ever a talker and a real extrovert, started talking

John W. "Bet a Million" Gates, who introduced
barbed wire to the cattle industry

Photo courtesy University of Texas Institute of Texan Cultures,
University of Texas Texana Collection, Austin, Texas

up the merits of the fencing material, stressing how it would keep their cattle in and their neighbor's cattle out of their property. And so it was that the two men built a corral to demonstrate the fine points of their barbed wire. It was erected on Alamo Plaza, according to an article that ran in the *San Antonio Herald* on February 27, 1910. Pete McManus, who stayed around San Antonio for many years after this event took place, told reporters during an interview:

> It was in 1876 that John W. Gates and I came to Texas for the purpose of demonstrating the practicality of the wire for fencing purposes. We went to San Antonio, taking several reels of wire with us. We made our first demonstration upon Alamo Plaza for the benefit of cattlemen who were gathered there from different parts of Southwest Texas. At that time Alamo Plaza was a mudhole. Mr. Gates and I set up the posts and strung four strands of barbed wire, making a corral of considerable size. Some of the cowboys were skeptical, and Gates and I were jollied a good deal as we went about our work of preparing for the test. A bunch of range cattle were driven into the corral and the ranchmen expected to see them go through or over the fence, but the wires held them without any trouble. Mr. Gates and I gave other demonstrations of the practicality of the fencing material and took some good orders for the wire. That was really the beginning of the barbed wire industry. Mr. Gates saw it was a good thing and he began its manufacture. I was with him for twenty-seven years.

This first demonstration must have been something to see! From all accounts, Gates and McManus sold a lot of barbed wire on that day, and they led the cattlemen into the lobby of the Menger, where they were staying, to fill out their order blanks.

After this successful beginning, McManus elected to stay in Texas, mostly around San Antonio, where he made a good living as a barbed-wire salesman. The ambitious and flamboyant Gates soon decided to go into the manufacturing business. Over the next two decades, he started up several successful factories, including the American Steel and Wire Company of Illinois, which he founded in 1897, and the American Steel and Wire Company of New Jersey, which was founded in 1898. (The two companies later became a part of a combine that grew into the world's first billion-dollar industry, the United States Steel Company.) Gates operated these wire companies for a number of years and became tremendously wealthy.

Because Gates had such an outgoing personality, he is better remembered than McManus, who actually started out as his "boss" when Gates was just getting started as a salesman. In fact, Gates became so successful in manufacturing that he put McManus to work for him. It was a wise decision. During the years he spent as a salesman, McManus sold more fencing than any other salesman in the whole world! He was well known in San Antonio, where he made his home most of the time.

Years later, in 1900, when Gates was on a business trip to London, the now very wealthy captain of industry was given a nickname. He and a business associate, named John Drake, had won a million-dollar racetrack bet. From then on John was called "Bet a Million" Gates! It is said he would bet on just about anything. It was just a part of his nature. And most of the time, he won. He successfully bought and sold stocks and made a great deal of money, eventually heading up several large corporations.

Ever the opportunist, when Spindletop oil field in Texas came in, Gates was there, too. In partnership with former Texas Governor Stephen Hogg and other prominent businessmen, Gates helped to found the Texas Company (later known as Texaco), one of the world's great oil companies. The now extremely wealthy Gates was one of the leading forces in the development of Port Arthur. He built and endowed Port Arthur College and gave it to the city and became a prominent civic leader. The colorful multimillionaire died while on a trip to Paris, France, August 9, 1911. He was only fifty-six years old.

Many historians have written about the introduction of barbed wire and of its having been first introduced to the cattle industry in San Antonio. For some reason, in 1971 a bronze plaque was erroneously placed by the Texas Historical Commission at Military Plaza, stating this was where the first demonstration of barbed wire was held. (The plaque is on the site of the City Hall.) The sponsors were the Texas Barbed Wire Collectors Association. Frank W. Jennings, a noted San Antonio historian, has long been at work to prove this event did not take place at Military Plaza, and to have the plaque removed from Military Plaza. He has worked tirelessly to have a new reworded plaque placed where it should be, on Alamo Plaza! Since the plaza is an open area, a suitable location for the plaque is on the wall of the Menger Hotel, where Gates and McManus stayed while they were demonstrating and selling their product.

Frank W. Jennings has composed the wording on the plaque, which marks the spot that is so important to the American cattle industry, where barbed wire and thus, fencing of the open ranges, was first introduced.

BARBED WIRE DEMONSTRATION

Once called "bobwire" by cowboys, barbed wire was a French invention first patented in the U.S. in 1867, but it did not gain favor with cattlemen until the late 1870s. Joseph Glidden of DeKalb, Illinois, received a patent for his barbed wire in 1874, and it was wire of his manufacture that was the first barbed wire fencing successfully demonstrated in Texas. In 1876, veteran salesman Pete McManus and his young partner John Warne Gates made their first demonstration of the "Glidden Winner" Barbed Wire. Though speculation has placed this demonstration in San Antonio's bustling Military Plaza, it was here in the quiet "mudhole" of Alamo Plaza that McManus and Gates set up a barbed wire corral and then drove cattle into the pen. It is said that after the corral held the thundering animals under the astonished eyes of cowboys and cattlemen, the flamboyant Gates invited spectators into the Menger Hotel to place their orders. After the theatrical demonstration in Alamo Plaza, the market for barbed wire fencing suddenly exploded with large sales to Texas ranchers and others along the frontier. Pete McManus reportedly sold more barbed wire fencing than any salesman in the world. John W. "Bet a Million" Gates became the world's largest barbed wire manufacturer. He helped found the Texas Company (later Texaco) and develop the town of Port Arthur. Barbed wire fencing changed the landscape of the American West and with it the industries of cattle and agriculture. It made possible the introduction of cultivated cattle stock into the beef industry and opened up the fertile land to farmers and other homesteaders. Within 25 years nearly all the open range had become privately owned and was under fence.

How interesting that, while a guest at the Menger Hotel, Gates and his colleague, Pete McManus, decided upon a scheme to introduce the product that would change the whole face of the American cattle industry and assure great riches for himself at the same time.

Captain Richard King

Another part-time resident of the Menger was the famous Captain Richard King. He kept a suite at the hotel to be available whenever he had to visit San Antonio on one of his frequent business trips. That suite, on the mezzanine adjacent to the Renaissance Room, is still known as the King Ranch Suite.

King was born in Orange County, New Jersey, on July 10, 1825, the son of poor Irish immigrants. As a youth, he had no schooling, living more or less from hand to mouth. At the age of ten, the youngster ran away from home. He stowed away in the hold of a cargo ship, the *Desdemona*, bound for the port of Mobile, Alabama. After enduring several hungry days at sea, the frightened little boy was discovered by seamen who delivered him to the ship's captain. The master gave him a good lecture, much as a parent might have done, and then gave him some fatherly advice that King still recalled in later years.

When the ship arrived in Mobile, young Richard met Captain Hugh Monroe, who was well known in those parts as a steamboat captain. He liked the plucky youth, and King stayed with him for some time, serving as a cabin boy and doing odd jobs about the boat. Later on, he steamboated on the Alabama River for a while with Captain Joe Holland. Holland was so impressed with King that he paid to send him north to school for a period of eight months. This short time was the only formal schooling that King ever received in his whole life. He must have applied himself well, learning a lot in those few months, because he made all the appearances in later life of a well-educated man.

By the time King was nineteen years old, he had become a fully qualified ship's pilot, serving on several riverboats.

For a time, King went into the military service during the Florida War, serving under Captain Henry Penny. After the war, King engaged in steamboating on the Chattahoochee River until 1847. He then left and joined Captain M. Kenedy on the Rio Grande in the Quartermaster Department of the U.S. Army, where he remained until the end of the Mexican War.

King loved steamboating. It was his first love, and he went into business for himself in 1850, establishing King, Kenedy, and Company. He had boats built specifically for service on the Rio Grande. The river must have been a busy place in those days! This firm stayed in business and was successful for a number of years.

In 1853 King visited Corpus Christi for the Lone Star State Fair. His route took him through the Wild Horse Desert, where he and his party stopped at the Santa Gertrudis Creek. It was the first water they had seen in days, a real oasis, with large mesquite trees for shade and cool, clear, sweet water to drink.

Captain Richard King

The University of Texas Institute of Texan Cultures at San Antonio,
photo courtesy of Mary Fearey

While he was at the fair, King met up with Texas Ranger Captain Gideon K. Lewis. The two men formed a partnership to establish and operate a livestock operation with headquarters at the site of the creek, which lay on a part of a 15,500-acre grant known as the Rincon de Santa Gertrudis. For just two cents an acre, the partners purchased the vast spread.

Earlier, when working on the Rio Grande, King had met the famous Robert E. Lee, who was then a lieutenant colonel in the U.S. Army. In pre-Civil War days, Lee was serving on the Rio Grande at the Texas-Mexico border. He gave the young riverboat captain some shrewd advice: "Buy land, and buy it cheap. Hold on to it. Never sell it. That's the way you'll make your fortune." Well, King and Lewis bought the Santa Gertrudis property and then slowly added ranch after ranch to the original land holdings. They set up their first cow camp right near the little creek.

Unfortunately, the partnership didn't last long. It broke up, not because of any dissension, but because Lewis was too much of a lady's man. He was paying too much attention to a pretty young married woman, whose jealous husband shot and killed the ranger.

In 1854, when he was twenty-nine years old, King married Miss Henrietta M. Chamberlain, the daughter of a Presbyterian minister. His father-in-law established the first Presbyterian church on the Rio Grande. Henrietta was a genteel lady and seemed to have had a calming, Christian influence on her rough, tough, self-made husband.

During the Civil War, the Nueces strip was the back door to the Confederacy and a way around the Union blockade of Confederate ports on the Gulf of Mexico. The King Ranch became a depot on what was known as the "Cotton Road." The Union navy had blockaded southern seaports, so thousands of bales of cotton were shipped overland to Mexico, and from there the cotton was trundled onto ships of foreign registry and shipped to European markets. Part of the old Cotton Road is in evidence even today on the King Ranch.

The ranch kept growing and growing until it reached around a million acres, and it was known as the real birthplace of the American ranching business. It still is a busy place today, with a huge herd of over 60,000 registered Santa Gertrudis cattle (named for the original land grant) and 1,000 quarter horses bred on the property, which has been cut back some to a "modest" 825,000 acres.

Captain King was a colorful, interesting personality. He was a big man and often outspoken. Once, when he'd been to the Menger Bar to slake his thirst after the long ride up from the ranch, he returned to his room to find that his wife, Henrietta, was extremely upset. Several times she had requested a pitcher of water so she could clean up, but none had been delivered. Probably because he'd had a few too many toddies at the bar, King picked up the empty porcelain pitcher from the washstand and headed for the gallery outside the doorway to his suite. He tossed the pitcher to the floor beneath, where it shattered into many pieces. "If we don't have any water, we don't need a pitcher," bellowed the impatient Captain. Water, in a new pitcher, arrived very promptly.

The story is told that one evening when the Captain returned to the Menger from a meeting with some of his friends, he happened to fall into step with a fellow cattleman. He had never met the man before, but they seemed to have a lot in common. They talked of cattle drives to the railheads in Kansas, and King judged the man to be very bitter. It seemed a banker had promised him a loan so he could put together a good-sized herd and drive the cattle to market, but at the last minute the bank reneged on the offer and the man was left both broke and embarrassed. King asked the rancher how much money he needed. "Ten thousand dollars," was the reply. Right in front of the Menger Hotel, King made the loan, right out of pocket (imagine carrying around that kind of money in those days), and handed it over to the startled cattleman. King had nothing to go by except the feeling that the man was honest and of high character. The man did not disappoint King. He bought the cattle, made the drive, and promptly paid King back, with goodly interest!

King made his last trip to San Antonio in the spring of 1885. He was not well. While at the Menger, he had to take to his bed. Physicians came to attend him, but there was little they could do. In those days there was no hospital in San Antonio, and many an illustrious individual slipped from the bonds of this earth while staying at the Menger Hotel because it was the most modern hotel of its time and the management provided well for its guests who were ill.

King's doctors told him there was no hope for curing the stomach cancer which was slowly sapping his strength. He had time to get his affairs in order and to visit with many friends and loved ones before time ran out. He died at 6:30 P.M. on April 14, 1885, in the big four-poster bed that is still in the bedroom of the King Ranch Suite. He was sixty years old.

There was a long and flowery obituary in the *San Antonio Express* of April 15, 1885. The following passage is a quote from it:

> While he had faults like most men, they were the outgrowth of a long life spent in the wilds of the frontier; yet they will be long forgotten ere his many acts of benevolence and charity shall fade from the memory of men.
>
> Capt. King has enjoyed the "luxury of doing good" with his wealth, and the consciousness of having done so will sooth his dying moments. Sir Walter Scott said that when men come to die, it is not the good that was done to them by others, but the good they have done that employs their thoughts, and Capt. King can look back without shame or regret on his life. May a merciful Providence sooth his last moments, and reward him a faithful steward of the money entrusted to his care.

King's funeral was conducted in the Menger Hotel's Victorian parlor, with Reverend J. W. Neil of the First Presbyterian Church conducting the services. Captain King was buried in San Antonio in the old city cemetery, but later his remains were removed to Kingsville. His widow, one son, and three daughters survived him.

By good authority, we are told the ghost of the great cattle baron still visits the King Ranch Suite at the Menger upon occasion.

Gutzon Borglum

One of America's greatest sculptors resided at the Menger Hotel for several years. Gutzon Borglum arrived in San Antonio in 1924. He was already an extremely successful sculptor, having been selected to design and execute a gigantic monument which was to commemorate the feats of early trail drivers who drove over six million beef cattle to the Kansas railheads from Texas. These drives netted over sixty million dollars for the state and the cattle industry when it was most needed. The work Borglum was commissioned to do was never done on the grand scale envisioned by the trail drivers, since sufficient funds could not be raised. It was to have been a massive forty-foot bronze statue to be placed on an island in front of the downtown telephone building. When the money was not forthcoming, the still impressive working model, which Borglum had made in his studio on the Menger property, was placed in front of the Trail Drivers Museum next to the Witte Museum on Broadway, where it still may be seen and admired.

Borglum was a complex and fascinating man. He was born on the border of Idaho and Nevada in what was then called "frontier country," on March 25, 1867. His father was Danish pioneer James de la Mothe Borglum. In his youth, Dr. Borglum had been a talented woodcarver before he turned to medicine as a better means of livelihood. Doubtless, Gutzon and his brother, Solon, who was also a famous sculptor, inherited much of their artistic talent from their gifted father.

Gutzon was sent to Europe to study, since his artistic abilities were evident from the time he was very young. After having first studied at the San Francisco Art Academy, his finishing touches came at the Academie Julien and the Ecole Des Beaux Arts in Paris, and for a time he was also a pupil of the famous Auguste

Sculptor Gutzon Borglum, with his son, Lincoln, reviewing plans for the Mount Rushmore faces, in a room at the Menger Hotel

Photo courtesy University of Texas Institute of Texan Cultures, *San Antonio Light* Collection

Rodin. When he returned to the United States after his studies abroad, he and his brother, Solon, traveled all over the western states. They roughed it, camping out in the Sierra Madres, where they studied wildlife at close range. Later, Borglum was able to produce amazingly life-like sculptures of animals. He loved doing extremely large works. He carved the head of Lincoln in the rotunda of the Capitol in Washington out of the biggest block of marble he could find. Other monumental works followed, including the Sheridan monument in Washington, D.C., a Lincoln, and one work he called *Wars of America*, which included forty-two bronze figures, in Newark, New Jersey. He did the Henry Ward Beecher statue in New York, heads of the apostles in the Cathedral of St. John the Divine in New York City, and the *Mares of Diomedes* in the Metropolitan Museum in New York. He also executed the beautiful North Carolina monument at Gettysburg. In addition to his sculpting, Borglum also painted a number of fine works, and in 1941 he designed and created the many faceted lighting system that illuminates the Statue of Liberty.

After he moved to the Menger in 1924, Borglum maintained a small studio located about where the swimming pool patio is today.

I found an interesting "letter to the Editor" which appeared in *Smithsonian Magazine*, the October 1992 edition:

Dear Sir: One of my earlier assignments in 1936 as a newly hired field representative for the General Motors Acceptance Corporation [GMAC] was to collect, from sculptor Gutzon Borglum, a long past-due balance on his Cadillac automobile. He lived at San Antonio's historic Menger Hotel and devoted a part of his quarters there to his work.

I found him chipping away on a partially completed room-size statue. While continuing to add to the deep litter of stone fragments on the floor, he told me that the car in question had been up on blocks for several years. He said, further, that his executive-level friends at GMAC were familiar with and sympathetic to his financial problems.

In fact, he said, when he had run low on funds in Europe

several years earlier, he had cabled GMAC and had been sent, as a loan, enough money to temporarily solve his problem.

Craig L. McNeese – Houston

Evidently, Borglum, although highly successful as a sculptor, still was not a wealthy man! After a few years, he did move from the Menger. First, he went to the St. Anthony Hotel, following a popular Menger manager who had changed jobs. He later moved to the Aurora Apartments, which were then considered very fashionable. Finally, he moved to a house on Graham Boulevard.

For many of the thirteen years he lived in San Antonio, Borglum maintained a studio in Brackenridge Park, having converted the old Pumphouse No. 2 on the San Antonio River into a studio. He spent over $7,000 on the building, which actually spanned a part of the river. It was here that he trained his young son, Lincoln, to work with him. Lincoln lived in San Antonio with his father most of the time that the sculptor resided here. Borglum was commissioned to do his most famous work, the monumental *Faces of Mount Rushmore*, while he lived here, and he executed the working model of at least three of the faces during that time. He and young Lincoln went to South Dakota to find just the right mountain on which to execute the work, which was carved into solid granite. The likenesses of Presidents George Washington, Thomas Jefferson, Abraham Lincoln, and Theodore Roosevelt still bring a thrill to thousands of Americans and many foreign visitors who visit the famous Black Hills of South Dakota every year.

Borglum was unable to see the completion of his greatest and most famous work. After working on the *Faces* project for over six years, he died on March 5, 1941, just a few days short of his seventy-fourth birthday. It is said he pushed himself too hard, neglecting his health, and he succumbed to kidney disease. His gifted son, Lincoln, whom he had trained well and who had been working with him on the faces, completed the project. Later Lincoln retired and became a rancher in the Corpus Christi area. In speaking of the gifted father-son duo, it was often noted that

Gutzon was a rancher who became a sculptor, while Lincoln was a sculptor who became a rancher.

Adina De Zavala

Another well-known person who resided for a number of years, from 1926 to 1932, at the Menger, was Miss Adina De Zavala, who was a devoted champion of the Alamo. She must have lived at the hotel in order to be close to the shrine which meant so much to her.

Adina was born on November 28, 1861, at Zavala Point, which was an estate belonging to her grandfather, General Lorenzo De Zavala, who became the first vice-president of the Republic of Texas. The estate was on Buffalo Bayou, a short distance from the San Jacinto battlefield. Adina, being able to read well by the time she was four years old, was a brilliant child, She was schooled at home and excelled in her studies. She especially loved history. Later, she graduated from what is now Sam Houston State University. All of her life she was passionately interested in Texas history and in the preservation of Texas landmarks. When it was feared that the Alamo would be sold to hotel interests and the old chapel would be torn down, De Zavala barricaded herself into the deserted long barracks for three days and nights without food until finally officials bowed to her demands. She first obtained an option on the landmark buildings and then she dictated a bill that was passed by the Texas Legislature in 1906 that appropriated $65,000 to purchase the mission and thus save it from destruction.

She is also credited with saving the Spanish Governor's Palace, which also faced the wrecking crew. For fifteen years she held an option on that building and advocated it be purchased by the state. Her continual efforts caused the city of San Antonio to purchase and preserve the old building, which was built in 1749. It is still maintained by the San Antonio Parks Department and is open daily to visitors.

Adina De Zavala, photographed March 1936

Photo courtesy University of Texas Institute of Texan Cultures, *San Antonio Light* Collection

It is interesting to note that although Miss De Zavala had a Spanish surname, she never learned to speak the language. Her father's mother was Anglo, and her own mother was Irish. She was well educated and spent the years between 1884 and 1907 as a schoolteacher. She retired early, devoting the rest of her life to preservation work. She served on numerous committees and founded several historic societies, including the Texas Historical and Landmarks Association. She was a fellow of the Texas State Historical Association, a member of the United Daughters of the Confederacy, the Texas Woman's Press Association, and other similar groups. She founded several Texas patriotic societies, including the Daughters and Sons of the Heroes and Pioneers of the Republic of Texas. She was president of the De Zavala Chapter, Daughters of the Republic of Texas, which raised the first funds for the purchase of the Alamo. Miss De Zavala worked tirelessly to establish libraries, art galleries, and art schools. As a young woman she was very attractive and no doubt had suitors, but she chose never to marry. She devoted all of her time, energy, and considerable means to keeping the memories of Texas heroes alive. She died in San Antonio on March 1, 1955, at the age of ninety-three. She was the last surviving member of her family.

Colonel Selah R. H. "Tommy" Tompkins

I first heard of Colonel Tommy Tompkins from my friends Lt. General (USA Retired) and Mrs. Beverley Powell. We were at a party and when I mentioned my Menger book project, General Powell said, "Then you must know all about Tommy Tompkins. He lived at the Menger for a time." I said, no, I really didn't know about the colonel, and since many of the old registers were gone, the Menger management probably didn't recall his stay, either. However, I added, I certainly would enjoy hearing about anyone who had once lived at the hotel.

General Powell was able to tell me quite a bit about the notable cavalry colonel. He also loaned me a fascinating book titled *The 7th*

U.S. Cavalry's Own Colonel Tommy Tompkins, a Military Heritage and Tradition, by John M. Carroll, from which I gained a real insight into a man who was considered the most colorful character who ever followed a cavalry guidon!

Colonel Selah R. H. "Tommy" Tompkins resided for a time at the hotel after his 1927 retirement from the military service. He faithfully served his country and his fellow soldiers for forty-three years. Born July 17, 1864, Tompkins was the oldest child of General and Mrs. Charles H. Tompkins, and like his father and two younger brothers, Frank and Daniel, he decided early on to pursue a military career. Failing the entry exam to West Point by only a tenth of a point, he still won a commission as a second lieutenant at the age of eighteen. The commission was granted by then President Chester Arthur.

As Tompkins' military career went on, he served at many stations. He distinguished himself as an Indian fighter. He was decorated for his bravery at the Battle of Wounded Knee. Then he fought with the U.S. Cavalry in the Spanish American War. In fact, he stayed on in Cuba after that conflict and met and married his wife, Dolores Muller, who was Spanish. Tommy and Dolores had one daughter, Augusta Mauda Del Carmen, whom they called "Nena." The marriage, which began in 1899, was short-lived. Dolores died from complications of pneumonia while giving birth to their second child in 1908. Tommy was devastated.

Tompkins also fought in the Philippines but later, during the World War I era, did not go overseas because the cavalry was not used in Europe, the age of mechanized vehicles having arrived. Instead, he and his troops of the Seventh Cavalry were stationed on the Mexican border at Ft. Bliss. They spent most of their time chasing Pancho Villa and his revolutionaries, who were warring with the Mexican government forces and at the same time making pesky forays into U.S. territory as they crossed back and forth over the Rio Grande.

At once respected, loved, and feared by his men, Tompkins was a soldier's soldier: hard living, hard riding, hard drinking, and tough

Colonel Tommy Tompkins photographed with W. Lee O'Daniel, General Claude V. Birkhead, and Texas Governor James V. Allred, on August 11, 1938

Photo courtesy University of Texas Institute of Texan Cultures, *San Antonio Light* Collection

talking. They said his vocabulary could wilt the spikes off a prickly pear! His colorful speech was peppered with profanity—strong words that soldiers understood. There were often deliberate attempts made to goad Colonel Tommy into an argument, just so listeners could enjoy a good display of some of the choicest cusswords one could ever hope to hear! His expressions were not spoken in anger or insult, because if he were truly angry he would revert to quiet, well-modulated, almost eloquent speech, totally devoid of profanity and totally out of character. This tactic often reduced his adversaries to trembling jelly! However, the old colonel was known to be extremely fair and even with his men and fellow officers.

Known for his reddish-tinged eight-inch-long mustachios and flowing goatee, which he wore in imitation of his alter ego, General George Custer, he was called "Old Pink Whiskers" by his men. A story often repeated about the colonel recalled what happened to a young trooper who failed to salute the colonel. When chastised, the soldier told Tompkins, "I just didn't see you coming, Colonel." Tommy replied, "When you see these whiskers coming around the corner, start saluting them, because I'll be right behind them!"

During the 1920s while he was stationed at Fort Sam Houston, Tompkins was asked to speak to a very genteel group of ladies from the Women's Christian Temperance Union, at a dinner held at the Gunter Hotel. His adjutant tried to persuade Tompkins to decline the invitation, but to no avail. He spoke to the ladies of the evils of alcohol, a subject upon which he was well versed since he was known to imbibe heavily at times. He succeeded in delivering his address without a single curse word being uttered and received a good ovation from the ladies. Then his closing remarks were, "Now ladies, I want you to know one thing. You didn't invite me just to hear me speak. You heard I cussed a lot! Well, I fooled you, didn't I, goddammit!"

And there was the time when President Taft was reviewing Tommy's troops at Ft. Bliss in 1909. He remarked to Tommy, "That's sure a fine body of troops," to which Tommy, according to officers who were on the reviewing stand, replied, "You bet your ass it is, Mr. President."

When Tompkins was stationed at Ft. Sam Houston in the 1920s and later at Camp Stanley, he had the habit of making a weekly visit to the Menger for drinks at the famous bar. Then he would have dinner and often would spend the night. He felt at home at the hotel, where he had many friends. It was not a surprise when he chose to live at the hotel in his later years, probably from the late 1920s to about 1936, according to some of his old cronies. Then he moved into the quarters of his younger widowed brother, Daniel, and their sister, Natalie, who kept house for her two brothers.

Colonel Tommy died at the Ft. Sam Houston General Hospital (now known as Brooke General Hospital) on February 6, 1939, after a long battle with stomach cancer. Tributes poured in from high-ranking military and government officials as well as enlisted men who served with him, from all over the country. Six military officers, including his brothers Frank and Daniel, served as pall-bearers at the crowded funeral held in the post chapel.

True to fashion, Colonel Tommy had made advance provisions for his pallbearers and nineteen honorary pallbearers to gather after the funeral to have a drink on him.

And so it was that this dedicated old soldier, a master of horse-manship, a military historian and poet, equipped with "glorious whiskers" and a razor sharp tongue, passed from this world into the next. Never was a man more loved or admired, feared and respected, than "Colonel Tommy" of the Seventh Cavalry.

Eddie Joseph

Eddie Joseph spent a lot of time at the Menger, beginning in about 1953, when the native of Ontario decided to escape the cold winters of his home and spend those cold months in San Antonio. Today, we call such winter visitors "snow birds," or "winter Texans." Joseph had previously made a visit to San Antonio with a friend of his, a sportswriter for the *New York Post*. The pair came to San Antonio to watch John McGraw's Giants working out in their winter camp here. Joseph fell in love with the city and with the Menger Hotel.

Joseph was the veteran of 159 professional fights. He used to laugh and brag a bit that he was responsible for giving Gene Tunney a cauliflower ear. Tunney repaid the gesture by bestowing three cracked ribs on Joseph in the same fight! He still lost the match to Tunney after going twelve rounds.

Ernesto Malacara recalls that Joseph loved to talk about some of his fights. He had fought numerous world champions including

Max Schmelling and Joe Louis. He served the boxing profession as both a fighter and an official for many years.

Eddie's lovely wife accompanied him on his Texas trips. She was legally blind, and a hotel employee recalled that Joseph paid careful attention to her comforts. He often came down to the lobby to watch TV so she could rest quietly in their room. A very outgoing individual, Eddie could be found there just about every evening, chatting with other guests who were staying in the hotel.

The Josephs' last winter visit to the hotel was in 1983.

Pola Negri

Pola Negri was a film star in the silent movie days when "stars" were really "stars." She looked and acted the part to perfection! And in the late 1950s, she was for a time, one of the most glamorous and eccentric residents of the Menger Hotel.

The actress was born in Lymo, Poland, in 1899 (some sources say it may have been earlier than that date). Her given name was Apolonia, but she preferred her nickname, Pola. She took her last name, her stage name, after Ada Negri, an Italian poet whose work she admired. She became an actress at a fairly early age. In 1922 she made a film in Europe called *Passion* which won her a Hollywood contract. She arrived in the United States in 1923 and made her first film, *Bella Donna*. She made at least nineteen films in the short period of six years. Not lacking in ego, Negri often said, "I was the star who introduced sex to the screen, but it was sex in good taste." These early films were then considered quite daring but today would probably be classified as PG. The sex scenes left a great deal to the imagination in those days. Miss Negri's counterparts and Hollywood rivals were Gloria Swanson and Greta Garbo.

Pola stayed very busy but not just at filmmaking. She had two short, tumultuous marriages. First, she married Count Eugene Dambski, a Polish career army officer, whom she stayed with for two years. This was before she came to America. She was already well known as an actress in Poland, and the count wanted her to

Pola Negri, during her silent movie days
Photo courtesy University of Texas Institute of Texan Cultures, *San Antonio Light* Collection

give up her career. This was the reason for the divorce. Then in 1927 she married a Georgian prince, Serge Mdivani, whom she divorced in 1931 after he grossly mismanaged her affairs. She lost over five million dollars in the stock market crash of 1929 and never quite recovered from this loss. The woman who referred to herself as a "living legend" once remarked she wished she had been half as good at managing her financial affairs as she was at attracting the attention and favors of men.

When she got to Hollywood, she soon became engaged to Charlie Chaplin and became his mistress for a time. She jilted him in a whirl of gossip column headlines. Then she fell head over heels in love with her leading man, Rudolph Valentino. She lived openly with him until his untimely death in 1926, and their romance was the talk of the country. Today, such a "relationship" would hardly cause a ripple, but in those days it was considered quite scandalous. She said of Valentino, "I loved him as I had never loved any other man."

However, Valentino had not been dead long when she married the prince. She was no doubt lonely and more or less on the rebound, looking for love and companionship. It did not work out.

Negri made a few more films after the death of Valentino. The first "talkie" she made was filmed in 1935 and was called *A Woman Commands*. It met with poor reviews, because her accent made it hard for the viewers to understand. She decided to return to Europe, where she made a number of films in Berlin until the outbreak of World War II. It was rumored at one time that she and Adolph Hitler were romantically involved. Both of them denied it. In fact, Miss Negri sued a French magazine for spreading the rumors and won a settlement of 10,000 francs.

By the end of World War II, Pola was no longer involved in filmmaking. Silent films were history. She never lost her heavy Polish accent, and of course, she was not getting any younger. She was reduced to living in one room of a small hotel in Manhattan, selling off her costly jewelry piece by piece in order to survive. Finally, she recovered some money and property that had been tied up in Europe during the war. Pola had a friend named Margaret L. West, who lived in California but who was a native of San Antonio. West was the first person to introduce country and western music on network radio, and for a time she had been the toast of Broadway, a great NBC star. She retired in 1935 at the pinnacle of her career. A member of a wealthy Texas family, Margaret, who was divorced, did not need money badly enough to keep working. The generous West, knowing Pola was in financial straits, invited her to move to California and stay with her in her palatial beach house in Santa Monica. There they could enjoy the beach, the swimming pool, marvelous ocean views, and the fine service of a staff of five that catered to their every need. Pola soon brought her mother over from Poland to join her. In 1951 Pola became an American citizen while living with Margaret West. Her mother died in 1955.

Margaret decided it would be nice for Pola to visit Texas. The two friends traveled to San Antonio in April of 1957, during Fiesta Week. They were caught up in a round of parties and attended a number of parades and special events. Pola was completely enchanted with the Alamo city and told Margaret she wouldn't mind living here one day. Finally, the two ladies decided they had had enough of California, and they decided to make a permanent move to San Antonio. In 1959 they picked up stakes and moved here, making the Menger Hotel a temporary headquarters. They resided at the hotel for almost two years while the house they were having built in Olmos Park was under construction. One can well imagine the stir they caused at the hotel. Both women had known lives of glamour and were used to living in the limelight and getting a lot of attention.

Unfortunately, the two friends had only a short time to enjoy their new home in San Antonio, because Margaret died suddenly of a heart attack in 1963, leaving her considerable estate to Pola. Soon afterwards, Miss Negri left the large home and moved into a more compact, but nonetheless luxurious, condominium in the Chateau Dijon, an exclusive apartment complex in Alamo Heights. She lived a life of semiseclusion, sometimes entertaining a few close friends and occasionally attending some of San Antonio's more glittering social events. She usually wore black gowns, kept her hair jet black, wore pale, theatrical makeup, and often wore black veils in her later years. Once asked why she dressed in this fashion, she replied, "My dear, so no one will notice me!"

The still glamorous silent screen legend died in 1987. It was said she was "around eighty-eight." Found among her personal effects was a photograph of her one great love, Rudolph Valentino, which was on the desk in her study.

Of her life in San Antonio, Miss Negri said, "I have come to call home a city which I had never even heard of as a child, in a foreign land in which I never dreamed I would one day live. And it is here, after the long odyssey, that I have finally found contentment."

Dr. Hubertus Strughold

A resident guest of the Menger Hotel from 1961 until 1970, German-born scientist Dr. Hubertus Strughold was a fascinating personality. He was born on June 15, 1898, in Westphalia, Germany, the son of well-educated parents. As a youngster, Hubertus was always fascinated with space...the sky...the moon and stars. He spent endless hours studying the constellations with his telescope. Later he studied natural science at the University of Muenster and in 1922 earned his Ph.D. degree from that institution. In 1923 he also became a doctor of medicine at the University of Wuersburg. In the late 1920s the young Doctor Strughold was appointed a fellow of the Rockefeller Foundation and came to the University of Chicago and later Western Rivers University of Cleveland, where he stayed several years. Then he returned to his native Germany, where he became director of the Berlin Institute until 1945. He served as a colonel in the German Air Force Medical Corps during World War II. He often stressed that he was never a member of the Nazi party. He said, "I was against Hitler and his beliefs, and sometimes I had to hide out because my life was in danger from the Nazis."

Dr. Hubertus Strughold with comedian Bob Hope
Photo courtesy Ernesto Malacara

At the close of World War II, Strughold was again the director of the Berlin Institute. A good friend of his told him that the Russians wanted him and intended to get him and take him to Russia. He had better get out of Berlin right away! Heeding this advice, he left in a hurry and in fact, began walking back to his old home in Westphalia where his sister lived. Sometimes he caught rides with farmers in wagons and hid out at night in barns and haystacks. He managed to outwit the Russians. Back in West Germany, he eventually associated himself with the University of Heidelberg. Strughold's widow, Mary, commented that although he gained great fame in this country, he was far more famous in Europe.

He was finally able to get to the United States with a group of the German scientific community that immigrated here after the war. Because he had stayed away from any Nazi affiliations, the Americans trusted him and treated him with respect when the war ended, and of course they utilized his great knowledge in the field of space medicine.

When Strughold came to the States, he was sent to the School of Aviation Medicine then located at Randolph Air Force Base, and he resided for a time in Schertz. Then the school moved to Brooks Air Force Base. He met Mary Webb in 1959 during the time he was making the long commute between Schertz and Brooks Field, and as their friendship blossomed, Mary urged him to move closer to his work. He was able to obtain suitable lodgings at the Menger where he lived in the original Sidney Lanier Suite on the fourth floor.

Strughold joined the School of Aerospace Medicine in 1947 and became chief scientist at the Aerospace Medical Division in 1962. He worked there until his retirement in 1968. In the meantime, in 1956, he had been naturalized, and he always said the day he became an American citizen was one of the happiest days of his life!

The scientist was recognized for literally hundreds of accomplishments in the field of space medicine, and he has often been referred to as the Father of Space Medicine.

Strughold predicted transoceanic flights, space flights to the moon, skylabs, and space shuttles. He was sometimes ridiculed for his predictions, but he lived to see them all come true. He developed the first space cabin simulator used to expose men to zero gravity. He was named to the Space Hall of Fame in 1978, and his native land, Germany, awarded him the Commanders Cross of Merit, the highest civilian honor that country bestows. Interestingly enough, when awarded the German medal, he had already become an American citizen.

On a more down-to-earth level, Strughold's studies in the 1950s resulted in yellow stripes being placed on streets, nationwide, as he ascertained this was the most visible color for striping highways and airport runway landing strips.

"Strugie," as the scientist preferred to be called by his friends, married his long-time good friend Mary Webb in 1970. The couple had dated for eleven years. Mary told me they wanted to be sure they were "well acquainted" before they married! Strughold was seventy-two at the time they said their vows in the downtown First Presbyterian Church and then celebrated later at the Menger Hotel. Shortly after their marriage the couple moved to Mary's home, but they still often dined at the Menger and visited with old friends there. Dr. Strughold died on September 26, 1986, at the age of eighty-eight, having lived a full, fascinating, and productive life. Mrs. Strughold was very helpful in sharing information about her late husband.

Ernesto Malacara recalls many visits he had with "Strugie." He said the only time he ever saw him lose his temper was when he was engaged in conversation with several people and someone remarked "Is that really true?" Strughold whacked the table hard with his walking cane and said in his still-thick German accent: "How dare you! I do not lie!" He never liked to be accused of telling a lie or even just a "tall tale," according to Mary.

Dr. Strughold loved being closely attached to the space program. Of course, he knew most of the astronauts and had been at a number of the launchings. He even had some little "space dollars" printed up to give out to people he met, and he always got a tremendous kick out of doing this.

Famous, fascinating, witty, and modest are words that best describe the famous scientist, and things were never quite the same at the Menger after he departed.

General William Hood Simpson

One of the most interesting and certainly one of the most famous residents of the Menger Hotel was General William Hood Simpson. The army officer came to live in the hotel soon after the death of his first wife, Ruth, to whom he had been married nearly fifty years. This was in 1971.

General Simpson was born in Weatherford, Texas, in May of 1888. As a child he always loved to play cowboys and Indians, and he always wanted to be a soldier. It was natural that he would attend West Point, where he graduated in the class of 1909. When interviewed by the press at one time, he said, "I held up the bottom of the class. I graduated three from the end, but remember George Patton was in that class, too, although he entered the academy a year before I did. He had to repeat the first year, so he took five years to get through. Still, he and I did all right for ourselves."

Simpson's distinguished career included service in the Philippines, time spent in pursuit of Pancho Villa's renegades around northern Mexico in 1916, and serving as a participant in General John Pershing's American Expeditionary Forces in World War I in Europe. Between world wars, he also served for a number of years as a professor at the Army War College in Washington, D.C. During World War II, Lt. General Simpson was given the command of the Ninth Army, the largest army ever assembled, numbering around 750,000 men. He led fourteen divisions beside his friend George Patton across Europe into the very heartland of Germany. His men were the first to reach the Rhine River and were the men who could have, would have, captured Berlin had not General Eisenhower stopped him short just sixty miles from that city. He said his

General William Hood Simpson
Photo courtesy Ernesto Malacara

men wanted to take it, but he could not go against Eisenhower's orders.

Simpson was forced to retire in 1946, due to medical reasons, as a lieutenant general. Then, by special act of Congress in 1954, he was given the permanent rank of four-star general. He was honored by King George VI, being knighted into the Order of the British Empire, and he also received the Legion of Honor from the French government for his distinguished service to our allies.

After Simpson retired from the army, he served as a vice president and member of the board of the Alamo National Bank. He retired from the bank position in 1963.

General Simpson loved to talk about the first time he ever had any contact with the Russians. His forces and theirs had met up on April 30, 1944. There was a big celebration, and the Russian troops gave him what was called the "Cossack toss," which was supposed to be a big honor. They tossed him up in the air, yelling the Russian equivalent of "hip, hip, hooray," and it all got pretty rowdy. He said he was so full of vodka by then he could hardly see, but a great time must have been had by all.

Ernesto Malcara, who visited often with General Simpson and knew him well, had this to say:

> General Simpson was a great man, and I was privileged to have known him. I can still remember the evenings when he would enter the Patio Room for dinner. Sid Fisher, the pianist, would play the "Field Artillery March," in honor of the General at the request of Mr. Lee Molpus, the Patio Room manager. As the music played and the General walked into the room, he would do his very best to straighten up to his full height and military bearing, walking with his cane, as he passed the piano. He was always every inch a general officer.

> I also recall one afternoon when we had a houseful of senior citizens, mostly older ladies. There must have been at least seventy-five of them gathered in the lobby. General Simpson walked up to me and announced in his booming

voice, "Mr. Malacara, I have a gift for you, my photo, which I have autographed for you." Of course, I thanked him profusely. The ladies in the lobby were all looking our way, because both of our voices carried very well. General Simpson then asked me, "Do you want to know why I gave this to you? It's because you are so G.. D.. good to me!" Seventy-five ladies nearly passed out in the lobby. I still chuckle when I remember this incident.

During a period of time in 1976 and 1977 General Simpson was pretty much confined to his rooms at the Menger, suffering from severe bouts of phlebitis and neuritis. He was popular with the hotel staff, and they did all they could to keep him comfortable.

Mutual friends introduced the General to Catherine Louise Berman, and they were married in 1978. At fifty-six, she was retired from government service and had never been married. She said the General just wouldn't take "no" for an answer, and though there was an age difference of thirty-three years, the couple was extremely happy for the brief two years they shared before the General's death. He had moved out of the Menger and into the home they built in the Windcrest section of the city.

At the time they were married, Simpson remarked, "Imagine, an old crock married to a beautiful gal of fifty-six!" Simpson was ninety at that time!

General Simpson passed away August 15, 1980, at the age of ninety-two. After his funeral services at Fort Sam Houston, his mortal remains were sent to their final resting place at Arlington National Cemetery.

Verna Hooks McLean

Verna Hooks McLean was another long-time resident of the Menger. Originally from the Beaumont area in southeast Texas, she came from a pioneer family who were early settlers of the Big Thicket area of East Texas. Verna Hooks married Marrs McLean, a native of Sherman in North Texas. He studied law at the University of Texas and, after receiving his degree, moved to live with an older sister and her husband, who was also an attorney, in Beaumont. There he first did a little farming, but he ultimately became heavily involved in the oil business. In fact, he was largely responsible for the second Spindletop oil boom in 1927.

Around 1927 the McLeans, with their only child, Ruth, moved to San Antonio, a city they had always liked. They also owned a Hill Country ranch, near Junction, where they spent much of their leisure time. The McLeans purchased a beautiful Spanish style home in Monte Vista. The prominent architect Atlee B. Ayres had designed the house, one of his first residential projects.

The McLeans lived in their elegant home until Mr. McLean passed away in 1953. The house was too large for the newly widowed Verna to live in, but it proved just perfect for her daughter, Ruth, and her husband, Jack Bowman. The Bowmans and their six lively children moved into the family home where Ruth had grown up.

Mrs. McLean decided a suite at the downtown Menger Hotel would meet her needs perfectly. She would not be alone, she would have all the room she needed, enabling her to bring some of her treasured possessions with her, and she would be close to her daughter and grandchildren. She wanted to spend part of her time at her Hill Country ranch, at another ranch the McLeans had acquired in far West Texas, and at her Gulf Coast home. She also planned to visit many of her East Texas relatives and friends in the Beaumont area. The hotel suite was a good place to come and stay whenever she was back in San Antonio.

The McLean suite consisted of an entry foyer, spacious living room, a nice-sized bedroom, dressing room, bath, and a full-sized kitchen, according to her daughter, Ruth.

Mrs. McLean especially enjoyed having Christmas Eve parties at the Menger, in one of the banquet rooms where she entertained her large family. The Christmas tree in her suite was always very

Verna Hooks McLean
Photo courtesy Mrs. William O. Bowers III

special, lavishly decorated with dolls from her travels to many places.

Mrs. McLean resided in the hotel from 1953 until 1978. She is remembered as a very pretty and always gracious lady. Unfortunately, in 1978 she fell and broke her hip, and after that she was largely confined to a wheelchair. She moved away from the Menger and came back to live in her original San Antonio home with her daughter, Ruth, and Ruth's second husband, William O. Bowers III. Mrs. McLean passed away in 1981.

Colonel George Wells

Colonel George Wells was a handsome, tall, and stately old gentleman who was the epitome of a retired army man. He had snow-white hair and a well-trimmed mustache. He was always well dressed and immaculately groomed.

After he retired from the military, he and his wife had bought a small place in Mexico, in the state of Morelos. There they raised horses and lived a relaxed, "mañana" sort of existence in the tiny village of Cocoyoc, near Cuautla. When Mrs. Wells died, the Colonel decided to leave his beloved little "rancho" behind. His friends had tried to persuade him to stay on, but there were just too many bittersweet memories, and the place had suddenly become too lonely. He sold his property and all but a few treasured mementos and headed north. He checked into the Menger Hotel in 1974, intending to stay just a short while. But the longer he stayed, the more content he became in his new surroundings, and the days stretched into weeks, then months, then years.

Wells' suite at the hotel was comfortable. There was a place for his few fine signed oil paintings by Mexican and Western artists, his lovely old Mexican hand-woven rugs, and a couple of really handsome Mexican leather saddles, heavily trimmed with silver. He also had some fine old Mexican spurs, reminders of his horseback riding days. He gave Ernesto Malacara a couple of pairs of the spurs, which he treasures.

Wells loved to talk about his paintings. Each one had its unique story and special memories for him. He talked about how he'd seen

Colonel George Wells astride his favorite mount

Photo courtesy Ernesto Malacara

one in a shop, another in a hotel, another in the market place, and how he had come to own them. He was especially fond of a painting the artist had given him. It was a portrait of the artist's wife, which Mrs. Wells had always admired.

Wells was quite a gifted artist himself. He especially liked to do caricatures for his friends, and a number of his cartoons were published.

Ernesto said the Colonel had "a heart as big as Texas." He was a gentleman's gentleman, a man born too late. By his own admission, Wells said he wished he could have lived in the days of the Old West, and he lamented how fast-paced life today had become.

Malacara recalls the day in 1979 when he drove his good friend the Colonel to the M. D. Anderson Hospital in Houston for tests. It was apparent he was quite ill. It was a very sad time for everyone at the hotel, as Wells died only two days later. "I still recall some of the last words the Colonel spoke to me," said Malacara. "Nothing lasts forever. You weren't promised anything when you were born."

Mimi Schreiner Rigsby and Myrtle Barton Schreiner

Mimi Schreiner Rigsby and Myrtle Barton Schreiner were sisters-in-law. They both maintained suites at the Menger at one time and lived on the same floor.

Mimi Rigsby was the sister of Walter Schreiner, who was Myrtle's husband. They were members of the influential Shreiner family of Kerrville, who founded the famous YO Ranch.

Mimi and her husband, William C. Rigsby, lived at 5200 Broadway for many years. The large family home has since been sold to the Catholic Church. After Mimi's husband died, she moved into the Menger Hotel around 1945 and lived there about fifteen years.

Myrtle Barton Schreiner came to the hotel around 1955 and stayed until around 1965 according to her son, Charles Schreiner III, in an interview. Shreiner still lives on the family spread at the 40,000-acre YO Ranch, where a herd of over eight hundred registered Texas longhorn cattle share the property with all sorts of exotic wild game specimens. Charlie said his mother, Myrtle, actually managed the ranch from 1933 until 1950. Even after she moved to the Menger, she still went back and forth from San Antonio to the ranch and kept an eye on its management. She deeply loved the YO, which had been founded by her husband's father, Captain Charles Schreiner.

Captain Schreiner was born in Riquewihr on the Rhine River, in Germany. He immigrated to Texas and founded the YO Ranch in 1880. At one time the Schreiner properties consisted of at least half a million acres and stretched over three counties. The name Schreiner became synonymous with Texas longhorns, and over 300,000 of the animals were driven to the Kansas markets.

Captain Shreiner served in the Confederate army as a sergeant. Many of the early German immigrants sided with the Union, and there were numerous rifts among German families over what side they would swear their allegiance to in those days just prior to the Civil War. Some members of the Schreiner family were killed trying to leave Texas to join the Union forces. After the war, Schreiner joined the Kerrville Mounted Rifles, organized to help quell Indian attacks. That is where the name "Captain" came from! The beautiful old Schreiner home is still in Kerrville and, like the YO Ranch, is open for tours.

Captain Schreiner's son, Walter, married Myrtle Barton, and it is she who lived at the Menger. She died on New Year's Eve, 1979, in Kerrville.

Charles also said that when he was married to his first wife, the mother of his children, their wedding reception was held at the Menger Hotel.

Schreiner, along with a few other ranchers, founded the Texas Longhorn Breeders Association (LBA) in the early 1960s. The cattle were registered for the first time, and the herds have gradually increased in both numbers and popularity. At one time they had slipped in popularity in favor of the Hereford breed. The Menger Hotel was chosen as the place where for many years the Longhorn Breeders Association had their offices, and they had many wonderful cattle breeders meetings there at the hotel.

The hotel always felt honored to have a close association with the Schreiners, one of Texas's most esteemed pioneer families.

Chapter 9

The Menger Bar and Teddy Roosevelt

⟨decorative divider⟩

The Menger Bar is undeniably famous. Its fame arises from the distinctive design of the room, unlike any other in the city, and from its historical association with one of America's great heroes. It has long been associated with Theodore "Teddy" Roosevelt and his famous "Rough Riders."

As an innkeeper for many years, Ernesto Malacara says a good hotel always needs a good bar to be a real success. The Menger Hotel has always had a bar, to be sure, from its 1859 beginnings. In fact, William Menger's business was begun with his brewery and his tavern and then just graduated into the opening of his fine hotel in 1859.

Just where the bar was located in the original hotel portion during the Menger years is not known. But it was there! According to old records, the best of libations were offered to its patrons. Of course, Menger's beer was featured. It had already established a reputation as being "good brew." The finest available wines were offered as well as Duff-Gordon sherry, London and Holland gin, Irish and Scotch whiskey, Swiss absinthe, and champagne.

When Hermann Kampmann took over the management of the hotel, he realized that his establishment did not have a saloon facility that stacked up to some of the other barrooms in the city. Travelers often mentioned that the bar facilities at the Menger lacked the elegance reflected in the rest of the hotel. The Kampmann family had already built a large lobby addition to the original hotel, and it was in this section that they decided to place the new saloon. An architect was sent to London to sketch and study the pub at the House of Lords, and these sketches later resulted in the Menger Bar that you see today. At the time of the addition of the new saloon, in 1887, there were two entrances. It could be entered via the lobby or from the courtyard. The new bar was divided into three sections and was much larger than the present Menger Bar. There was a poolroom, which held two large tables; an assembly room, which gave the appearance of a private mens' club; and the barroom itself. Each room was connected to the other by means of archways partioned off by heavy portieres of elegant fabrics.

The assembly room was twenty-two feet square and contained eight solid mahogany tables, which were complemented by Vienna bent hardwood chairs. At the rear and at either side of the room, large beveled glass mirrors set into mahogany frames of a cherry tint were placed to reflect the light of the incandescent electric lights and gaslights, which were set into oxydized silver fixtures.

There was a paneled ceiling of cherry wood and booths and beveled mirrors from France in the saloon. Beautiful decorated glass cabinets were installed as well. Around $60,000, which was an exorbitant sum in those days, was spent on these fittings. The massive bar was constructed entirely of mahogany, except for the brass footrests, and it was said to be more costly than even marble would have been. No expense was spared to make the new bar, which formally opened in 1890, the equal of any fine drinking establishment in the South.

Special compartments were fitted out for ice, and all the beer and wine was kept at just the right temperature. The crystal glasses were imported and were as fine as money and good taste could make them. A summer specialty of the bar was the mint julep, served in frosted sterling silver goblets. Hot rum toddies warmed the constitutions of winter drinkers.

The *San Antonio Express,* October 12, 1890, noted:

The glassware is all of the very finest obtainable by a conjunction of money and taste, and is imported. There are two mirrors in the front room exact in size and pattern with those in the assembly room. One of the beauties of the place is that gentlemen, who are not disposed to drink, and are disposed to admire themselves, can drop in and pose in some half dozen reflectors at once.

Hermann Laux, who was widely known to the gentlemen of San Antonio, became the head bartender in the new establishment.

Sometime during the Kampmann's ownership, the serving of a light lunch was included in the price of liquid refreshment, making the bar a very popular gathering place. Not much has changed in that regard, actually, because today's Menger still offers a delicious "happy hour" selection of food offerings to those who might drop in for a late afternoon cocktail.

In 1908, due to extensive renovations in the hotel, the bar was moved to a place overlooking the garden area. Later, during Prohibition in 1918, the bar was completely closed down. The bartender at that time, George La Motte, insisted all the component parts be safely stored away, because he felt that Prohibition was to be only a temporary situation. Of course, he was right!

After Prohibition was over, the bar again reappeared at the Menger. Then, while the National Hotel Corporation was building their new addition in 1948, the bar components were pulled down and put into storage once more. After several years it was put together again in its current location off Crockett Street. It may be entered via Crockett or through double doors leading off a corridor that runs from the registration desk to the valet parking garage. This location might indicate its preservation is more for the historically minded than for general walk-in trade, but the bar does a brisk business and is a favorite place for local residents as well as hotel guests.

Menger Bar, showing bartender George H. La Motte, August 16, 1932
Photo courtesy Texas University Institute of Texan Cultures, *San Antonio Light* Collection

There are many points of trivia about the bar. For instance, there is a triangle of wood in the mahogany bar that fills the gap left by the flying ax of a chief of police. It seems that sometime in the 1920s a bartender was dispensing more than legal beer from behind the counter, and the policeman's ax is said to have rattled a couple of bottles of bootleg whiskey!

Although the story has been bandied about quite often, we can find no real evidence that Carrie Nation ever chopped on the bar with her little hatchet. As previously mentioned, she briefly visited the bar in 1908 but only verbally chastised the bartender and his patrons for imbibing in alcohol.

While many famous people have enjoyed a drink in the old Menger Bar, by far the most talked about visitor to the bar was Theodore "Teddy" Roosevelt. The hotel has, in fact, named the bar for the late president, and much emphasis is placed on the ties of Teddy and the Menger Bar. There are numerous photographs of Roosevelt on the walls of the bar itself and in the corridor leading from the hotel lobby into the bar.

Menger Bar, circa 1970

Photo courtesy Menger Hotel

To say Theodore Roosevelt was a "colorful" individual would be an understatement. He was that, but much, much more. He was born on October 27, 1858, the son of a prominent New York family. He was a frail youngster, suffering from acute attacks of asthma. In addition, he was extremely nearsighted and wore wire-rimmed glasses all of his life. He was tutored at home, because he was too sickly to attend regular school. He developed a keen interest in reading and studying natural history. As he grew into his teens, he took up physical training with great dedication, much against the advice of his physicians. By sheer force of will and great determination, he took up boxing, learned to be an expert horseman, an excellent marksman, and became a tireless walker. Through his constant efforts, he developed a fine physique and was able to enter Harvard College in 1876. He received a bachelor of arts degree in 1880. While still in college he began to write *A History of the Naval War of 1812*, which he completed after graduation. This was the first of many books he wrote during his lifetime.

In 1880 Roosevelt married Alice Lee of Boston. In 1881 he ran for the New York assembly, was elected, and served that body until 1884, the year his wife died. Just a few hours after her death, his beloved mother, Martha Bullock Roosevelt, also expired. The young Roosevelt was devastated, and for a few years, he left public life and moved to a Montana ranch, where he thrived in the mountain air he loved. He also had time to engage in writing. He returned to New York in 1886 and soon married Edith Kermit Carow. He ran, unsuccessfully, for mayor of New York and continued to write. President Benjamin Harrison appointed him to the Civil Service Commission. There he battled the "spoils system," until he became head of the New York City police. He became a real reformer, substituting the merit system for the money-politics method of promoting police officers.

It was right around this time that Roosevelt first visited San Antonio. He signed the guest register at the Menger Hotel in April of 1892. Still a young man of only thirty-four, he had already gained a national reputation as a genius of extraordinary literary merit. He wrote for a number of magazines and periodicals and authored several books on hunting, an interest that brought him to San Antonio. He later reported after his trip to South Texas that "a successful hunt for peccary, better known as javelina, was executed."

In 1897 Roosevelt became assistant secretary of the navy, advocating preparedness for an ultimate war against Spain. He resigned this position when the war broke out in 1898 after the sinking of the U.S. battleship *Maine* off the coast of Cuba. Teddy was ready for action!

The United States rapidly mobilized 200,000 volunteer troops and deployed them to face off with 60,000 Spanish troops stationed in Cuba. The Spanish fleet was blockaded, and when it attempted to run the blockade, the U.S. fleet, under Admiral Simpson and Commodore Schley, sank the Spanish ships.

As a part of the U.S. involvement in the conflict, a group of volunteer cavalry was rapidly put together. A news story announcing the formation of the "First U.S. Volunteer Cavalry Regiment" ran in a number of papers all over the country, and Washington was bombarded with applications for enlistment. The authorized strength of the unit was increased from 760 to 1,000 men. After about fifty men were accepted from Maryland, Virginia, and the northeastern states, it was determined that the balance of the regiment would be recruited from the "territories." This area included Oklahoma, New Mexico, Arizona, and the Indian Territory. Because the actual training was to take place in San Antonio, Texas, a few Texans just naturally slipped into the ranks as well.

When Theodore Roosevelt resigned as assistant secretary of the navy to become second in command of this cavalry unit, he was given the rank of lieutenant colonel. He was to serve under his good friend Colonel Leonard Wood.

The cavalry unit was described by a Washington correspondent as a "rough riding outfit." The new organization had found a name! The Rough Riders were what they were and what they were called, although once the men had begun to arrive in San Antonio some of the local townspeople referred to them as "Teddy's terrors," as well. This bunch was a real melting pot of young American manhood, all spoiling for an adventure. Native Americans, Texas cowboys, New York social leaders (some of Teddy's Harvard classmates and best friends), rangers, miners, and drifters made up the ranks. They were a rough, tough, bunch of hard-riding, hell-raising young men, and while their stay in San Antonio was short, it was certainly memorable.

Colonel Leonard Wood arrived in San Antonio on May 5, 1898. He set up his recruiting table in the patio of the Menger Hotel, right next to the famous Menger Bar. Many recruits had already arrived and had their own horses, firearms, and bedding. Most of them bedded down on the grounds of the old Alamo mission. They were ready for action! The next day Wood decided it would be wise to move the whole recruiting operation out to the training grounds. This site is now known as Roosevelt Park, but in those days it was the grounds of the International Fair. There the conscripts were assigned to tents in a hastily erected encampment. They were more or less segregated by the territories they represented.

Roosevelt arrived at 7 A.M. May 16, 1898, having come via the Southern Pacific Railroad. A valet carrying several suitcases accompanied him. He took a cab (cabs in those days were horse-drawn conveyances) and drove to the Menger Hotel where he had breakfast immediately. Then he waited until Colonel Leonard Wood arrived by phaeton to take him to the training grounds. It was reported that Wood wore a light brown suit and a campaign hat when he went to meet Roosevelt, and Roosevelt was dressed in very much the same manner. As soon as Wood's carriage drove up to the Menger, Roosevelt embraced his commanding officer and good friend, and the two men drove off to the training camp, where Roosevelt addressed the recruits.

Roosevelt was delighted to see some of his old college classmates, who had already arrived from the East. They were serving as "kitchen police" and digging trenches, falling into the spirit of getting the outfit ready for combat. This group of twelve young men arrived in San Antonio on May 10, and they headed straight

Lt. Colonel Theodore "Teddy" Roosevelt
at Rough Rider encampment, May 1898
Photo courtesy Menger Hotel

for the Menger Hotel. They lunched at the hotel their first day in San Antonio. The local papers reported that the Menger register looked like "an invitation list to a New York society ball." Among the highly pedigreed young recruits were Cornelius Vanderbilt, Woodbury Kane (cousin of John Jacob Astor), Hamilton Fish Jr. (scion of the old Knickerbocker family), William Tiffany (grand nephew of Commodore Oliver H. Perry), Reginald Robards (descendant of Pierre Lolliard), and J. B. Trailer. They were the creme of New York society! They were all Teddy's friends, and they were ready for action!

The troops were supplied with food and equipment out of Fort Sam Houston's warehouses. Their uniforms included slouch hats, blue flannel shirts, brown trousers, leggings, and boots. They wore handkerchiefs knotted around their necks and looked just like a "cowboy cavalry" ought to have looked!

Lt. Colonel Theodore Roosevelt and two of his Rough Riders
mounted on horseback in front of Mission Concepcion, May 1898
Photo courtesy University of Texas Institute of Texan Cultures, *San Antonio Light* Collection

Colonel Roosevelt later wrote about the men who formed the Rough Riders:

> These men were what gave the regiment its peculiar character and reputation. These Southwesterners, naturally, many from Texas slipped in, gave us a ready-made group of fighters who could ride and shoot and take orders. They were hardy, sinewy, and resourceful. They could hit what they shot at with anything that would shoot. They did their best fighting on an empty stomach. They knew the value of discipline, and orders to them were sacred.
>
> Many enlisted under their right name. Many improvised. Many were men whose lives in the rugged Southwest had not been entirely free of the taint of fierce crimes. But they were superb fighters. Every one, whether fighting under his right name, or an alias.

One former Rough Rider, whose name was Clifton David Scott, from the Oklahoma Territory, wrote his memoirs years later and sent these reminiscences to his relatives. Peggy Green, of Weatherford, Texas, was kind enough to send a copy of one of them to Ernesto Malacara at the Menger. He wrote at length about the hasty training they received at the camp, and he had a few interesting remarks about Teddy Roosevelt. Evidently, Roosevelt, short and stocky, with wire-rimmed glasses, did not cut a very military-looking figure. He was a New Yorker, and these men were mostly from the Southwest. They had heard he was just a "New York cop." This rumor probably stemmed from his having been head of the New York City police. He didn't seem to fit the mold of a hard-riding cavalryman, and the men were suspicious. This is what Scott had to say:

> I was on the detail that went after the horses, and it was a wild bunch, there were about 1500 head and not over one out of a hundred had ever had a rope on him. There was an iron gray in the bunch, which seemed to be the leader. We figured that he would kill somebody, for you could see that

he had fight in him. After they had been rounded up the boys were looking them over and Roosevelt came out and after looking them over made the remark that he wanted that iron gray. We all rather wondered who would have to break him for him, but he got a rope, made an underhanded throw, which is the most difficult to make, and got him the first throw. It surprised us, and some of the boys thought that it must have been an accident, but when he began to hip him down we knew that he knew horses. As soon as he got up to him he took off his bandanna handkerchief and blindfolded him and saddled him. He mounted and took the blindfold off and I never saw such bucking and such riding in my life, and we all knew then that he couldn't be a New York cop, and began to inquire around about him and found out that he had been a Montana ranchman. We all felt rather cheap and felt that we had not treated him the way we should, and most of the boys went up to him and apologized. He pretended he didn't know what it was all about, but I know that he did. We soon found out that he was a great guy and there wasn't a man that wouldn't have gone through fire for him. No bunch of men ever served under a better or more understanding officer than Teddy Roosevelt. Cheap politicians called him a grand stand player, but if he had not been the kind of a man that he was he never could have won out with a bunch of men that he had to work with, for no man who did not have the right kind of stuff in him could have ever led that wild bunch.

The whole bunch of Rough Riders were only in San Antonio about a month. Teddy Roosevelt was here just short of two weeks. Now where does the Menger Hotel figure in all of this? It has been said, time after time, that the Menger Bar was where Teddy Roosevelt recruited some of the Rough Riders and where he enjoyed having libations with the troops. I questioned a friend, a well-respected military historian, about this.

Colonel John Manguso is one of San Antonio's primary military history authorities. He is the curator-director of the Fort Sam Houston Military Museum. I asked him about the validity of Roosevelt's troops being allowed to drink at the Menger Bar during their training period in San Antonio. He reminded me that "times have changed." There was not the strict military discipline attached to the hastily gathered group of recruits that one would associate with the regulars. These were men who could shoot and who could ride, and that was what was needed. Military discipline was no doubt sadly lacking, and the word "protocol" was probably foreign to these men. After a long hot day on duty, it was highly likely they headed into town, about a four- or five-mile ride, for a cool libation or two, just to wind down.

Roosevelt was friendly and informal. Although he had come from a socially prominent background and was extremely well educated, he was a very down-to-earth individual. The men loved him. He had a charismatic personality and probably would have made a great salesman! He could convince anybody to do anything he suggested. And while it might not have been "proper" to drink with his troops, it is said that Teddy did, although Colonel Wood did not approve.

As persuasive as Roosevelt could be (an acquaintance of his once said after spending time in conversation with Roosevelt, you had to go home and literally wring the personality out of your clothes), he just might have talked a few cowpunchers into "joining up" with his outfit. There is a definite connection with the Menger Bar and Roosevelt.

Cecilia Steinfeldt, in her book *San Antonio Was,* says:

When the Rough Riders trained in San Antonio, Teddy Roosevelt and Cornelius Vanderbilt were known to gallop their horses up to the hotel entrance to partake of its hospitality.

In his book *The San Antonio Story*, author Ted Fehrenbach remarks:

The regiment gained national prominence by their charge up San Juan Hill, but, comprised of Western cowboys, toughs and New York "millionaire clubmen," it also made local legend with exploits from the Menger Bar to less savory sections of the city.

The troops shipped out of San Antonio May 28, 1898. Their stay had been short, but they had made an indelible imprint on the city of San Antonio. The war was almost as short as their training had been. Trained as cavalrymen, they found, upon arrival in Florida, there were not enough ships to transport their mounts. Most of the men arrived as foot soldiers, and only the officers were able to take their horses. Teddy stayed with his troops, valiantly leading them into battle. His dear friend Sgt. Hamilton Fish Jr. was one of the first casualties. The Rough Riders lost many brave young men, and many others were wounded. All had fought valiantly, and Teddy was proud of his troops.

After the war Roosevelt returned to New York. He ran for governor and was handily elected. Later, in 1900, he was nominated on the Republican ticket for vice president of the United States. On September 14, 1901, President William McKinley was assassinated while in office and thus Theodore Roosevelt, not yet forty-three years old, became the twenty-sixth president of the United States. He ran for the office of president in 1904 and was elected. A wise and brilliant president, he was the first incumbent to leave U.S. soil, to visit the construction site of the Panama Canal, which was constructed during his administration. His was the fundamental dictum in foreign policy to "speak softly and carry a big stick." And while Roosevelt was known as a fighter, he also won the Nobel Peace Prize.

While Roosevelt was president, the Rough Riders had a reunion at the Menger Hotel, in 1905. An elegant banquet was served to the president and his men, and a grand time was had by all.

Another "reunion" was held at the Menger on October 30-31, 1998, when the Theodore Roosevelt Association met to commemorate the one hundredth anniversary of the founding of the famous Rough Riders. The Theodore Roosevelt Distinguished Service Medal was presented to former President George H. W. Bush, and his wife, Mrs. Barbara Pierce Bush, for many years of tireless service to their country in fields reflecting the works and interests of Theodore Roosevelt.

Theodore Roosevelt was a brilliant man, a compassionate man, a man of his word, and one who did not run from confrontations. This is a man who could ride, shoot, and confront all types of foes, both in battle and politics, and yet he was such a gentleman that the most beloved toy a toddler can own was named for him. The "teddy bear" was so named when a cartoonist sketched a little bear cub that the president had compassionately spared on a hunting trip out west, calling him "Teddy's bear." The name stuck, and there are few children in this country who have not owned a cuddly teddy bear.

Because of the impression Teddy made on San Antonio during his short stay, the Menger Bar is called the Roosevelt Bar in his honor. I believe he would have been delighted!

Ode to the Rough Riders
Docia Schultz Williams

They were rough, and tough, and ready,
Those men who served with Teddy;
   In the war they fought in Cuba a hundred years ago.
They could shoot and they could ride,
And they served with utmost pride;
   Their valor and their courage they well knew how to show.
Now this war they fought with Spain
Gained them nothing much but pain,
   Many of their number remained behind in Cuba, dead.
But their country bade them fight . . .
So they did, with all their might,
   On the slopes of San Juan Hill their blood was bravely shed.
Now, we believe their spirits are

Still in this mirrored Menger Bar,
    Where they first came together in that spring of '98.
Their leader's name was Teddy,
And his men were rough and ready
    Their training it was hasty; there wasn't time to wait.
Now their lusty spirits linger
At the bar here at the Menger
    Their ghostly apparitions have been seen by quite a few.
If you stop and stay awhile
You may glimpse a ghostly smile
    Of a uniformed Rough Rider as he downs a beer or two.
Here we welcome them with pleasure,
Brave men who gave full measure;
    Teddy's volunteer Rough Riders! They were brave, and
tough, and true!

Chapter 10

Specialties of the House

The Menger's reputation for superb cuisine all began with Mary Guenther Menger, who was noted for the fine table she set at the boardinghouse that she and her husband, William, operated prior to the opening of the hotel in 1859. Now, over a hundred and forty years later, the Menger Hotel is still recognized for its excellent food and service.

From the opening days of the hotel, food served in the dining rooms has always been of the highest quality. Soon after the hotel opening, the San Antonio newspapers reported that the Menger was the headquarters for genial hospitality and its patrons were served the best foods the market offered. Even though it was expensive for those days, they purchased the finest quality beef at 4 cents a pound, chickens at 15 cents apiece, and fresh country butter which ran from 15 to 20 cents a pound! Eggs at 20 cents a dozen were purchased for the restaurant as well. Mr. Menger bought such diverse delicacies as stuffed olives, almonds, Sultana raisins, English currants, imported teas, pie fruits, fresh cranberries in season, tomatoes, guava jelly, cod fish, herrings, and Goshen butter at the grocery market operated by Groesbeck and Smyth.

Gentlemen guests were well taken care of as well. The finest whiskies and wines and the very best cigars for after dinner enjoyment were provided. These quality smokes, especially made for the hotel, included the San Pedro Springs, Vista Del Casino, and Vista Del Menger Hotel brands.

Mr. Menger made his own beer, and the "Brew of Gamrinus" beer was so famous he received orders from all over the state of Texas and had to hire wagoneers to deliver the beverage by ox cart and wagon train. An equally popular beer was Menger's "Degen Beer," named in honor of his first brewmaster, Carl Degen. At the hotel, the beer and wine was stored in the cellars, which had thick limestone walls. These cellars were so well insulated that beer stored there would frost the glasses the year round! Sometimes Menger cooled his beer and wine in the waters of the old acequia, which once flowed through the patio gardens.

William Menger raised his own pork on a little farm that was managed by another German immigrant, Gustave Schmelzer. The farm was located about where the infantry barracks at Fort Sam Houston were later located. Menger took great pride in the cured bacon, pork chops, hams, spareribs, and freshly ground sausage that were served to the guests at his hotel.

One of Menger's hogs was so huge the newspaper reported on the size of the creature. The *San Antonio Herald,* March 15, 1867, reported the hog was "the talk of the town." The beast weighed 1,011 pounds and was 6 feet, 8 inches long, and stood 3 feet, 7 inches tall.

One time Menger is reported to have bet a friend that he could raise a bigger hog than his friend could, and the winner of the contest would be host to a dinner and invite all their mutual friends. Menger's entry in this contest grew to the size of 750 pounds, and Menger was just sure his animal would win the bet. But alas, the obese animal broke out of its pen, got into the corncrib, and literally ate itself to death.

In order to keep meat from spoiling, ice had to be shipped to San Antonio from Boston. It was shipped to the port of Indianola, and from there it was transported to San Antonio in specially designed "ice wagons." Other meat was cured or smoked, since there was so little refrigeration. Some game was kept chilled in the thick-walled beer cellars under the ground floor of the hotel. Often the Menger courtyard was filled with wild game hanging from the trees waiting to be cured. There were sides of venison, antelope, bear, and buffalo. Mr. Menger often gave liberally of this meat to the poor, who could not afford the price of a Menger meal. In those early days, a diversity of wild game was featured in the hotel menus. Haunch of venison, wild turkey, buffalo steaks and tongue, braised quail, and a variety of gamebirds stuffed with oysters were regularly served. Turtles, caught in the San Antonio River, were transformed into a delicious soup that was a specialty of the house. At one time, as many as twenty-six cooks were employed to serve a diversity of guests distinguished in the literary, military, theatrical, financial, and social circles of the day.

Local housewives frequently visited the Menger brewery to purchase yeast cakes for use in making their breads, rolls, and coffeecakes.

Local businessmen enjoyed dining at the hotel because of its excellent food and service. The enterprising Mengers outfitted a wagon with benches, which they called a "talley ho." A team of four horses pulled this wagon, which held about thirty passengers. It would go every day, at noon, down Commerce Street to Main Plaza, then up Soledad to Houston Street, and thence back to the hotel, picking up patrons along the way. After the customers had dined on the Menger's delicious fare, they were delivered back to their places of business.

We were fortunate to uncover a Menger dinner (noon meal) menu among the Menger memorabilia at the San Antonio Central Library's Texana Collection. The menu, which is dated August 23, 1880, shows why the local businessmen patronized Mary Menger's table. The front cover of the menu reads as follows:

BILL OF FARE
Mrs. W. A. Menger, Proprietress

Hours for Meals

Breakfast 7 - 9 1/2
Dinner 1 - 3
Supper 6 - 8

Meals sent to the rooms will be charged extra

Guests having friends to meals will please give notice at the office

*For guests leaving by early train, breakfast at 5 a.m., and by
Eagle Pass, Laredo and Bandera stages, 5:30 a.m.*

*All fruit or luncheons taken from the table
or sent to rooms will be charged extra*

Children occupying seats at the public table will be charged full price

The inside sheet of the menu listed the following bill of fare available to hotel guests and local diners who ate at the hotel on a regular basis:

BILL OF FARE

SOUP
Vermicelli

BOILED
Ox tongue, tomato sauce, or Beef, plain

COLD DISHES
Sugar cured ham   Fresh tongue   Pressed corn beef

ENTREES
Round of beef, braised with new carrots
Stewed lamb, with dumplings
Baked macaroni, Italian style
Rice with cream   Stewed California pears

ROAST
Ribs of beef   Loin of beef
Mutton   Veal, brown gravy

VEGETABLES
Mashed potatoes   Roast sweet potatoes
Lima beans   Ochra   Cabbage

RELISHES
Worchestershire sauce   Pepper sauce   French mustard
Chow-chow   Tomato catsup   Pickles   Horseradish

DESSERT
Cocoanut and Green apple pies
Cornstarch pudding, wine sauce
Golden jumbles   Sponge cake   Spice cake

Times and eating habits have changed over the years that the Menger has presided over Alamo Plaza. In the last century the main meal, called "dinner," was served at noon. A lighter meal, or "supper," was served in the evening. Today, we seem to enjoy light noon lunches and we dine in a more leisurely and elaborate fashion in the evening when we are served "dinner." Food habits have changed a great deal also. For instance, the wild game, which was once an important item on the Menger menus, is no longer evident at all, and today there are a lot of frozen and ice cold confections that would not have been available in those early days.

We read from the files of the Daughters of the Republic of Texas library an interesting article clipped from an unidentified newspaper. The clipping bore no date. The column, written by Ruth Massey, was called "From an Army Wife" and must have been a regular feature in the newspaper. Mrs. Massey had interviewed a former Menger waiter, one Aaron Townsend, who first began working at the hotel at age fifteen as a bellhop. Later he became a waiter. Townsend was quoted as saying the breakfasts in the old days were very bountiful. At the tables there were bowls of fruit, and guests ordered two or three meats, which they ate with hot cakes and milk. He said they served coffee in big thick white coffee cups that "you couldn't break if you tried." The dinner menus (noon meal) consisted of soup, fish, four meats, four vegetables, a salad with a cooked dressing, four desserts, coffee, and cheese.

Menger Hotel patio with tables set up
for a party, postcard, circa 1935

Ilse Griffith collection, courtesy Ingrid Kokinda

Townsend told Mrs. Massey that in those early days the elevators were run by water, and if the water pressure gave out, there were no running elevators. He said big fans were used for ventilation in the early days. He recalled that around 11:30 every morning the waiters would shoo all the flies towards one end of the dining room and then force them out of an open window. The men sang as they shooed, and the lobby often filled with people who came to hear the "shoo fly" chorus.

Sidney Lanier, the famous Southern poet, wrote to his family of a dining experience he had at the Menger in 1872. He mentioned a cook known as "Mammy Hannah," a former slave, who was famous for her old Southern-style cooking. There was also another cook named "Uncle Manasseh," who made absolutely incomparable "shore dinners," featuring fish cooked over a charcoal grill or a broiled pompano with melted butter poured over it.

Patio, the Menger Hotel, date unknown
Photo courtesy University of Texas Institute of Texan Cultures, Zintgraff Collection

Early day newspapers often mentioned the Menger cuisine. A reporter for the *San Antonio Express* wrote in 1879; "A Mexican meal at the Menger really sets a man up. He feels like getting on a pony and roping cattle right off."

The late Texas folklore writer J. Frank Dobie once told the story about the time trail boss Gus Schreiner, up from his big ranch at Kerrville, decided to treat his cowhands to a nice dinner at the Menger Hotel. Schreiner ordered quail on toast. All the cowboys, who had never seen a written menu in their lives, followed his example and ordered the identical meal the boss had ordered. One of the fellows spent the rest of his life complaining: "It wasn't a damn thing but a little old pa'tridge on a slice of scorched light bread. No other meat, and not a thing was fried."

Often hunters brought in game they killed to the hotel kitchen. Bear, venison, buffalo, and wild turkey were traded in exchange for a free meal or a free room. In 1879 one such bear ended up barbecued for the staff of the *San Antonio Express* newspaper. The glowing report read, in part:

> The grave should cover all resentment. That bear is dead, and we helped bury him. We dropped a tear over his tenderness, while engaged in the melancholy duty. While we think of his tenderness even now, it is more than we can bear. Excuse our emotion, but we cannot proceed.

For a time, the hotel employed a German baker named William L. Richter. He became the chief baker at the hotel and was known for his special pastries, breads, tantalizing sponge cakes, tortes, pies, and rolls. Richter, who not only was a great baker, but an exceedingly handsome young man as well, eventually established the Richter Bakery. He was the originator of the still produced and still delicious Buttercrust Bread.

In the late 1890s the American Plan was implemented at the hotel. Guests paid for their rooms, and the room rate included meals that were most often served family style. Diners could eat all they wanted, but if they missed a meal, they still had to pay for it. We were fortunate to find, at the historical archives at the University of the Incarnate Word, some old Menger ledgers. These handwritten records were kept, in detail, on each guest. Every item was listed and then itemized when the guest checked out. Not only were the room rates listed and the number of meals consumed by the guests, but also there were numerous other services included in the tabulations. These included the bathhouse, washing (laundry), the stable (some guests had more than one horse) with grooming, blacksmith service, bar bill, and cash loans. Would you believe that guests often borrowed money from the hotel and repaid the loan at the time they checked out?

During the late 1800s the major hotels in San Antonio began to cater to local diners as well as hotel guests. Many people began to eat out and take their guests to a favorite hotel to dine on special occasions like Christmas and Thanksgiving. For such events, the Menger offered a lavish array of dishes, such as Benedict Bay oysters, green sea turtle, baked filet of trout au gratin, prime roast beef with Yorkshire pudding, turkey with oyster dressing, and young pig with homemade applesauce.

In our day brunch has become a favorite meal at the Menger, and the Menger brunches, served on Sundays and special days such as Christmas, Thanksgiving, Easter, and Mother's Day, are especially noteworthy. Today's Colonial Room bill of fare includes a daily buffet selection as well as a very large a la carte listing.

Special Menger Menus From the Past

We are fortunate that many of the early Menger menus were preserved, so we can get a good idea of the dining preferences of the hotel's guests down through the years.

For instance, a dinner served on Sunday, March 28, 1880, which honored former President Ulysses S. Grant and his party, included:

MENU

Beef Filet   Fresh Trout   Fowl with Mushrooms
Fresh Asparagus   Potato Croquettes
Charlotte Russ   Apricot Torte   Strawberry Meringue
Lady fingers with Oranges filled with cream

It is fairly certain that calories were not counted in those days, and no one had ever heard of or worried about cholesterol!

The San Antonio Daily Express on October 19, 1950, ran an article about the Menger's food service over the years and printed the following menu from the Colonial Room:

Colonial Room, Christmas 1893
MENU

Oysters
Puree of Game   Consomme a la Chiffonade
Salted Almonds   Celery   Olives
Whitefish a la Joinville
Sliced tomatoes   Potatoes Victoria
Small Patties au Salpicon
Sirloin of Beef, Yorkshire Pudding
Turkey, Chestnut Dressing   Cranberry Sauce
Suckling Pig stuffed with Oysters
Suprement of Chicken, a la Richelieu
Epigramme of Lamb, Parisienne
New Peas   Orange Fritters, Glace   Mashed Potatoes
Cauliflower   String Beans   Asparagus
Cardinal Punch
Mallard Duck, Currant Jelly
Boned Turkey, au aspic   Russian Salad
English Plum Pudding   Charlotte Russ
Mince Pie   Pumpkin Pie
Coconut Meringue Pie   Assorted Cakes
Strawberries in Cream   Peach Ice Cream
Oranges   Bananas   Malaga Grapes   Assorted Nuts
Roquefort and Edam Cheese
Water   Crackers   Cider   Coffee

The Menger has long been used to serving distinguished guests. In 1905 there was a reunion of the famous Rough Riders at the Menger, and President Theodore "Teddy" Roosevelt was the honored guest at a gala banquet prepared by Chef Adolph Metrovitch. One might wonder if the Rough Riders understood the menu any better than we might understand it today:

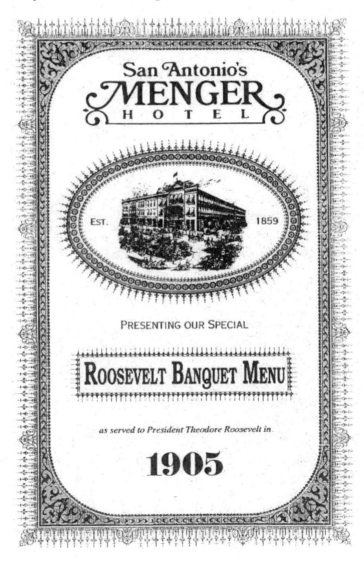

San Antonio's
MENGER
HOTEL

EST. 1859

PRESENTING OUR SPECIAL

ROOSEVELT BANQUET MENU

as served to President Theodore Roosevelt in

1905

Canapés aux Anchois
Anchovy Canapes

Tartines de Caviare
Caviar on Rounds of Toast

Consommé de Gibier
Game Consomme

Soft Shell Crabs à l'Américaine
American Style Soft Shell Crabs

Cailles en Aspic Belle–Vue
Belle–Vue Quail in Aspic

Riz d'Agneau aux Pointes d'Asperges
Lamb Rice with Asparagus Tips

Grouse Farri aux Truffes
Grouse Stuffed with Truffles

Salade Jardinière
Garden Salad

Glace Diplomate
Layered Ice Cream

Fraises　　　　Gateaux Assortis
Strawberries　　　*Assorted Cakes*

Fromage Roquefort
Roquefort Cheese

Café Noir
Black Coffee

Whether the Rough Riders understood the French menu or not, I am sure they enjoyed the delicious food that was served. The four wine courses served with the meal must have added to the merriment at the tables as well! First, Chateau Yquem was served with the crab, Royal Scharzburg with the aspic course, Chateau

Larose with the asparagus, and Louis Roederer Grand Vin Sec with the grouse and truffles.

Robert Fairley, one of the waiters, recalled that the president gave him a piece of elephant tusk (ivory) which Fairley greatly treasured. Fairley stated that many of the meals served around the turn of the century consisted of fifteen to twenty courses.

On Friday, October 20, 1950, there was a public open house, followed by a gala dinner to commemorate the reopening of the "new" Menger Hotel, which had been extensively remodeled, repaired, and had generally undergone a complete "face-lift."

This red-letter occasion was marked by the arrival of the governor and his party, who came in carriages pulled by palomino horses, escorted by the Bexar County Sheriff's Mounted Posse and the San Antonio Charro Group. An assemblage of impersonators attired as former guests of the hotel greeted the governor's party.

After the dinner a historical pageant was presented by the San Antonio Conservation Society in collaboration with the San Antonio Little Theatre. The pageant, directed by Mr. Joe Salek, featured descendants of pioneer San Antonians modeling authentic period costumes. An honored guest was the famous French designer, Christian Dior, who presented his winter collection.

Menu For Menger Gala

Champagne
Hors d' oerves Parisienne
Jellied Green Turtle Soup au Caviar
Cheese Straws
Baked Oysters de Souvien
Melba Toast Fingers
Charcoal Broiled K.C. Sirloin
Sauce Bernaise
Or
Broiled Main Lobster, Drawn Butter
Souffle Potatoes   Giant Asparagus Tips Hollandaise
Cloverleaf Rolls   Menger Hot Biscuits

Half Avocado stuffed with Grapefruit Sections
French Dressing
Brandied Fruit Sundae
Merangue Glace
Demitasse
Salted Nuts   Raisins   Mints

Famous Menger Recipes

The current executive chef at the Menger, Winfried Heumann, continues to execute incomparable menus in the traditions established by out-standing chefs of the past, such as Adolph Metrovitch and Hipolito Garcia. It is most appropriate that Mr. Heumann, a native of Germany, is now established at the hotel that was founded by a German hotelier, William Menger. Mr. Heumann was born in Wissen Sieg, West Germany, and educated in that country. He received his hotel and restaurant training in Sinzig, Rhein, West Germany, between 1967 and 1970. Later

Executive Chef Winfried Heumann

Photo by author

he worked in several fine restaurants, hotels, and clubs in Germany, Bermuda, Atlanta, Houston, and League City, Texas. For a time he owned his own restaurant, the Edelweiss, in Humble, Texas. Mr. Heumann has collected many culinary awards at International shows in Bermuda and in Texas. He won a gold medal in the Texas Culinary Arts competition, and has won three gold and two silver medals in Gulf Coast seafood cook-offs. He is also a prizewinner in chili, Irish stew, and fajita cook-offs. He has pre-sided over the kitchens at the Menger since 1993 and originated many outstanding recipes now featured on the Menger bill of fare. Mr. Heumann has kindly permitted us to include some of the most popular Menger recipes, both his own innovations and some old favorites from years gone by, in this chapter. We hope you will enjoy them! Bon Appetite!

Rinder Rouladen
(Stuffed Beef Rolls)

By Chef Winfried Heumann of the Menger Hotel

Ingredients:
> 6 to 8 oz. top butt steaks
> Dijon mustard
> 8 bay leaves
> Juniper berries
> Garlic, salt, pepper mix (equal parts salt, pepper, and garlic)
> Flour
> 2 cups Burgundy wine
> 1 cup water

Stuffing:
> 6 slices of lean bacon
> 2 whole onions
> 1/2 lb. sliced mushrooms

Directions:
> Pound the top butt steaks flat. Season with salt and pepper mix. Then paint with Dijon mustard. Stuff with bacon, onion, and mushroom stuffing, and roll into rolls. Roll the rouladen in flour and then saute in oil until golden brown. Add Burgundy wine and water, bay leaves, and juniper berries, and bring to a boil. Cover with aluminum foil and let simmer in 325-degree oven for about 1 hour. Take the rouladen out of the pan and thicken gravy with flour. Add salt and pepper to taste.

Menger Schnitzel

By Chef Winfried Heumann of the Menger Hotel

Ingredients:

Veal cutlet, 4 to 5 oz. quarter-inch thick, cut from leg

Flour as needed

One egg, well beaten

Toasted bread crumbs, coarse crumble

Clarified butter; cover bottom of saute pan with about an inch of butter

Directions:

Remove all fat and any other tissue from veal. Pound lightly with mallet and make small incisions around edges to prevent curling. Place each ingredient in a separate, flat container. Dip and coat veal in the following order: flour, egg wash, and bread crumbs. Shake off any excess. Saute cutlets a few minutes on each side until golden. Top with Menger Sauce and serve immediately.

Menger Schnitzel Sauce

Ingredients:

2 large mushrooms, thinly sliced

4 oz. heavy cream

White pepper and salt, to taste

2 oz. demi glacé

1 oz. cognac

Directions:

Saute mushrooms for a few minutes (can be done in advance). Bring cream, cognac, and demi glacé to boil. Add mushrooms and reduce by one third. The consistency of the sauce should lightly cover a spoon. Cover schnitzel with sauce, serve on a warm plate, garnish with parsley, and enjoy!

Original Menger Chicken Salad

Courtesy Chef Winfried Heumann of the Menger Hotel

Ingredients:

    2 lb. chicken breasts, which have been grilled and diced
    2 tsp. cilantro
    4 tsp. diced green onion
    2 tsp. fresh minced garlic
    4 tsp. minced Thai pepper
    6 tsp. sugar
    8 tsp. fish sauce
    2 cups diced cucumber
    2 tsp. lime juice
    Salt to taste
    24 thin slices of lime, for garnishing

Preparation:

    Mix all ingredients together and marinate for at least two hours. Serve in a pineapple boat on a bed of lettuce. Garnish with thin lime slices.

Menger Golden Cheese Soup

A long-time hotel favorite

Ingredients:

    1 cup finely diced carrots
    1 cup finely diced celery
    1/2 cup diced onions
    3 Tablespoons butter
    3 Tablespoons flour
    1 tsp. seasoned salt
    2 cups milk
    1 quart chicken broth
    4 oz. diced American cheese

Preparation:

Put celery, carrots, onions, and butter in saucepan and saute over slow flame until vegetables are soft. Be very careful not to scorch them. Add flour, salt, milk, broth, and cheese. Stir well until cheese is melted. If too thick, add more milk or broth.

Menger Tortilla Soup

By Executive Chef Winfried Heumann of the Menger Hotel

Note: This delicious tortilla soup, which I consider the very best tortilla soup I have ever tasted anywhere, is often featured on the noon buffet lunches in the hotel's famous Colonial Room.

Ingredients:

2 1/2 lb. ground beef
1 lb. yellow onion, diced
3/4 lb. Anaheim peppers, diced
1/2 lb. poblano peppers, diced
2 16-oz. cans diced tomatoes
1/4 lb. tomato paste
1 gallon chicken stock
1/2 oz. ground cumin
1/2 bunch fresh cilantro, chopped
1/2 oz. fresh garlic, chopped
1/4 oz. ground black pepper

Preparation:

1. Brown meat and drain well.
2. Add onion and peppers and saute.
3. Add diced tomatoes, tomato paste, and saute.
4. Add chicken stock and seasonings.
5. Bring to a boil and reduce to a simmer.
6. Simmer for 1 hour.

When ready to eat, top with tortilla strips (red corn tortillas) and white and cheddar cheese mix.

Menger Spinach Pudding

This is an old favorite Menger recipe!

Ingredients:

3 cups cooked spinach
1/2 small onion
1/2 green pepper
1 1/2 garlic buds
4 eggs
1 tsp. salt
1/4 tsp. pepper
Dash nutmeg
2 cups finely ground bread crumbs (no crusts)
1/2 cup softened butter

Preparation:

Put spinach, onion, green pepper, and garlic through grinder (food processor) using a fine blade. Add eggs and seasonings, mixing well. Mix in 1 1/2 cups of the crumbs. Take a clean dish towel and spread the butter onto it, forming a 9- to 10-inch square. Sprinkle with remaining bread crumbs. Drop spinach mixture in center and form into a roll about 1 1/2 inches thick. Wrap cloth loosely around roll and tie ends and middle securely with string. Steam this 20 minutes. Yields 10 to 12 portions.

Hot Cheese Puffs

These are delicious, easy to do hors d' oeuvres

Make rounds out of sliced white bread. Lay flat on large baking pan. Make ahead of time and let stand out in the open for about two hours. Place a thin slice of green onion in the center of the round of bread, then a mound of mayonaisse. Sprinkle the top and sides with Parmesan cheese, covering surface well with cheese. Just before serving, put under the broiler and allow to lightly brown. Serve at once.

Famous Menger Chess Pie

This recipe makes five pies.
You will have to figure out how to divide it!

Ingredients:
   5 lbs. sugar
   26 eggs
   2 lbs. butter, melted
   4 oz. cornmeal
   6 oz. lemon juice

Preparation:
   Break eggs in a bowl and mix in sugar and cornmeal and stir for three minutes. Add butter and lemon juice. Pour into unbaked shells and bake for 45 minutes in 325-degree oven.

Caramel Topped Apple Torte

A delicious German torte courtesy Chef Winfried Heumann
of the Menger Hotel

Crust:
   1 cup sifted all-purpose flour (sift flour first, then measure)
   2 teaspoons sugar
   1 teaspoon salt
   1/2 cup (1 stick) butter, chilled
   1 Tablespoon vinegar

Preparation:
   To make crust: Grease bottom and sides of a 9-inch spring-form pan. Combine flour, sugar, and salt in a medium-sized bowl. Cut in cold butter using pastry blender until mixture

resembles coarse meal. Blend in vinegar. Press dough evenly over bottom and partially up the side of the pan.

Filling:
    1 21-oz. can apple pie filling
    2 large or 3 small apples, peeled, cored, and diced
    1/2 cup sugar
    2 Tablespoons all-purpose flour
    Juice of 1/2 lemon
    1/2 teaspoon cinnamon
    1/2 teaspoon allspice
    1/2 teaspoon nutmeg

Preparation:
    To make filling: Preheat oven to 375 degrees. Put apple pie filling, diced fresh apples, sugar, flour, lemon juice, and spices in a large bowl and blend well. Spoon filling into crust and bake until top is golden, about 45 minutes. Allow torte to cool to room temperature.

Caramel Sauce

Ingredients:
    1 1/2 cups sugar
    3/4 teaspoon lemon juice
    1 1/2 cups water
    1 1/2 cups heavy cream

Preparation:
    To make the caramel sauce: while torte is cooling, melt sugar in a heavy bottomed aluminum, stainless steel, or unlined copper saucepan over moderate heat and cook, without stirring, until it turns golden brown. You can shake the pan to distribute the heat, but don't stir. Add lemon juice, water, and cream. The caramel will harden initially. Slowly bring the mixture to the boiling point, stirring. Continue stirring until all of the caramel has dissolved and the sauce has thickened. Remove from heat and let the hot

caramel cool.

When torte has cooled and caramel sauce is still slightly warm, spread the prepared caramel sauce evenly over the top of the cake and refrigerate. Serve, garnished with a dollop of whipped cream.

Menger Mango Ice Cream

Rich and creamy, with a delicate sweetness, mango ice cream is, without a doubt, the hotel's most famous dessert! It has been served at the Menger for over 100 years.

Ingredients:
    2 large ripe mangoes
    1/2 cup sugar
    1 Tablespoon lemon juice
    1 cup heavy cream

Preparation:
    Scoop out the mango flesh and chop roughly, discarding peel and seed. Put chopped mango, sugar, and lemon juice in food processor and process until smooth and thick. Pour puree and cream into an ice cream canister and freeze according to freezer instructions.

Mango Sauce

Ice cream can be topped with this, as it always is served at the Menger. Puree canned mangoes, without adding any juice or sugar, in the blender or food processor until of sauce consistency.

During a visit to the Leagues of United Latin American Citizens Convention in 1992, then presidential hopeful Bill Clinton took time out to make a quick trip to the Menger Hotel. He dropped in to get a taste of its signature dish, the mango ice cream. He declared, "It's unbelievable, like a creamy peach." Clinton had first tried the delicacy some twenty years before when he made a visit to San Antonio on behalf of George McGovern's unsuccessful bid for the presidency. During his 1992 visit, Clinton told his entourage that "Mango ice cream at the Menger Hotel is one of the great treasures in American life." He arranged to pick up enough mango ice cream for himself, the twenty-seven members of the national press (news media) traveling with him, plus his staff and various other hangers-on.

When Mr. Clinton was elected president, the hotel shipped forty gallons of this delicious dessert to Washington, D.C., for his 1993 inauguration celebration!

President Clinton is not the only devotee of the dessert. Mrs. Mary Moody Northen, the daughter of W. L. Moody Jr., who purchased the hotel in 1943, always ordered the ice cream when she visited the Menger.

Chapter 11

Down Memory Lane with Ernesto Malacara

Ernesto Malacara is a native San Antonian. He served a four-year tour of duty in the U.S. Navy. Then, in 1960, he began his forty-year career in the hospitality business. He started from the "ground up," serving in various capacities and at numerous hotel properties in the city of San Antonio. For the past twenty-three years, he has been employed at the Menger Hotel. He is extremely devoted to his duties as assistant general manager of the famous hostelry. Mr. Malacara loves to meet people and takes the greatest of pleasure in making the Menger guests feel comfortable, welcome, and "at home."

Ernesto often accompanied me to various research libraries, helping me to ferret out the facts that were needed to tell the Menger story. We went through pages and pages of musty, fragile old ledgers, faded old newspaper articles, hand-written accounts, and various history books and journals. Most of the hotel registers have been lost, however the library on the grounds of the Alamo, operated by the Daughters of the Republic of Texas, owns the 1874 register. Mr. Malacara shared all of his personal files, correspondence, and photographs with me.

The following are some of his personal recollections of incidents that have taken place during his years of service at the hotel.

Ernesto Malacara
Assistant General Manager, Menger Hotel

In my over twenty years at the Menger I have met many interesting people, guests, employees, and San Antonio residents who drop in from time to time to visit, enjoy our bar, or to dine in the Colonial Room. Some of my experiences have been humorous, and others have been sad, interesting, exciting, frightening, you name it. In the hotel business, there is never a dull moment. I just wish I had written down all the things that have happened that might now make interesting reading. Never did I dream that Docia Williams and I would one day collaborate on a book such as this.

I can recall the "what" of the incidents I am relating far better than the "when," so you will just have to believe they really did happen!

Ernesto Malacara photographed in Colonial Dining Room

Photo by author

A Case of Mistaken Identity

I was once called to the motor drive-in area, where I was told a guests' red Cadillac automobile was missing. The car could not be found anywhere, and of course, the guest was very irate. He believed his car must have been stolen. We had to send the gentleman out to a business appointment in a taxi, after we finally convinced him that his car might have been taken in error. Naturally, this guest was very upset, the valet parking driver was extremely nervous, and I was almost ready to have a nervous breakdown myself. The police were called, and the car was reported missing (I hesitated to say "stolen"). I just knew I would be fired, and the valet parking driver looked like he was awaiting his execution!

After nearly five hours of worry and agonizing anxiety over the whole thing, the red Cadillac showed up. A little elderly lady stepped out of the car. The guest to whom the car belonged had returned from his business engagement, and we summoned him at once to tell him his car had been returned. Of course, he was furious—with the lady, the hotel, the valet driver, and me.

The poor little lady just couldn't understand what all the fuss was about. She volunteered her valet parking ticket and gave it to the valet driver. When he brought her car around it was a blue rental Buick. She had driven around for hours not realizing she was in the wrong car! We could only surmise she was color-blind or just totally oblivious to the world around her. Believe me, I prayed a month of rosaries over that one.

All That Glitters is Not Gold

One afternoon my now deceased friend and co-worker, J. W. MacMillan, and I were in the Menger Bar enjoying soft drinks. We discussed the bar in general, its history and great age, famous patrons that had enjoyed refreshments there, etc. Two men sitting near us were obviously listening in on our conversation. Suddenly Mac said, "You know, Ernest, we have to remove those solid gold spittoons as they are just too valuable to leave unguarded." (They were brass.) He elaborated on the "gold spittoons" a bit longer, and then we finished our sodas and left the bar. The next day the early shift at the bar reported that one of the brass spittoons was missing.

Worries About Who Pays

One of our service employees was not feeling well. He was sweating profusely and yet he said he was cold. This was in July. We called EMS and explained the situation. They arrived within minutes (the hotel is conveniently located just about a block from the Central Fire Station). All the man's vital signs were taken, and the EMS attendants told him he must be taken to the hospital immediately. I escorted the employee to the ambulance, and he stopped just as we got to the vehicle. He hesitated to get in and turned to me and asked, "Mr. Ernest, if I get in the ambulance do I have to pay them right now?" I told him to get in the ambulance! He was taken to the nearest hospital and was diagnosed as having had a heart attack. I do believe his guardian angel was working overtime that day.

The Creep

I'd like to preface this incident by saying almost all the employees we have had since my association with the Menger began are wonderful people. But I suppose, along the way, you have to expect to meet someone like this particular employee.

It was Christmastime, and this hotel employee seemed to be having a difficult time. He had no money with which to buy Christmas gifts for his children. Several of us went down to Walgreens and bought some presents for the children. We were happy and felt good about providing a little joy to the youngsters. The employee was happy and seemed to be grateful.

We found out the next day that the gifts never arrived at his house. On the way home, it seems, he stopped at a bar and traded off all of our presents for beer!

Trouble on Five

Once I was called up to the fifth floor by a guest, who said, "There is much loud talking and maybe a fight about to start up here." When I arrived, I recognized the guest who was involved in the heated conversation. I asked his female companion, who was there with him, "What is this all about?" She said her friend had gotten involved with two men on a drug deal. The guest decided he wanted his money back, and the two men said they didn't have his money. Things seemed to be getting out of control. I attempted to calm the situation, but the two men told me I could get hurt if I interfered in their business.

I realized we were about to have an ugly incident here, and I needed some help. I used my passkey to gain entrance into a room, hoping it wasn't occupied. I called the switchboard operator, explained the situation, and asked her to call the police. I then called the other assistant manager, but he was not in his room. I went back into the corridor. The elevator door opened and our garage supervisor, Frank Santellan, stepped out. The operator had called him, telling him, "Mr. Malacara needs some help." Frank sized up the situation and proceeded to tell the two men, whom we presumed to be drug dealers, that they were about to "get their tails kicked." The two ruffians seemed to think that over. The odds were even now. There was silence for a minute, and then the elevator opened again. This time a couple of police officers stepped out. The officers took the guest and one of the "street men" into a room. Shortly afterwards the policemen escorted the whole group out of the hotel. The police timing was good, but I still thank Frank to this day for his actions. If the police hadn't arrived when they did and Frank hadn't come to my rescue, I might not be here now.

A Surprise in the Coffee Shop

We had an elderly male guest who lived at the hotel for some time. He was getting up in years, so we always had one of our young male employees go to his room and escort him down to his meals in the hotel's dining rooms, returning to take him back to his

room about an hour or so later. This particular morning the employee had left the guest in the hotel coffee shop, which used to be located at the front of the building, overlooking Alamo Plaza, where several shops are now located. The employee was very busy that morning, and he did not return for the old gentleman after the hour had elapsed. The elderly guest got impatient and finally decided he would wait no longer. He rose from his table and started to walk away. Suddenly his trousers fell down around his ankles, and the old gentleman was wearing no underwear!

The coffee shop was enjoying a brisk trade that particular morning. Most of the diners were elderly ladies. Rosie, one of the waitresses, had to pick up his trousers, get him reasonably presentable, and then escort him to his room.

Recollections of Dr. John Moore

I will never forget Dr. John Moore, one of our resident guests. He was a well-known pathologist. Moore was a wonderful man to be around, always an interesting conversationalist. He was also quite a colorful character. He was a good friend of Dr. Hubertus Strughold and General William Simpson, who also lived at the hotel at that time.

I vividly recall how Dr. Moore dressed up every Fourth of July. He would strut off the center section elevator all decked out in his red, white, and blue necktie!

Towards the end of his life, I helped to get him ready to go to the hospital one time, as he was not feeling at all well. As the EMS crew was placing him on the gurney, Dr. Moore called me over and said, "Mr. Malacara, would you please bring me that paper sack in the corner. I want to take it with me." Mary Strughold, who was there in the room with us, said, "No, John, you don't need that sack." Dr. Moore replied, "Yes, I want that sack!" I took his sack with me as I accompanied him to the hospital. Upon arrival I asked the doctor in attendance if Dr. Moore could keep his sack. The physician said that at Moore's age (he was in his nineties) he could have whatever he wanted. The sack turned out to contain a big bottle of vodka!

We all miss Dr. Moore.

Poor Pepe

I used to stay at the hotel during the weekends, relieving the general manager so he could get away from the hotel. Sometimes I had the morning room service waiter, Pepe, bring me a small pot of coffee to the room at 6:45 A.M. I would hear the elevator door open and then I would know that Pepe was on the way.

That particular morning I heard the elevator door open and I went to my door, opening it slightly. Pepe was walking past my room with an order of coffee. It was extremely quiet, and the only sound was Pepe's little low whistle as he walked along. I don't know what on earth made me do it, but I decided to have some fun. As Pepe walked past my room, I spoke his name in a low authoritative voice . . ."PEPE!" He stopped, looked around, and then started to walk on by. I again called, "PEPE." He stopped, looked around again, and stood still. I then announced, "PEPE, THIS IS GOD!" He dropped the tray and the coffee hit the floor. He had a very scared look on his face; I could no longer hold back the laughter as I opened my door. There was coffee and cream all over the place. Pepe was not upset with me, but he was relieved that he had not really gotten what he referred to as "The Call." I then called the guest who had ordered the coffee and apologized that the coffee order had been delayed.

An Attempted Theft

I do have the date on this occurrence. It was September 23, 1991, at 9:45 P.M. I was paged to call the hotel operator. Loretta answered the phone and informed me a lady had been robbed in the lobby, and that Carlos Ortiz, the front desk clerk, and Frank Hayslip, from security, were in pursuit of the individual who had snatched a guest's purse. Loretta was very excited. She said that Carlos had actually jumped over the desk in pursuit of the man!

When I arrived outside the hotel, I saw Carlos and he informed me the man had been captured. A construction worker and another man had caught the individual. They held him until the police arrived. The police officer, whose name was Brown, Badge No. 67, also referred to the individual by name and informed everyone that this man had a long police record. He had snatched the purse in the lobby from Mrs. Bill Jack Hurst, a hotel guest. The lady immediately yelled out "Stop that man!" About fifteen men from a group staying at the hotel and four hotel employees took out in hot pursuit of the man. He dropped the purse as he tripped in the lobby, retrieved it, and then dropped it again when he got out on Alamo Street. He was apprehended close to the corner of Alamo and Commerce Street and taken off to jail.

Our "Prizefighter"

I vividly recall the antics of one of our permanent guests whom I shall not name. Suffice it to say, he enjoyed drinking, most often choosing to imbibe in one of the local rough, tough bars a few blocks from the hotel. He always wore a gold-colored sweater, and we all called this garment his "fighting uniform," because when he'd return from a trip to the bar, his face was generally bruised, cut, and covered with various and sundry abrasions.

He generally went to the bar at about 3:30 P.M. and would return to the hotel around 7 P.M. pretty well "oiled." Then he would go off to bed.

On this particular afternoon he returned from the bar about 5:00 P.M. I guess no one was in a fighting mood that day. At around 8:30 the clerk at the front desk called me and informed me that our pugilist had departed the hotel in his shirt, sox, and shoes, and of course, the gold sweater. But he was wearing no trousers! I ran out the front door and managed to bring our man back to the hotel, took him to his room, and tucked him in bed.

Another time, I recall it was a Sunday, it was rather quiet at the hotel. Most of the guests had checked out, and we had a slow house. One big wedding reception was scheduled for the Colonial

Room later on, and the catering staff was quite capable of handling that. I decided to take off at 4:00 P.M. and informed the desk clerk where I would be, and of course, I had my beeper as I always do. I was just settling down to enjoy a little TV when the beeper went off.

The manager on duty at the hotel informed me that our version of a champion prize fighter (we called him "the Great White Hope") had just passed out in front of the entrance to the Colonial Ballroom where the wedding reception was about to be held. He was clad in his shoes, sox, undershorts, shirt, and of course, the famous gold sweater, but he was minus his pants. Our fighter was very inebriated.

The manager on duty could not awaken him and wanted to know what to do. I told her to get five of the biggest maintenance men we had on duty, secure a large linen cart from housekeeping, and have our sleeping guest placed in the cart, put on the elevator, and delivered to his room.

There was never a dull moment during the time that gentleman used the Menger Hotel as his permanent address!

Part 2

The Menger Hotel: Its Haunting Mystery

Haunted Hallways
Docia Williams

Hotels, like houses, can haunted be,
By ghosts one can both hear and see.
In cozy rooms and trysting places,
Spirits dwell in hidden spaces.
Why, there's a wraith that walks the halls,
Where shadows play upon the walls.
Doorknobs turn, and lights go out
To tell us spirits are about.
No need to fear, or have alarm,
Our friendly spirits mean no harm.
They loved this inn, and so they cleave
Close by its shelter, loathe to leave,
Please, dear friends, do not feel fright
When 'ere you stop to spend the night!

Chapter 12

Ghostly Visitations

That the Menger Hotel enjoys an illustrious and fascinating history, there is no doubt. You have read, in preceding chapters, that the history of the Menger Hotel is an integral part of San Antonio's heritage. However, the "mystery" pertaining to this historic inn is just as fascinating, although not as well known as its historical background.

It is a well-accepted fact that the hotel is home to a plethora of spirits from various historical periods. These ghostly visitors, who seem to come and go at will, fall into several categories. They have, during their lifetimes, been hotel employees or guests. Or they may have simply occupied or passed through the land upon which the hotel is situated, prior to its construction. They have separate and distinctive "personalities" just as they would have had during their lifetimes.

At the Menger, there have been numerous sightings of actual entities. Some of them have appeared to be as solid as you or I, and others appear to be transparent or misty as is the case with many ghostly sightings. Easily identifiable manifestations that indicate the presence of disembodied beings are frequently reported. Interviews with executive staff members, the housekeeping and security staff, and various former guests, all point to the fact that the hotel is, and long has been, inhabited by ghosts!

To better understand the succeeding chapters, let's dwell for a few minutes on just what ghosts are. Although I am not a psychic, I have read a great deal, and I've interviewed many fine psychics who have the unique gift of being able to connect with souls who have passed on. My conclusion is that there are, indeed, such things as ghosts or spirits of former mortal beings who can return to this earthly environment at times. Some of these souls of people now dead have not been able to accept the fact of their death, and so they are earth-bound. Some of them have somehow taken up residence, for the time being at least, at the Menger Hotel. Sometimes when I am conducting a tour group over the lobbies of the Menger, pointing out the beautiful paintings and antique furnishings, I am asked why such a beautiful place has ghosts attached to it. My stock reply is: "If you aren't good enough to get into Heaven, the Menger Hotel certainly isn't a bad second choice!"

Seriously, I believe that many restive spirits who have not yet made it to "the light," or the place most us refer to as "heaven," will return to places they loved and which figured importantly in their lifetimes on earth. Although a common belief seems to be that spirits come back to the places where they died, and in some cases this may be so, this is not always the case. More often than not, spirits will return to places where they were very happy in life. Others come back in search of something or to complete a task they were unable to finish during their earthly sojourn.

The anniversary of their deaths or of an event that played a very important role in their lives will call forth some ghosts or spirits. A real "haunting" is usually the re-enactment, over and over again, of a particular event, and it will often happen only on the anniversary of that particular occurrence. The ghosts who appear during these recurrent times pay no attention to mortals and show no interaction. Almost robot-like, they go through the paces of that particular time in their lives and then disappear, only to reappear at some future time when they will do the same thing all over again.

There are some spirits that are known to appear at only certain hours. There are some that appear during daylight hours, others at dusk, some at midnight, all for reasons known only to themselves. These appearances are usually very brief, just a few seconds, and then the apparitions disappear as suddenly as they first appeared. Often it was reported, "We could see right through them. They were transparent, and yet we could make out their features and what they were wearing." These are the most typical ghosts. Others are completely solid and look like any human being one might see. What gives them away is generally the period clothing they are wearing or some eccentric habit they might have which is not the norm in today's world. These spirits no doubt have a great deal more energy than the wispy, smoky, ethereal creatures we glimpse for just a few fleeting moments.

The truly shy, rather lackluster spirits have ways of making their presence known. They don't seem to have the energy to manifest themselves in human form. But they can cause the page of a book to turn or a window to open or close. They can turn a radio or television set on and off, and they do seem to enjoy toying with electronic items and appliances. A curtain might suddenly start fluttering in a breeze that does not exist. Their footsteps may be heard walking along hallways or climbing stairs. These illusive spirits are the most difficult to identify, just because they do remain unseen.

Some spirits make only one earthly appearance after their deaths and never reappear. They have made their peace and have moved on. Others remain restive because they left this world before some task was completed, before a final goodbye was said or an apology made for an unkind deed.

Psychics have told me that a full moon phase seems to bring out restive spirits, and they also seem to prefer warm weather. This has always been a bit puzzling to me, since the British Isles are known to be home to so many ghosts, and the weather is cold in that part of the world for much of the time.

The Menger Hotel is over one hundred and forty years old. It has housed many hundreds of people over the years. There have been births and deaths in the old inn. Whether or not these events have led to manifestations, we cannot be sure, because numerous spirits have been sighted and recognized that did not die in the hotel. On the other hand, a number of people have passed away in the hotel, and their ghosts have never returned at all to the scenes of their demises.

The Menger management does not try to hide its ghosts from current guests. And most guests find the whole idea of the hotel having resident spirits most fascinating. Many people actually request "a haunted room." Therefore, the spirits seem to feel welcome. Their presence is not threatened, and so, at will, they return when they so desire. No attempt at exorcism has ever been made. They are not the types of ghosts one would want to shoo away. They are totally friendly and benevolent, and they just make up a part of the personality of the hotel.

Of course, these spirits are not trained seals. They cannot be summoned to appear at the whim of those who are still alive and who would like to see them. However, on October 31, 1997, Halloween night, the Menger management gave a most unusual party! This was the brainchild of Ernesto Malacara, who has actually seen some of the Menger ghosts, and he planned a very entertaining evening, which was titled "The First Annual Ghost Disclosure Gathering." Numerous friends of the hotel were invited to the gala affair, which took place in the Patio Room. Delicious refreshments were served, including a huge ghost-decorated Halloween cake. Psychic and noted parapsychologist Marie Simpson, a well-known talk-show hostess, and Sam Nesmith and Robert Thiege, historians and gifted psychics, were honored guests and spoke about the phenomena known as ghosts. Numerous hotel employees who had experienced ghostly encounters also spoke to the assemblage, and Marguerite McCormick, great-great-great-granddaughter of William and Mary Menger, brought some fine family memorabilia, photographs, and jewelry that had belonged to the first owners of the hotel. Although no ghosts appeared in persona, the psychics said they had "seen" several of them hovering in the background, evidently well satisfied they were receiving such a warm welcome from the hotel management!

Speakers at the October 31, 1997 Halloween Ghost
Disclosure Gathering including: Robert Thiege, Sam Nesmith,
Ernesto Malacara, Docia Williams, and Marie Simpson

Photo by Roy Williams

Numerous employees, past and present, have seen the ghosts at various times. Guests have also had encounters with them. These events have been reported to the front desk, and Mr. Malacara keeps a sort of running diary of these appearances. No particular patterns have been formed. The spirits just come and go at will, and the Menger is happy to welcome them as long as they don't frighten the guests or upset the daily routine.

The next chapters will identify some of these spirits and their favorite habitats in the hotel. Actual room numbers of guestrooms where manifestations have occurred are not mentioned or have been changed, since these rooms are still assigned to hotel guests.

Chapter 13

The Menger's Most Famous Ghost: Sallie White

$\mathcal{P}$robably the most famous and most often reported ghost at the Menger Hotel is the wraith of Sallie White, a mulatto chambermaid who worked at the hotel in 1876. She was employed in the second floor guest section of the original hotel and must have loved her work there very much. At least, that is why we believe she still returns to her place of employment.

Sallie was tragically killed by her common-law husband, Henry Wheeler, who shot her on March 28, 1876. The local papers featured several articles about the shooting. The *Daily Herald,* dated March 28, 1876, ran the following article:

THE GREEN EYED MONSTER

A Discharged Negro Soldier's Attempt at Murder

This morning, about six o'clock, the citizens living in Alamo City in the vicinity of the Laborer's Association, were startled by a succession of pistol shots and piercing shrieks. It seems that a discharged negro soldier by the name of Henry Wheeler was attempting to murder his wife. The facts in the case are as follows:

For some time past Henry Wheeler, who is a large heavy-built dark mulatto, has been exceedingly jealous of his wife, Sallie, who by the way was the widow of Solomon White, another discharged soldier, and who died of hydrophobia while in the employment of the City as a policeman. She is a chambermaid at the Menger Hotel, at least she has been employed there in that capacity, and last night her husband came to the hotel, and they had one of their customary quarrels. The woman, however, was terribly afraid of her husband, who threatened to murder her, and consequently she went to the Courthouse, and slept there, instead of going to their home, which is on the west side of Bonham Street, opposite the residence of Judge Klocke.

THE TRAGEDY

After passing the night in the Recorder's office the woman went home, and there she found her husband waiting to carry out his fiendish plan. She started to run and he pursued her, overtaking her before she had run thirty steps. Seizing her by the throat he fired, the pistol being so close as to burn her clothing, the ball penetrating the lower part of the abdomen. She tore away from him, ran around the corner, across the street toward the Menger Brewery. The would-be murderer then walked backward into the street until she was fairly in range and fired again, the ball striking her in the back to the left of the spine. She fell within a few steps of where young Wesenberg met with his fatal accident during the Mardi Gras procession. Wheeler then turned, walked slowly up Bonham Street toward the Laborer's Association until he was arrested by policeman Fox. The wounded woman was carried to her home, and medical assistance obtained, but little hopes are entertained of her recovery.

The *San Antonio Daily Express* also wrote of the shooting in its March 29, 1876 edition:

ANOTHER OUTRAGE

Malicious and Probably Fatal Shooting of a Negro Woman by her Crazed Husband

The peaceful neighborhood to the rear of the Menger Hotel was yesterday morning suddenly disturbed by pistol shots, succeeded by the shrill shrieks of a female. A negro by the name of Henry Wheeler was murdering his wife. The tale runs thus:

Wheeler and his wife have been very quarrelsome for some time, and complaints of abuse from her husband have been carried to the Recorder's court, where the offender has met justice. Monday evening, Wheeler seemed to be very angry about something, and finding that his wife was absent from home, proceeded to search for her in the surrounding neighborhood. He was successful in his search, and immediately upon meeting her, began to abuse her to the extent of his calumnious capacity. On returning to their dwelling, Wheeler made the open and bold declaration that

He Would Murder Her

Storming and swearing all the while. The woman could bear his threats and abuse no longer, and sought the protection of the police. The house was searched, but no arms found, but still the woman said, "he will kill me if I stay here tonight." Finally, arrangements were made for her to spend the night at the Recorder's office, where she went in peace, and slept until yesterday morning, undisturbed. She awoke between the hours of six and seven, and proceeded to go home. Arriving near the dwelling, she was again met by her husband, who, with a six-shooter in his hand, proceeded to carry out the determined

Work of Her Death

He seized her, he fired, the ball wounding her severly in the bowels. She ran, and after her he went, firing two other shots and felling the partner of his bosom on the south side of the Menger brewery. The act from beginning to end is a most revolting one, the man being actuated by pure malice aforethought, making him, it would seem, if the woman dies, subject to the highest punishment the criminal offender has to bear.

Both of these articles stated the couple lived on Bonham Street. In those days, Bonham, which now terminates at Crockett Street in front of the Crockett Hotel, ran right behind the Menger Hotel and the Menger brewery, which was also on the hotel property in those days. Bonham ran through to Commerce Street, and there were a number of dwellings, both large and small, on that part of the street, which has been closed off for many years. This is where the couple lived, very close to the Menger Hotel where Sallie was employed. Hotel records show she was working there at the time of the shooting.

The *San Antonio Express*, April 1, 1876 made mention:

The negro woman, Sallie White, who was shot by her husband Tuesday morning, died yesterday at 9 a.m. This places the criminal in a very dangerous position.

Sallie must have been well thought of by the Menger management and her fellow employees. There is a glassed-in case in the lobby that displays some old hotel ledgers. In one of them a page is turned to an entry made by Mary Menger's accountant, Frederick Hahn. Still in very clear handwriting, into the "cash paid" column is inscribed:

To cash paid for coffin for Sallie White, col'd chambermaid, deceased, murdered by her husband, shot March 28, died March 30, $25 for coffin, and $7 for grave, total $32.

Just for the record: Evidently, when Sallie did not die immediately, Henry was released from custody. As soon as he was freed, he left San Antonio. In spite of attempts made to trace his whereabouts by law enforcement authorities, he was never brought to justice.

The story is generally known that the hotel paid for her medical care and tried to see that she had whatever she needed, but the shots hit vital organs, and she lost far too much blood to recover. Sallie must have known that her employers loved her, because her spirit continues to come back to the hotel. She comes to the section where she worked as a chambermaid, cleaning rooms, changing bed linens, and tending to her regular duties. A number of housekeepers, chambermaids, and guests have seen Sallie's apparition.

Sallie was a fair-skinned mulatto, and it is said she was quite pretty. This is probably why Henry Wheeler was so insanely jealous. When her spirit is seen in the hotel, she is either working in one of the guestrooms in the oldest section, or she is walking down one of the hallways. She wears an ankle-length skirt with a long white apron over it. Her hair is caught back under a bandana kerchief. Some say she wears a string of beads around her neck. She is usually seen carrying either a broom, a feather duster, or a stack of clean, white linens.

Debbie Taylor works as a clerk in a dress shop where I like to buy my clothes. She said in 1990 she was employed as a temporary helper at the Menger, in the fourth floor sales office. Debbie had heard the stories about Sallie White, so she recognized the apparition when she saw it. Sallie was walking along the fourth floor hallway about thirty feet ahead of Debbie. The figure was wearing a long skirt and had a bandana handkerchief around her head. The wraith was transparent, not solid, but the clothing and the figure were clearly discernable. Debbie was unable to see the face, since she was following the figure from the rear. Debbie told me the figure seemed to be carrying a stack of white linens or towels in her arms when she suddenly stepped into one of the guestrooms along the corridor and vanished. I asked Debbie if she tried to follow the wraith and she said, "Are you kidding?" She hurried back to the office, instead, to tell her fellow workers what she had seen. She said she would never forget it.

Some Menger guests had a similar experience. Prior to moving to San Antonio several years ago, Cesar Gonzalez and his wife stopped at the Menger. The IBM executive and his wife attended an evening concert at the Theatre for the Performing Arts and then returned to the hotel, as it was quite late. They went straight up to their room, which was located on the third floor in the oldest section of the hotel. As they got off the elevator, they started down the corridor. Suddenly, a young woman appeared, coming down the hallway towards them. She was wearing a dark dress, topped off with a long white apron with a bib front, which had wide straps over the shoulders. A bandana kerchief was wrapped around her head. She carried a stack of clean linens in her arms. She seemed to almost float towards them, and then suddenly, poof! right in front of their eyes, she disappeared!

The couple were certainly nonplussed over the experience, but they did not mention it to anyone at the hotel before they checked out.

Later, Mr. and Mrs. Gonzalez moved to San Antonio. They purchased the book *Spirits of San Antonio and South Texas* which Reneta Byrne and I co-authored in 1992. They read the story I had written about the Menger, which included a description of the ghost of Sallie White. Recognizing the similiarity to the apparition they saw at the hotel, Mr. Gonzalez got in touch with Mr. Malacara to tell him what he and his wife had seen. Gonzalez said he is convinced they had a close encounter with Sallie White.

The housekeepers say towels often start falling out of their storage area for no apparent reason. One logical answer might be that Sallie just wants to let them know she is still around.

Chapter 14

Two Ladies in Blue

I first read about one of the "blue ladies" at the Menger some years ago, when I bought a copy of David Bowser's book *Mysterious San Antonio*. Bowser, an interesting young man, is quite a historian, and he likes to ferret out all sorts of little known but fascinating trivia about San Antonio. He mentioned having heard of the "blue lady" thusly:

> For some time, there have been vague rumors of odd occurrences in a certain second floor room in one of the old sections of the hotel. The door to the room faces on a long, dimly lit hallway where the wooden floorboards creak as you walk over them. The rear of the room has long floor-to-ceiling windows. Outside, there is a little balcony with a green painted railing of iron grillwork. From these windows, you can look down upon the famous Patio Garden of the Menger.
>
> Several of the hotel's personnel assigned to this room have experienced bizarre incidents; strange noises, room lights flicking on and off inexplicably, doors closing of their own accord, and a general feeling as though someone was watching.
>
> The most eerie incident occurred one day while one of the maids was routinely cleaning the room. She had a strong feeling as though someone was in there with her. Thinking it was one of the guests, she turned and was

stunned to see a woman in an "old fashioned" long blue dress sitting calmly in a chair a few feet away. The maid described the apparition as an attractive-looking woman with blondish shoulder-length hair, worn in a style of the '30s or '40s. She also related that the figure in the chair appeared "real" but had a very odd look about her because of the way she was dressed, and also, because of her silence and unusual facial expression. At any rate, as the awe-struck hotel worker gazed at the woman, the figure suddenly disappeared. The maid told her story with conviction and sincerity. She was not kidding around, not in the least.

I have since spoken to several of the chambermaids, and they have told me they had "rather work in twos" when it comes to cleaning that particular room. A number of employees have also seen the mysterious "blue lady" strolling in the patio. Perhaps she is waiting to meet someone there...someone who never comes. She is dressed very much in the style of the World War II years. Maybe she is waiting at the Menger to meet her sweetheart who never came back from the war. Who knows?

There is another lady dressed in blue, a very different type of figure. This is a middle-aged woman who has been seen sitting in the Victorian lobby, the main lobby, and on the mezzanine near the Renaissance Room. She is a solid-looking spirit, not at all ethereal or transparent. She sits, and sometimes she knits or reads a newspaper. She is clad in a blue print dress with little red star patterns all over the material. The dress has a sailor collar. She is wearing a little beret with a tassel on top, rather like a tam-o-shanter. She wears small glasses with metal frames. Ernesto Malacara has actually seen her and spoken to her. He described her shoes as the most unfeminine footwear he has ever seen. She wears brown lace-up oxfords with medium high heels very much like the Womens Army Corps (WACS) wore in World War II.

Ernesto walked up to her the first time he saw her, thinking she looked rather strangely dressed, but he certainly didn't think about seeing a ghost. He greeted her, saying, "Good morning. I'm Ernesto Malacara, the assistant manager here. Is there anything I can do for you?" She replied, "No, I'm just fine, thank you," and promptly disappeared! Not long after this initial appearance, she was seen by another employee on the mezzanine. She has appeared several times and just as quickly disappears. She seems to be very contented, doing her knitting and enjoying the nice atmosphere of the Menger lobbies.

Chapter 15

Identifiable Entities

*O*ver the years, there have been appearances of ghosts or spirits of many different individuals. Some have been identified as former employees. Some were former guests of the hotel. Then, there have been sightings of individuals who are a little more difficult to identify. They look as solid and "alive" as you and I, and yet they can appear and disappear in the twinkling of an eye. They are not as well known as Sallie White and the blue ladies and they do not appear as frequently, but they are still a part of the ghostly population of the Menger.

Captain Richard King

As you read in chapter eight, Captain Richard King stayed at the Menger Hotel many times, and the hotel named the King Ranch Suite in his honor. He died on April 14, 1885, in the big canopied bed in the suite. His funeral service was conducted the next day in the Victorian lobby of the hotel. Some believe he still returns on occasion to the hotel suite where he died.

A number of years ago, when I was working on a story about the Menger for *Spirits of San Antonio and South Texas*, a young security guard at the hotel told me he had an unnerving experience very late one evening when he was making his rounds of the hotel. He got off the elevator on the mezzanine and saw a tall figure in a dark suit, wearing a broad brimmed hat, walking towards the King

Ranch Suite. When the man got to the door, he did not attempt to use a hotel key. He just seemed to float through the door, as if he had "melted into the door," the young man told me. He said he very quickly went downstairs to report to the main desk what he had seen. A check through the reservations revealed that the suite was not occupied that evening!

Several guests have reported seeing a large man wearing a very broad brimmed hat who just seemed to walk through the wall to room 2052 (the King Ranch Suite). In 1998 a military officer who was staying at the hotel reported seeing such an apparition, not once but twice, during the same evening. This was the last report of a sighting of Captain King.

The Confederate Officer

A figure wearing what has been described as a gray military uniform, probably a Confederate uniform, has been sighted by a number of employees. The night room service person, Karen, was walking from the room service department to the front desk one evening when she saw the figure of a man walking in the patio. He was wearing an old-fashioned gray military uniform, and Karen said he looked like pictures she had seen of Robert E. Lee. He was wearing high-topped boots, and a sword hung at his belt. She watched him as he strolled from the patio into the lobby and then disappeared.

On another occasion, a couple of staff members saw a similar gray-clad figure standing in the corridor leading to the new wing where the grand ballroom is located. His broad brimmed campaign hat, his white beard, and the sword at his belt were clearly discernable.

A number of people at the Menger have voiced the opinion that the figure must be General Robert E. Lee, who stayed at the hotel soon after it opened in 1859. He came to the hotel from his station at Fort Mason, north of San Antonio, and was a guest several times. This was before the Civil War broke out, and Lee was a lieutenant colonel in the Union army at this time. He would have worn a dark blue Union uniform during his Menger stays. I believe if he were to return to the Menger for any reason, his shade, or apparition, would be wearing the same uniform he wore during his last stay at the hotel. It is more likely that the gray clad military figure might be General Kirby Smith, one of General Lee's most trusted officers. His photographs bear a remarkable resemblance to Lee.

Smith came to San Antonio and stayed at the Menger right after the war. Broken in spirit, he was seeking some seclusion before going into exile. He was still wearing his Confederate gray when he came to the Menger. I believe his spirit is a likely candidate for the ghostly figure in gray that has been sighted.

A Solicitous Maitre D'

A number of hotel employees have seen him. They all believe, from his actions, he was a former maitre d' at the hotel. When custodians are cleaning the Colonial or Minuet Rooms, late at night after the rooms have closed, sightings have been reported of a portly, bearded gentleman wearing a cutaway frock coat and formal trousers. Sometimes he wears a high crowned top hat. Other times his head is bare. He goes from table to table, nodding and smiling at unseen guests. He seems to be asking if everything is to their satisfaction, much as a maitre d' would do. After "visiting" with a few of his patrons, he generally just disappears through one of the walls, or in the case of the Minuet Room, he floats through the big mirror and vanishes!

The Man in Buckskin

A couple of years ago, a guest reported an unusual occurrence in his room. The gentleman had just gotten out of the shower, and he wrapped his towel around his waist and opened the bathroom door. As he started to step out into his room to get dressed, he was startled to see a man there! The figure stood between the bed and the window. The guest said he plainly saw the man and could describe what he was wearing, except for his footgear, which he could not see from his vantage point. The figure wore a tan buckskin shirt, gray trousers, and an old, floppy brimmed brown felt hat. He had long, stringy, dirty-looking hair that was about shoulder length. He had an untrimmed beard, or, the gentleman recalled, "Maybe it wasn't so much of a beard as just a number of days he had gone without shaving."

The hotel guest first demanded, "Who the hell are you, and what are you doing in here?" The figure did not reply to the gentleman, but he was talking to someone else...someone the guest could not see. "Are you going to stay, or are you going to go? Make up your mind," the figure said. And he mumbled something about "Walker" which didn't make any sense to the startled guest. He took no notice of the guest and just stood by the window still talking. The guest, who didn't want his name mentioned, stepped back inside the bathroom and just sort of peeped out at the strange, uninvited visitor. When he did this, the figure suddenly disappeared.

It only took the guest a few minutes to dress and dash downstairs to the front desk to report what had happened in his room. He described the figure he had seen in great detail and then added, "And, yes, he smelled like he had been riding a horse for a long time, and he needed a bath." When questioned, he declared the figure was just as solid as any living being and did not look "ghostly" at all, just unkempt and dirty.

Ernesto Malacara told me about this occurrence right away. We called our good friends Sam Nesmith and Robert Thiege, both gifted psychics, to come check out that room and see what they might find. The two spent some time one evening in that room, and they sensed the presence of someone who had been there just around the time of the beginning of the Civil War. They said the man was the spirit of someone in deep discussion with someone who was having difficulty deciding where to place his allegiances.

This wasn't unusual in those days, as many people felt pulled between their love of Texas, which they knew would secede, and their love for the United States.

There is another possible explanation. The Menger was built on land that belonged to the Mission San Antonio de Valero, where the famous Alamo chapel is located. The figure in buckskin might have been standing in the spot where he had his discussion with "Walker," and they might have been discussing whether to stay and defend the Alamo against the overwhelmingly large Mexican army, or go while they could get away. Buckskin shirts were common attire in those days. And there was a Jacob Walker, from Tennessee, counted among the defenders at the Battle of the Alamo.

Could This Ghost Be a Spaniard?

Mrs. "G," a maid on the fourth floor of the original section of the hotel, was once startled by the sudden appearance of a ghostly figure. The apparition was dressed in a silk shirt with billowing, full sleeves, a dark-colored tunic over the shirt, dark, tight fitting trousers, and a funny peaked hat. He was rather short of stature, with a dark, swarthy complexion, and he had very broad shoulders. Mrs. "G" was waiting for the elevator when the figure briefly appeared and then disappeared right in front of her eyes. When she arrived on the first floor, she was quite visibly shaken. To our knowledge, this was the only time this particular apparition appeared dressed like someone from the Spanish period of our city's history. This isn't really so strange. The land on which the Menger is located was part of the earliest Spanish mission in San Antonio, the Mission San Antonio de Valero. Many soldiers, grandees, and notables of that era walked all over the property where the Menger now stands.

Phantom Chambermaids

Sallie White is not the only loyal former chambermaid who comes back to the hotel on occasion. There are others.

Ernesto Malacara once strolled down a hallway, checking on the rooms, when he encountered an open door to one of the guestrooms. He glanced inside and was startled to see a maid dusting and straightening up a room. She was wearing a uniform that had not been in use at the hotel for many years. As Malacara started to say something to her, the figure totally vanished. She was obviously the spirit of a former chambermaid who had just come back to check one of the rooms she used to clean.

One gentleman guest reported his strange experience to the front desk. It seems he called to ask for some extra towels, and when the housekeeping department did not deliver them quickly enough to suit him, he called a second time. Then he decided to look out into the hallway, and he spied a maid's cleaning cart about halfway down the corridor. He walked down and asked the maid who was inside the room, cleaning, if she would bring him some extra towels. She didn't answer him or acknowledge his presence. He asked her a second time, this time just saying he would like to take a couple of towels from her cart, and again, she took absolutely no notice of him. He went back to his room, puzzled by the strange and, what he considered, rather rude behavior of the maid. He called the front desk and told the person who answered that the maid up on his floor cleaning was certainly rude. He gave the desk clerk the room number where he had seen the maid. He was asked to describe the maid's appearance. He told the desk clerk that the maid was wearing a pink uniform with a little white apron.

He was then told no maid was working in that area and all the rooms had been cleaned and made ready on that floor. Further, he was told the uniform he described was not worn by any of the current Menger housekeeping staff.

When the man hung up the telephone, he looked outside his door. There was no cleaning cart in the hallway.

Who Was Mr. Preston?

Yvonne Saucedo reported that many of the waitresses who work at the hotel during early morning hours have mentioned they have seen a spirit they refer to as "Mr. Preston." He appears in broad daylight and has been seen sitting on a bench on the patio. He always wears a top hat and a dapper dress suit of the late 1800s era. I wonder if he might be the same figure that others have referred to as the maitre d' ghost.

The Sleepwalking Spirit

Alma Gutierrez, a former Menger employee, said while she was working at the hotel, several employees reported seeing a lady walking around the swimming pool very late at night. They believed she might be sleepwalking. Concerned the woman might fall into the pool and drown, several employees decided to watch for her one evening. They decided if they saw her making her evening rounds of the patio, they would follow her and see what room she came from. They had heard it was best not to awaken a sleepwalker, but they wanted to keep the woman from harm's way.

Their vigilance paid off. The lady did make an appearance, and since the employees had taken up "stations" at the entrances to the pool-patio, they were startled when she just suddenly appeared at the side of the pool. They were even more taken back when she just as suddenly disappeared! They, no doubt, had the opportunity of seeing still another of the hotel's ghostly guests.

The Woman in White

Mike and Ginger Cave were with me on a tour that I conducted a couple of years ago. After I finished my talk about the history of the Menger Hotel, we were standing in the lobby, chatting. Reverend Cave is the associate pastor at the Coker United Methodist Church. Prior to entering the ministry, the Caves lived in Austin, where Mike was engaged in the advertising business. Ginger recalled a pleasure trip to San Antonio when the couple spent a few nights at the Menger back in 1973.

Ginger said they had twin beds in their room, which was in the older section. In the middle of the night, she heard a noise. She awoke to see the figure of a woman clad in white standing at the foot of her bed. She quickly jumped out of bed and crossed the few feet to Mike's bed to awaken him. By the time she could shake Mike to wake him, the figure had disappeared. Ginger said she knows she was not dreaming. The figure was very real. And she has never forgotten that night.

Dr. Nancy Frances is a physician who stayed at the hotel in April 1999 while attending a nursing convention being held there. She said she turned on a small lamp and left it on so she could see, should she need to get up in the middle of the night. However, sometime during the night, the lamp turned itself off. Later, she clearly saw a woman in a white gown standing beside her bed. She said she firmly believed her middle-of-the-night visitor was another of the Menger's famous ghosts!

Chapter 16

Spirits at the Bar

Although alcoholic spirits are certainly available at the famous Menger Bar, there are other spirits that seem to hang out there as well. Over the years various phenomena have been reported in that part of the hotel.

Four or five years ago, on a quiet April night, one of the custodians arrived to clean the bar. It was in the wee hours of the morning, when both patrons and bartenders had called it a night. The young janitor, a husky man of about six feet, three inches in height, was the kind of fellow you'd want on your side in a fistfight. He looked like he wouldn't be afraid of anything or anybody.

Well, that night he opened the inside double doors to the bar and put the kick-stools in place to hold them open so he could wheel his cart of cleaning equipment down the center aisle of the barroom. He started getting his cleaning items organized and just happened to glance towards the bar over to his right. He noticed one of the barstools was on the floor. All the others had been placed, as was customary, upside down on the bar to facilitate cleaning the floor. A glance to the end of the bar revealed a man, dressed in what the custodian later described as an old-fashioned military-looking uniform. The figure, which had suddenly materialized, was transparent, but the janitor could make out the features and the clothing. And as he watched, the strange figure beckoned to him with his index finger, a "come here" sort of gesture.

Realizing he was seeing what was definitely an otherworldly being, the young man hastily headed for the open double doors.

But something was very wrong. The double doors had slammed shut and were locked! It took a few minutes for the shaken janitor to gather his wits, yell, and make enough noise to attract the attention of someone to come and get him out of the locked barroom. The unusual guest still sat upon the barstool.

Yvonne Saucedo was the night manager on duty that evening. She was at the front desk chatting with one of the security guards, when they heard the shouts of the janitor coming from the bar. The guard hastened to go and let the young man out of the bar. Yvonne said he was as white as a sheet and was breathing hard, visibly shaken. He came stumbling into the lobby and slumped down into one of the big overstuffed chairs. Yvonne feared he might be having a heart attack. The terrified young man was gasping for breath and shaking violently. He managed to blurt out, "I think ... I think I must have seen a ghost. He was a soldier. ... " Because he seemed to be in shock and was so deathly pale, Mrs. Saucedo called 911. In only a few minutes the EMS crew arrived and escorted the man to a nearby clinic for observation.

Later that night Yvonne and the security guard went into the Menger Bar and looked all around. They stayed there for at least half an hour, just hoping for a reappearance of the ghost, but the strange spirit did not make another appearance that night.

The young custodian did not return to his job at the Menger.

Mr. Malacara said there have been some other incidents connected with the famous bar. Another night employee was in the bar around 1:30 A.M. He happened to glance up to the little balcony area. He noticed a man dressed in a dark gray suit and wearing a little hat. He just sat there a few minutes at the railing on the side closest to Crockett Street. The surprised custodian ran out to summon another staff member. When the men returned to the bar just a few minutes later, the apparition had disappeared, and he did not return.

In September of 1996 a couple remained until closing time, chatting with the bartender. As they were preparing to leave, the woman stood in the center of the barroom and her husband was standing slightly off to one side. He saw a man enter the bar and head right towards his wife. He stepped in front of the man, since he seemed to be purposely approaching the woman, and the astonished couple and the bartender were shocked to see the man vanish in front of their eyes!

One time Denise, the bartender, was setting up the bar prior to opening. She had not yet unlocked the doors. After she got everything set up, she slipped into the uniform changing room to dress. She heard a voice that clearly said, "We're gonna be late...we're gonna be late." She hurried into the bar area, but no one was there and the doors were still locked.

The late Rodney Miller, who for many years managed the valet parking area, told me he understood that one night all the glasses in the bar began to violently tremble and shake, and this was witnessed by several hotel guests.

Bartenders, both male and female, have reported things such as lemons and limes for drinks suddenly being found out of their little baskets and rolling around on the counter or floor. Several times, they have witnessed glasses falling off the bar onto the hard cement floor, and yet they did not break!

Bar attendants cut off the music before closing, but it turns itself back on even louder than it was before. This happens often.

Listening to '50s type music while alone in the bar, the attendant reported, when she turned off the music, she heard someone in the bar softly humming the tune that had just been playing.

When one of the bartenders started cleaning up the bar late one evening, he glanced into the mirror and was startled to see a man sitting in the balcony intently staring at the television set as if he were watching it. Only the TV set was not turned on, and there was no one in the balcony!

A kindly old gentleman visits his son here in San Antonio about every other year. This elderly man is from Ireland. He loves to visit the Menger Bar and enjoys his beer. Probably because the bar is a copy of a British pub, he feels at home there. On several occasions in the bar with only the bartender, the voice of a third person has been heard, grumbling as if upset with the service. No one can explain why this just happens when the old gentleman from Ireland is in the bar.

As was previously mentioned in chapter nine, there is a tie between Teddy Roosevelt, the Rough Riders, and the Menger Bar. Perhaps the figure in the military uniform the young custodian saw was one of the Rough Riders, or even Teddy, himself. Or, to pose another theory, it is a well-known fact that at one time the U.S. Army used the Alamo as a sort of headquarters building. The building also served for a time as a police headquarters back in the late 1800s. All these men wore uniforms. They all probably enjoyed dropping by the Menger Bar for a cool libation on a hot day, so any one of them might be the perpetrator of some of these ghostly hijinks.

Chapter 17

A Miscellany of Manifestations

$There are identifiable spirits that have been seen off and on in the hotel over a period of many years. There are also "manifestations," which take various forms, but all are indicative of some supernatural activity. There are the spirits that sometimes are only heard. Or, if seen, they generally are not identifiable entities but are more like vapor or smoke. Sometimes they do take on a more or less human shape. They are sometimes the most frightening, because they appear and disappear so quickly. The Menger has some of these mysterious manifestations on record and shares them here with you.

Suicidal Spirits

Several psychics have told me that generally, suicides regret their hasty acts within seconds after their accomplishment. Their spirits become very restive and often do not venture towards the "light," fearful they will not be accepted on the other side. Some suicides "live out" what would have been their natural life spans by staying in the environment they last knew before their death for a certain number of years and then moving on. In other words, the spirit of a man thirty years old, who ordinarily would have lived to

be seventy, might wander and make appearances or cause manifestations in the place where he terminated his life for at least forty
years. In some cases, tormented spirits continue to cling to the
place where their life ended at their own hands and make no
attempt to move on.

Like many other large hotels, there have been suicides at the
Menger over the years. Ernesto Malacara says there was one
woman who jumped from the fourth story facing Blum Street. She
hit a bicycle stand with her head. Then, there was another suicide
that took place in a fourth floor room. This room has been the
scene of numerous manifestations. The bathtub often mysteri-
ously fills and empties all by itself, the television set loses its
picture, and the lights flicker on and off for no reason.

The Frisky Ghost

A couple attending a high-tech convention reported an unusual
occurrence that happened to them while they were staying in the
hotel. The wife saw the apparition of a male spirit grinning at her in
their room. Then he got "frisky" and tried to pull the bedcovers off
her. The couple was promptly moved from their historic suite to a
room in the new part of the hotel.

Was This a Time Warp?

A lady from Austin was assigned a room overlooking the swimming pool. It was the end of the day, and she was resting on the bed.
The television set was turned on, and she had a number of magazines on the bed beside her that she was leafing through.
Occasionally she changed the channels on the TV. She said the
curtain over the glass door facing the patio was partially open. She
also mentioned that her room had two double beds, and the bed to
her left was fully made.

The next thing she realized it was morning! Her phone was
ringing. Her husband was calling to wish her a good day. She got

up, turned on the light, and then it hit her! She recalled lying in bed with the magazines by her and having the TV set turned on. Now the lights were all turned off, the television set was off, and the curtain, which had been partially open, was closed. The bed next to hers, which had been fully made up, was now turned down. But it wasn't turned down as the maids do nowadays with just one corner of the spread turned down; the entire bedspread had been neatly folded to the footboard. Her pile of magazines had been arranged in the shape of a cross. Then the TV remote control and her eyeglasses had been laid on top of the magazines.

She thought she realized what had happened, and the first thing she did was loudly call out, "Are you still here?" She said she felt like she had been caught up in some sort of "time warp" that night, and she would never forget it.

Swinging Doors

One evening as Ernesto Malacara stood at the front desk chatting with three employees, all four men noticed the big double front doors of the hotel slowly swing open. But no one came in! These doors are extremely heavy, made of brass and beveled glass, and they just would not blow open. According to Ernesto, there was no wind at all that night. These doors do not open to the outside of the building, either. They are located in a covered and protected entryway that also has doors. There is no earthly way they could just blow open. There is no explanation why those big heavy doors opened that evening. Since then I have spoken to several other employees who have seen the doors open, and no one is there.

The Leaking Ceiling

Hazel Davis told me about an experience some friends of hers had while they were in San Antonio for a convention. She said it was about 1996 or 1997. The couple, telephone company executives, stayed at the Menger. They told Hazel they were awakened about 2 A.M. by what they thought was rain pouring on their bed from the ceiling. This sudden deluge only lasted a few minutes, just long enough to thoroughly soak their bed. When they reported this to the desk, the room on the floor above where they were staying was carefully inspected but showed no leaks in the bathroom or other plumbing. There was no way to explain the drenching they received. No explanation at all, except—well, you figure it out!

Moving Jiggers

One of the women who operate the gift shop off the main lobby reported she actually witnessed a display of little shot glasses, which she had just arranged on a counter, get up and move, one by one, from the left to the right side of the counter. They were apparently lifted, moved, and then set down by careful invisible hands as the astounded shopkeeper watched.

The Telephone Bill

Several years back, a gentleman who was checking out of the hotel questioned some items on his bill. There were a number of telephone calls billed to his room, and he said he had made no calls at all. Then, glancing again, he noticed that the phone number he had supposedly called and which appeared on the room charge was his mother's old telephone number. But she had been dead for many years! When I mentioned this strange occurrence to one of my psychic friends, he interpreted it to be a signal that the spirit of the man's mother was trying to reach him.

The Busy Buzzer

I recall one incident I personally witnessed a few years ago. Before a recent remodeling job done on the front registration desk, there used to be a little electric bell that guests could ring to summon a room clerk. It had been disconnected for some time, but they just left it out on the front desk, perhaps to lend "atmosphere" to the Old World look of the registration desk. Periodically, even though it was not connected, it would ring loudly as if an impatient guest was trying to summon a clerk. The desk staff paid no particular attention to it. It even went off during an interview I was conducting with some front desk personnel in 1990, so I can attest to its performance. The bell has now been removed, so it's no longer available for any impatient spirits to ring. I miss it.

Who Was There?

A couple of years ago I was at the hotel early one morning to do a radio interview about the history of the hotel with a crew from KTFM. I ran into Ernesto Malacara, and he told me he had just had "an incident." It seems he and Tom Brady, the chief of security, were strolling down the hallway leading to the parking garage. They both happened to glance through the glass doors to the executive offices, and they saw a man sitting in the office, which they knew had not yet opened. They'd passed the door when they stopped, looked at one another, and said, "Who was that?" They backed up a few paces to glance into the office again. The man they had both seen had vanished into thin air!

The Bedspread Smoother

Robert Cordova, a long-time bellman, recalled an experience related to him by a guest.

The gentleman had a very disturbing night. He and his roommate had slept in separate double beds. He was awakened in the middle of the night by feeling someone running their hand over the bedspread as it to "smooth it out," he said. He presumed it was his friend doing this, but he found it most odd he would be doing this in the middle of the night. He said, "What do you want?" When there was no answer, he turned on the bedside lamp, only to discover that his friend was sound asleep in the other bed! He turned off the light and again felt the invisible hands running over the bedspread. This continued, off and on, for the remainder of the night, much to the dismay of the guest. He could give no explanation for the strange presence of an unseen "bedmaker" in his room.

Vaporous Forms

About a year ago, banquet captain Hector Solis and his assistant, Juan Chavez, had just finished putting the final touches on a meeting room on the third floor in the original section of the hotel. They secured the room and started to walk toward the service elevator at the east end of the third floor. Suddenly, they saw this shapeless form of vapor or smoke moving towards them. They stopped, and the vapor passed right between the two men. They felt chilled. The vapor headed towards the west end of the floor where two French doors were located. Silently, without speaking, both men moved together as if they had been instructed by the vaporous shape to follow it. The smoke-like vapor went right between the French doors, and as the men approached the doors, the section on the left opened all by itself. Needless to say, Solis and Chavez left in a hurry.

Then there was Rosie, a long-time maid, who was busily making up a room on the third floor in the section overlooking the swimming pool. She had already finished making the bed nearest the pool door and now was making up the second bed, the one nearest the wall. Suddenly, she felt hot breath on the back of her neck as she was bending over making the bed. She thought it was one of the other maids, and she scolded, "Now, I don't have time to play; we are too busy." She resumed her work, and once more she felt the hot breath on her neck. She turned to admonish what she thought was a fellow housemaid and was startled to find there was no one in the room with her. At that moment a shapeless cloud of smoke or vapor appeared and moved towards the pool door. As the vapor passed in front of the large mirror, she noted it was not reflected in the mirror, although she could plainly see it. The vapor got to the balcony door, and it was evidently solid enough to move the sheer curtain as well as the heavier curtain over the door. Also, the door itself started to move.

Rose left the room and found Mr. Malacara. He had to sit in the room with her while she finished making up the room, as this experience had greatly unnerved her.

Ernesto Malacara said two of the maids, Amaya and Margaret, recently went to the dumpster in the basement. As Amaya started to open the dumpster door, it opened all by itself as if someone was pushing on it from the inside. Amaya, a small lady, grabbed the dumpster door and was hurled against the body of the dumpster. Then, she said, a cloud of smoke in more or less a "human form" just floated up out of the dumpster!

A Quick Room Change

Sylvia, one of the night maids, told Mr. Malacara that on August 21, 1994, the night manager called Robert Petryk, the security officer on duty. Petryk was told to come immediately to the front desk. It was 1 A.M., and a guest was standing at the front desk clad only in his underwear. The man said he had been sound asleep and had been awakened by the sound of someone beating on his second story window and trying to open the window from the outside. The guest was so nervous he left his room clad only in his undershorts. He was quickly assigned a room on the fifth floor. He asked the security guard to accompany him to his old room to get some things he needed. He said he would return in the morning to get the rest of his things.

The Lady on Camera

A new man in the security department was at work recently in the monitoring room. Here several TV screens are located, so that what the surveillance cameras placed around the hotel pick up can be monitored from one central area. It was after midnight. There was very little activity in the hotel that late at night. Suddenly, the image of a lady, dressed in old-fashioned clothing, appeared, momentarily, on the screen. She disappeared and almost immediately appeared on another, then she disappeared from view. The screens were picturing different parts of the hotel, and no one could possibly have moved into view from the area shown in the first picture and the area shown in the second in such a short period of time. No one, that is, except a ghost. The security man was quite shaken up and requested he be transferred to daytime duty.

There's Something about TV Sets

A PBX operator, who still works at the hotel, went to the storage room to retrieve some forms. There is a small television set in this room, and it was turned off when the operator went into the room. As she was getting ready to leave the room, the set came on, and a "woman's face with a man's eyes" came on the TV. Also, she saw a man's hand reaching out, beckoning her to come closer to the TV set. The operator ran out of the room! She still gets a cold, shivery feeling when the incident is mentioned, and she does not like to talk about it.

In 1997 a teen-aged guest reported to the front desk that she awoke in her room to find a woman playing with the knobs on the television set. She told the woman to stop, and the figure disappeared.

There was a lady from Knoxville, Tennessee, who was a guest in the hotel for four days. She reported that every night the radio and television would both keep coming on although she had turned them both off. This happened the entire time she occupied the room.

One evening Loretta, the rooms division manager, was sitting at a desk in a room right back of the front desk. Suddenly she heard a lot of loud voices as though a number of guests had gathered at the front desk. She went to the front, and the only people there were the two desk attendants. Then the same loud voices were heard again, and she went back a second time to see what the disturbance was. No one was there other than the attendants. It happened a third time, and this time, since no one was in front, she decided to follow the noise to a television set (which was not plugged in) in the storage area. She firmly spoke out to the TV, "Go away and leave us alone," and since then, there has been no noise coming from that particular TV set.

Cigar Smoke

Cindy Shioleno, who lives in Kennedale in North Texas, had a strange experience at the Menger. The whole time she occupied her fifth floor room in the newer section, she had the feeling there was a presence of someone there with her. Several times she smelled the unmistakeable aroma of cigar smoke in the nonsmoking room. The smell of the smoke would come and go and was especially noticeable in the early morning hours.

Half a Face

PBX operators have reported they often feel as if they are being watched by unseen eyes. In the restroom in their area, several ladies have reported that they've seen half of a man's face staring at them while they are in the restroom. The other half of the face seems to be hidden by the doorframe. It's a little unnerving, to say the least.

Pardon Me!

Former Menger executive Gil Navarro told me about an incident he had a couple of years ago. He was up in the older section of the hotel on the second floor one evening. As he stood outside of room 205, he distinctly felt someone pass by him very closely, actually brushing his shoulder. He whirled around to see who had collided with him, saying "Pardon me" at the same time. But, of course, no one was there. There had not been enough time for whoever it was to have disappeared. When ghosts at the Menger were mentioned, Gil never laughed. He just took them for granted as being hotel fixtures.

Slamming Doors

Stephanie, a sales manager, reported she went into the restroom to wash her hands. She left the door open, but then it slammed shut with tremendous force. There were no winds to cause this, and no one else was in the sales office or anywhere around. She said it did not just close, it slammed shut hard!

One of the engineers was up in the Victorian section, painting one of the rooms. It was a lovely room with a big chandelier and a sleigh-bed. The room had very thick carpeting. In fact, he said the carpet was so thick it was difficult to shut the door. But while he was painting, the door suddenly slammed hard, and it really frightened him.

On Friday, September 3, 1999, at 2:30 in the afternoon, two of the maids were cleaning a guestroom. They had been discussing a former manager, now deceased, speaking of what a nice man he was. The door to the bathroom started to beat back and forth against the closet doors, which were alongside the wall leading to the bathroom. One of the maids got extremely flustered and called Mr. Malacara to come up to the room. They showed him how the door had banged, and there was just no way to explain the strange "activity" of the bathroom door. Perhaps the spirit of the former manager was there and just wanted to acknowledge the flattering remarks he had heard the maids making about him.

A Jolt of Energy

In 1998 Donna Hartsfield, who works as a sales representative for Globus Tours, said she stayed at the Menger on the second floor. She recalled her room overlooked the Alamo and that it had a little kitchen. She said in the night an "energy" went through her, like a shock jolt, and the room suddenly became very bright. She was terrified! However, she did not mention this occurrence to the management before she checked out the next morning.

Broken Bed Slats

I was recently the guest speaker for an organization called the Friendship Force of San Antonio. I spoke of many of San Antonio's most interesting haunted places, and I brought up the Menger Hotel during my talk. At the close, a number of people came up to speak to me, as is usually the case after my programs. A nice gentleman, Jack Bowden, introduced himself to me. He said it suddenly dawned on him, after many years, what was the cause of a strange incident that occurred while he was a guest of the Menger back in the 1950s. At the time, Bowden was living in Belton and was a traveling salesman. He had a number of accounts in San Antonio. He usually stayed at another less luxurious hotel, but he had had a very successful trip and decided to reward himself for all of his hard work.

He was assigned a nice room in the older section of the hotel and soon settled down for a good night's sleep. He was startled out of his slumber by the sudden collapse of his bed. The slats had broken, and the mattress and springs had fallen to the floor, jolting him awake in a hurry! He called the front desk to tell them what had happened. He recalled it was about 2 A.M. Someone was dispatched to his room, and they certainly could not explain how or why all the slats had quite suddenly broken. Mr. Bowden was quickly transferred to another room where he finished off his night's rest without further incident.

Bowden said he had often wondered what on earth caused the sudden upheaval in the middle of the night. He had not tossed or turned, and there was no explanation for all of the slats to have broken at once. As he listened to my talk, he thought, "Aha! At last I know the answer! I was just staying in one of the Menger's haunted rooms, and the spirit assigned to that particular room just decided to have a little fun at my expense in the middle of the night."

Red Lights and Cat Calls

I spoke at a dinner in the Minuet Room on September 12, 1999. The group to whom I spoke were women of the Overseas Service League. After my speech, one of the ladies came up to the lectern to speak to me. She said she had been fascinated by my talk about the spirits of the Menger, and she had her own personal experience to add. She said the night before she had first seen a strange red streak of light go across the ceiling of her room. Actually, this happened twice, some minutes apart. Then she and her roommate both heard the yowling of cats, and they sounded as if they were coming from within the walls. They looked out the window of their third floor room, which faced the Alamo. They said that Crockett Street was well lit, and they had seen no cats in the street at all. The sounds went on for some time and were very puzzling to the ladies.

A Disturbing Night

This story was told to me by Ernesto Malacara the day after it happened. There were three ladies staying together at the hotel. The two older ladies were sisters, and one of their daughters was with them. When they went to their room, one of the sisters felt something caressing her hand. She sort of shook her hand to get the strange feeling off and then put on the light to illuminate the closet. She thought maybe she had felt a moth or something brushing her hand. Of course, there was nothing there.

That night as they lay in their beds, the sister who had felt her hand being caressed suddenly felt a great weight on her as though someone was lying on top of her, pinning her down. She was attempting to speak but could only mutter little groaning sounds. She heard her niece say, "My aunt must be dreaming." The other sister clapped her hand, and at this, the pinned-down sister felt the weight leave her.

Then there was suddenly the sound of footsteps, a sound like a loose floppy houseshoe hitting the heel of a foot as the person walked. As the sound moved, it levitated, and only the sound of the slipper hitting the heel could be heard. But the sound went higher than the bed! The three ladies said they were so puzzled by all of this that they turned on the lights and stayed up the rest of the night. Ernesto said they had a long talk about the incident the next day.

Seeing Things?

One evening the night hotel manager and the night food and beverage auditor were both hard at work. The food and beverage auditor was working at the front desk. The night manager was in an office located behind the front desk. Out of the corner of his eye, the manager saw the auditor walk past him, or at least, so he thought. Just a half minute later, the auditor appeared—from the front desk. The manager still wonders who it was he saw walk past him that evening!

The Lady in Black

Robert Cordova, a hotel employee, told me that one of the painters, whose name is José, was painting an elevator door about 2 A.M. This is the elevator nearest the Colonial Dining Room. He happened to look up, and there, standing right beside him, was a woman clad all in black. He said he didn't know where she had come from. She just smiled and said, "Goodnight," and promptly disappeared!

Strange Goings-on

In the reservation department, the office lights come on and go off for no reason. The cabinets open alone. The combination lock to the office door is punched in and the door partially opens, but no one is there. Often books simply fall out of the area where they have been placed.

Phantom Phone Calls

About fifteen years ago there were two rooms at the east end of the hotel that were being redecorated. The rooms were empty while painting was being done and new carpets were being installed. Margaret Solis, the PBX operator, reported that every night the switchboard lit up. When she answered the call, the voice came from one of those empty rooms. It was the voice of a very elderly lady, with a very raspy voice. She always wanted to make reservations for dinner in the Colonial Room. But what was most strange, there was NO PHONE in either of the rooms that were undergoing redecorating, and the Colonial Room at that time was being used for a ballroom, not the restaurant it had been and now is.

When Alma Gutierrez (she is now Alma Rodriguez) worked at the Menger on the switchboards in 1980, she had a most peculiar experience one night while she was working the 11 P.M. to 7 A.M. "graveyard" shift.

In those days, the hotel switchboard lit up on the room number that was calling the operator. This particular evening, sometime after midnight, the phone from room 354 rang. Alma answered in her usual manner: "Good evening. Hotel operator. May I help you?" The lady answered, saying she wanted to be connected with room service. Alma explained that room service closed at midnight and could not be reached. She did offer to tell the woman where there were some nearby restaurants that might be serving that late. No, the woman was adamant she wanted room service, and again Alma explained it was not available. Then the woman hung up.

Just a few minutes later, the same lady called back and made the same request. Again, Alma explained she could not get room service at that hour. And then, once more, the lady called. After the third call, Alma called the front desk and asked who was in room 354. The reply was the room was unoccupied.

After Alma told the front desk manager what was going on, she got the security guard and the two of them went up to the third floor and knocked on the door. When there was no answer, they opened the door with a passkey. The room was unoccupied, but a window, which opened onto Alamo Plaza, was open. There was water on the window ledge and also on the floor beneath the window. It was a clear evening and there had been no rain. The guard and the desk clerk mopped up the water, closed and locked the window, and returned to the lobby.

In the meantime, Alma was still answering calls from room 354! There were three more, one after the other, from the same woman. Again Alma called the front desk and once more the desk manager and the security guard went up to the third floor, knocked on the door, and admitted themselves with the passkey. The window was again open, and there was again water on the windowsill and on the floor! They cleaned up the water, securely locked the window, and once more headed downstairs.

Alma said the calls kept coming, and she finally just quit answering any calls from that room. She is firmly convinced that she had a number of telephone conversations that night with one of the Menger ghosts! Certainly, no one can think of a better explanation.

Chapter 18

A Summation of Spirits

In my personal collection of books dealing with the paranormal or supernatural, there are many, many ghost stories about hotels. Famous old hotels all over the world appear to literally crawl with ghostly inhabitants. In fact, several of San Antonio's finest hotels are, like the Menger, inhabited by ghosts. It is as if an old hotel hasn't really "arrived" unless it can boast the presence of a ghost or two!

All sorts of spirits inhabit the Menger Hotel, as you have read in previous chapters. Because we are here in this mortal world and they are there in their own world of the afterlife, we cannot communicate well enough to explain their presence. We can only suppose that they are still capable of thought as well as of action. They are apparently happy where they are and therefore have made little effort to move on to another level of existence.

If I were a psychic, perhaps I could sense their presences and even communicate with them, finding out why they seem to have taken up long-term residency in the hotel. However, I must be satisfied to only guess at why they seem to want to remain at the Menger.

The management welcomes them. As long as they do not frighten or upset guests, they are welcome to stay. Most guests seem more fascinated than frightened by the spirits. Often they ask for not a "room with a view," but a "room with a ghost." Since there's no telling when or where a ghost might appear, this is not an easily filled request.

The Menger is a beautiful place. It has hosted countless people, many of them famous personalities. I believe spirits cling not only to buildings but to things—paintings, beds, furnishings. And to rid the Menger of its spirits, one would have to have an all-out house clearing, and the hotel would then be devoid of many of its treasured antiques. It's far better to just keep the ghosts!

By the time this manuscript goes to the publisher, I am sure other incidents will have taken place at the Menger. That's the way it is when one is writing about ghosts. They don't seem to slow down. They are totally unpredictable. I am sure these friendly, benevolent spirits will continue to enjoy the hospitality of the beautiful Menger Hotel. There is absolutely nothing to fear from them. In fact, an occasional manifestation just adds a spicy note of mystery to the elegant old inn, another fascinating facet to that precious gem that so beautifully adorns Alamo Plaza!

At the Inn We Call the Menger
Docia Williams

Spirits dwell within these walls;
Footsteps echo in the halls,
As in the courtyard, darkness falls.
At the Inn we call the Menger.

In the bar we've seen appear
Uniformed, from by-gone year
A soldier-ghost, who quaffs a beer;
At the Inn we call the Menger.

A lady seen by quite a few
Clad in her gown of royal blue
In a room with courtyard view;
At the Inn we call the Menger.

There's the wraith of Sallie White
Who walks the halls with steps so light
In the middle of the night.
At the Inn we call the Menger.

In the dining room, we might see
Frock-coated, he's the maitre d'
Who speaks to guests we cannot see.
At the Inn we call the Menger.

When the maids have come to clean
In his suite on the mezzanine
They know he's there; old Captain King!
At the Inn we call the Menger.

Wearing buckskin shirt and trousers gray
"Will you go, or will you stay?"
Is what this phantom had to say.
At the Inn we call the Menger.

A soldier ghost we sometimes see
Tall and courtly as can be;
Kirby Smith? Or R. E. Lee?
At the Inn we call the Menger.

A lady in a tasseled hat,
She's not too thin, and not too fat,
She speaks and nods. Imagine that!
At the Inn we call the Menger.

A ghostly crew, more than a few,
Content to roam and linger.
They like to haunt, it's all they do,
At the Inn we call the Menger!

Epilogue

$\mathcal{F}$or over one hundred forty years the Menger Hotel has proudly presided over Alamo Plaza, sheltering countless numbers of travelers during their visits to San Antonio, while offering fine dining and meeting room facilities to local residents as well. And doubtless, when we have long departed, gone to our eternal resting places, the Menger Hotel will continue to flourish. The chandeliers will still sparkle and glisten in the lobbies, and butterflies will continue to sip sweet nectar from the flowering borders in the patios. Fiesta queens will sparkle under the lights as they dance at countless Queen's Balls to come, and newlyweds will find its gracious suites a perfect place to spend a honeymoon. Yes, it will all still be there, in place for future generations to enjoy, and they will all come to cherish their own special memories of this grand hotel.

Ageless Lady
Docia Schultz Williams

Just as a dowager duchess, perfumed and attired in satins and lace,
Holds court in her chosen place,
So our lady waits for her subjects to arrive.
She will, as always, receive them with courtly grace
Born of years of stately adherence
To rules of conduct and genteel decorum,
Which might be considered, by some, to be old-fashioned,
Even out of step, amidst the artificial, neon-lit, chrome plated
Conformity of this day.

Her pristine garments are arranged in starched-lace splendor,
Their colors scarcely faded in this century past.
There is no shabbiness in her attire, only charm and gentility
Made more gracious still by its antiquity.
Like fine vintage champagne, this grand lady
Has grown more cherished in her maturity.

Just as she has welcomed countless visitors before,
She awaits your arrival even now,
Offering up the gracious hospitality
Of her many-roomed abode;
Knowing she may soon number you
As still another loyal subject soon to be cast beneath her spell.
Approach this ageless enchantress
With the respectful courtesy due one's elders.
She will return your expectations a thousandfold.

Then, after having satisfied your hunger
At her bountiful table,
And having refreshed your body and soul
In her tranquil bowers,
You will find that you, too, have cast your heart and your homage
At the feet of the gracious Lady Menger.

You will bid her farewell with reluctance
Coupled with a solemn vow to return.

And she will still be waiting.

Sources

Newspapers

San Antonio Daily Express
Dec. 12, 1867; Sept. 20, 1869; March 18, 1871; March 21, 1871; March 28, 1871; Sept. 17, 1871; May 24, 1875; March 29, 1876; April 1, 1876; Feb. 20, 1877; April 15, 1885; Sept. 18, 1889; Oct. 12, 1890; Aug. 12, 1897; May 2, 1898; May 10, 1898; May 11, 1898; May 17, 1898; May 29, 1898; May 30, 1898; Jan. 10, 1905; Nov. 18, 1906; May 18, 1908; Nov. 26, 1940; Sept. 20, 1959; Jan. 27, 1966; Dec. 5, 1968; Oct. 14, 1971; Aug. 30, 1985

San Antonio Semi-Weekly Express
May 6, 1898

San Antonio Evening News
July 30, 1943

San Antonio Freie Presse Fur Texas
March 27, 1880

San Antonio Light
Sept. 11, 1938; Woolford's Tales, by Sam Woolford on Feb. 1, 1959, Feb. 8, 1959, and Feb. 22, 1959; Sept. 20, 1959; March 22, 1980; April 7, 1986; May 2, 1986; Sept. 28, 1989

San Antonio Herald
Jan. 18, 1859; Feb. 1, 1859; Sept. 13, 1859; May 2, 1863; March 15, 1867; Jan. 12, 1872; May 12, 1875; March 28, 1876; Feb. 27, 1910

San Antonio Express News
Nov. 18, 1906; Oct. 19, 1950; Sept. 20, 1959; Jan. 27, 1966; Oct. 10, 1974; March 4, 1979; Sept. 13, 1989; Oct. 15, 1989; March 20, 1992; May 15, 1992; June 5, 1992; Oct. 20, 1993; Feb 1, 1994; Oct. 26; 1997; Oct. 31; 1997, Nov. 2, 1997

The Galveston Daily News
Aug. 26, 1986; Aug. 28, 1986; March 23, 2000

Texas City Sun
   Aug. 26, 1986

Magazines and Periodicals

In Between Magazine: Galveston, Clear Lake and Points Between #238
   Aug. 14, 1986

San Antonio Express Magazine
   Dec. 24, 1950

Southern Messenger
   San Antonio, Texas, April 16, 1936: "Texas Pioneers Made Use of Houston Ship Channel Ninety Years Ago."

The Pioneer Magazine of Texas
   Feb. 1924

Life Magazine
   Sept. 1959

Southern Living
   Sept. 1987

San Antonio Semi-Weekly News
   April 4, 1865

Philanthropy in Texas
   Aug. 1996, "The Moody Family of Galveston," by E. Douglas McLeod, attorney of Galveston

Southern Homes and Gardens
   Sept. 1941

Smithsonian Magazine
   Oct. 1992; Letters to the Editor: re: Gutzon Borglum

San Antonio Magazine
   Jan. 1951; March 1979: "The Ghosts of the Menger," by Grant Lyons; July 1976, "Those Charming Hostelries of History," by Marjorie George

Texas Highways
   Oct. 1997

Commemorative Program
Brooks Air Force Base, 75th Anniversary, 1917-1992, "Sidney J. Brooks Jr."

Books

American Historical Society Vol. III, Chicago and N.Y., 1914; "A History of Texas and Texans" by Frank W. Johnson, edited by Eugene C. Barker, Ph.D.

Bishop, Merrill. *Chromotropes.* San Antonio: Naylor Publishing Co., 1926.

Bowser, David. *Mysterious San Antonio.* David Bowser, 1990.

Bushick, Frank H. *Glamorous Days in Old San Antonio.* San Antonio: Naylor Publishing Co., 1934.

Carroll, John M. *The Seventh U.S. Cavalry's Own Colonel Tommy Tompkins: A Military Heritage and Tradition.* Mattituck, New York: J. M. Carroll and Co., 1984.

Emmett, Chris. *In the Path of Events.* Waco, Texas: Jones & Morrison, 1959.

Encyclopedia Americana, N.Y., Chicago: Americana Corporation, 1940.

Encyclopedia of Military History, Second Revised Edition. New York City: Harper and Row, 1986.

Everett, Donald E. *San Antonio, the Flavor of its Past.* San Antonio: Trinity University Press, 1975.

Fehrenbach, Ted. *The San Antonio Story.* Tulsa, Oklahoma: Continental Heritage Inc., 1978.

Griffin, S. G. *History of Galveston, Texas.* Galveston, Texas: n.p., 1931.

Jennings, Frank W. *San Antonio, The Story of an Enchanted City.* San Antonio: San Antonio Express News, 1998.

Johnson, S. S. *Texans Who Wore Gray.* Tyler, Texas: n.p., 1907.

Morrison and Fourney's General Directory of the City of San Antonio. compiled by Morrison and Fourney, 1881-82.

Ramsdell, Charles. *San Antonio: A Historical and Pictorial Guide.* Austin: University of Texas Press, 1985.

Silverthorne, Elizabeth. *Christmas in Texas.* College Station: Texas A&M University Press, 1991.

Southwestern Historical Quarterly, Vol. 63, July 1959-April 1960.

Steinfeldt, Cecilia. *San Antonio As Seen Through a Magic Lantern.* San Antonio: San Antonio Museum Association, 1978.

Stumpf, Mrs. Franz. *San Antonio's Menger.* self published, 1953.

Complete Works of O. Henry. Garden City, N.Y.: Garden City Publishing Co., 1937.

The Texas Historian, Vol. XLIX, #1, Sept. 1983.

Webster's American Military Biographies. Springfield, Massachusets: G.C. Merriam Co., 1978.

Wendt, Lloyd and Kogan, Herman. *Bet a Million! The Story of John W. Gates.* Indianapolis and New York: Bobbs-Merrill Co., 1948.

West Texas Historical Association Year Book, Vol. XXXII, Oct. 1956, "The Menger Hotel, San Antonio Civic and Social Center, 1859-1877" by Inez Strickland Dalton.

Articles and Essays

"From an Army Wife," article by Ruth Massey, which appeared in unidentified newspaper, no date, from Menger Hotel vertical file, Daughters of the Republic of Texas Library, San Antonio

Reminiscences of 1898, memoirs of Clifton David Scott, Oklahoma Territory Rough Rider, provided to us by his relative, Peggy Green, of Weatherford, Texas.

Personal Interviews and Contacts

I want to thank those individuals who gave me leads to stories that I had not previously heard, and to those people who granted me their time and their information, by means of personal or telephone interviews or through personal correspondence:

Bryan Snyder III, Austin, for information regarding the Celeste Willis Snyder portrait in main lobby

Mrs. Marguerite McCormick, great-great-great-granddaughter of William and Mary Menger, interview and allowing me to photograph her family heirloom furniture

Mrs. Lewis Moorman, interview regarding 1959 Centennial Ball

Mr. Frates Seeligson, interview regarding 1959 Centennial Ball

Mrs. William O. Bowers III, interview regarding 1959 Centennial Ball and the information about her mother, long-time Menger resident, Mrs. Verna Hooks McClean

Mr. Maury Maverick Jr, helpful suggestions on research material

Mr. Ike Kampmann Jr., descendant of former Menger owners, interview providing information about the Kampmann family

Mr. Charles Schreiner III, YO Ranch, for telephone interview regarding his mother, Myrtle Barton Schreiner, and his aunt, Mimi Schreiner Rigsby, who were Menger residents

Lt. Gen. Beverly Powell, USA Rtd., for information about Colonel Tommy Tompkins

Colonel George Weinbrenner, for information about Spanish American War

Lt. Colonel John Manguso, for information about Theodore Roosevelt and Rough Riders

Natalie Tompkins Gooch, Alburqueque, for information on her uncle, Colonel Tommy Tompkins, and her father, Colonel Daniel Tompkins

Frank W. Jennings, author of *San Antonio: The Story of an Enchanted City,* for information on John W. Gates and the barbed wire story

Index

About the Author

Author, lecturer Docia Schultz Williams is an avid student of history and a long-time resident of the city, Mrs. Williams leads tours of San Antonio sites and is the owner/operator of Spirits of San Antonio Ghost Tours. She is also a published poet, member of the Texas Poetry Society, and has been named one of the Outstanding Women in San Antonio by the Express News Publishing Company.

Docia Schultz Williams is the author of several previous books, including:

Best Tales of Texas Ghosts
Ghosts Along the Texas Coast
Phantoms of the Plains: Tales of West Texas Ghosts
Spirits of San Antonio and South Texas
*When Darkness Falls: Tales of San Antonio Ghosts
    and Hauntings*